Land Of Rivers And Trees

Craig Briggs

Copyright © 2025 Craig Briggs

The moral right of the author has been asserted. This is a work of non-fiction that recounts real events and experiences. Some names, places, conversations, and identifying characteristics have been changed to preserve anonymity of those concerned.

Copy editing/proofreading by Louise Lubke Cuss
Cover design and photography by Craig Briggs
Portrait photo by Melanie Briggs
All rights reserved.

ISBN-13: 979-8316399468

By the same author

The Journey series

Journey To A Dream

Beyond Imagination

Endless Possibilities

Opportunities Ahead

Driving Ambition

The Discerning Traveller

A Season To Remember

An Excellent Vintage

Life In A Foreign Land

The Accidental Explorer

Seasons To Be Cheerful

Here To There And Back Again

Land Of Rivers And Trees

Fiction

Pandora's Box

Short story

Roast Pig and Romance

Hardcover

**Journey To A Dream
Special Tenth Anniversary Edition**

In Memory

Pilar Carnero Fernández
(1917 – 2023)

Andrea Jones
(1966 – 2024)

CONTENTS

	Introduction	1
1	Found without Trace	14
2	You Know Who	30
3	Repairs and Renewals	46
4	The Price Is Right	58
5	Acronyms Rule OK	74
6	The Mind Boggles	93
7	The Final Act	106
8	Two-Minute Updates	120
9	First Impressions	136
10	Weather or Not	149
11	If You See Cid…	166
12	Love at First Sight	179
13	Back in the Big Time	193
14	Terry on Tour	204
15	Down to This	218
16	The Art of Being Patient	231
17	Parple Rain	247
18	Where's Jesus?	260
19	Well I Never	273
20	Table Toppers	287
21	What's for Dinner?	300
22	Don't Mess with Lola	312
23	Bumps in the Road	325
	What Next?	336
	About the Author	347

Introduction

For those who are new to my work, the Introduction will bring you up to date with The Journey so far. For those who are not, you might prefer to start on chapter 1.

If life deals you a bad hand, don't fold, take a chance; a good player will always come out on top.

I entered this world on the 12th of July 1962, in St. Luke's Hospital, Huddersfield. The second child, and only son, of Donald and Glenys Briggs. Donald, a humble lathe operator, worked for one of the town's largest employers, David Brown Tractors of Meltham.

The birth of their first child, Julie, had been a joy. The arrival of a son would make the family complete. Donald couldn't wait to groom his boy for sporting success. Notification of my arrival came via a phone call to his work, a call that dashed his parental hopes. Young Craig was not a 'normal' lad: he'd been born with congenital feet deformities. I cannot imagine a crueller message.

Unaware of my disability, I got on with life as any infant would. My first birthday brought a gift that would change my life forever. Not a cuddly toy from Mum and Dad, nor a silver-plated trinket from friends or relatives. My life-changing gift was a marvel of modern engineering, manufactured by J. E. Hanger and Co. of London for and on behalf of the National Health Service. Bespoke footwear gave me what the Vespa had given the youth of the fifties: freedom and independence. They weren't quite as stylish as an Italian built scooter but I didn't care. From now on, Master Briggs was on the move and no one would hold me back.

Over the next five years a series of surgical procedures changed the way I moved. Recollections are few but these infant experiences would influence the rest of my life. In the 1960s bedside visits were restricted to one person for one hour per day. The anguish of a young mother listening to the tortured screams of her infant son begging her to stay must have been horrific; it wasn't much fun for me either.

When the time came, Mum walked me to school like other proud mothers. For his part, Dad gave me his first and only piece of worldly advice. 'If anyone hits you, hit 'em back.'

With one exception, my mind proved sharper than my boxing prowess. Kids can be cruel, particularly to those who stand out, but only once did I break down in tears and ask, 'Why? Why me?' It's a question I sometimes ask myself today, but for very different reasons. Academia was not my thing. I found it difficult to concentrate on anything that didn't interest me.

I left secondary education with a mediocre haul of four 'O' levels and drifted aimlessly into an 'A' level course. It seemed preferable to starting work. If my 'O' level tally was disappointing, my 'A' level results were pitiful. I blamed a perforated appendix, two months before my finals, but if truth be known I'd had my fill of education.

In May 1980 I left college and entered the employment market. Margaret Thatcher was busy dismantling British industry and unemployment was running at a post-war high. I signed on to receive unemployment benefit and spent the summer lounging around the house watching the Wimbledon Tennis Championship on telly. As the tournament drew to a close, parental pressure to find work intensified. In September, during one of my many visits to the Job Centre, a job card caught my eye: 'Wanted: trainee retail managers'. The idea of becoming a manager appealed, so I applied.

Five hundred and sixty applicants chased six positions. I pleaded my case at an interview and ended up being selected. After a two-week training course in the seaside town of Southport, I passed with honours, achieving the rank of assistant manager. When asked where I'd like to ply my newfound retail skills, I chose London, a city paved with gold.

In October 1980, I left Huddersfield a naïve child and returned three and a half years later a wiser and more mature young man. A brief period of letting my hair down followed, catching up on lost time and lost youth. During these wild and hedonistic months, I met the love of my life and future wife, Melanie.

My career in retail panned six and a half years with five different companies. Each one expanded my experience and knowledge but to realise my dream I would have to go it alone. Not long after my twenty-sixth birthday, I handed in my notice. My future lay in leather jackets. Unfortunately, no one shared this vision and my aspirations fell at the first hurdle.

The prospect of returning to the retail trade pushed me into pursuing a different path. I reached a compromise and worked as a self-employed agent for one of the nation's largest insurance companies. The job title, Financial Consultant, exaggerated the role. In reality I was nothing more than a desperate insurance salesman. Life was hard and the insurance industry ruthless. Trying to sell a product that nobody wants, and which by its nature will never benefit the payee, is not easy. Unlike most recruits, I managed to survive and learnt some difficult but valuable lessons.

My 'Big Break' came when two of my clients asked me to invest in their fledgling printing business. The first year's accounts showed greater losses than actual sales. Against all professional advice I jumped at the chance, remortgaged the house and bought an equal stake.

By accident rather than design, I'd finally found my true vocation. The company was losing money hand over fist. The bank had taken a second charge on the partners' homes and my investment was swallowed up in a black hole of debt. Just when things couldn't get any worse, the bank called in the overdraft. While others worried, I applied myself to the problem. Through hard work and determination, we weathered the storm, but casualties were high.

After thirteen years of blood, sweat, and holding back the tears, I ended up owning a modestly successful little business. The time was right to begin my journey to a dream.

In May 2002 my wife Melanie and I decided to sell up and chase our dream. We packed all our worldly belongings, including our dog Jazz, into my ageing executive saloon, and headed off to Spain.

Not for us the tourist-packed Costas of the Mediterranean or the whitewashed villages of Andalucía. Our destination was Galicia: a little-known region in the northwest corner of Spain.

The contrast in lifestyles from England's industrial north to Spain's rural interior proved far more traumatic than either of us had imagined. Three and a half years at night school studying the Spanish language was little help. Galicia has its own language, galego. A proudly spoken tongue that has more in common with Portuguese than Spanish.

Dubious estate agents and questionable property descriptions turned our search for a new home into a lottery. Clear objectives became blurred and after several failed attempts to buy a property, we were forced to reassess our goals.

Eventually, we found our dream house, a tiny bungalow on the outskirts of the sleepy village of Canabal. Coping with Spain's laid-back approach while managing a building project tested our resolve. What could go wrong did and by Christmas we were ready to throw in the towel and head back to Blighty. But Yorkshiremen are made of sterner stuff.

A timely visit from my dad re-energised our ambitions. Twelve months and ten days after arriving in Galicia, we moved into our new home and completed the first part of our *Journey To A Dream*.

Choosing a name for our renovated property proved difficult. After much deliberation we decided on El Sueño (The Dream). After the challenges of the first twelve months, we settled into a more relaxed lifestyle. Drinks at sunset, or Teatime Tasters, became an integral part of our daily lives and the warmth and generosity of our village neighbours made us feel at home.

With Melanie's help, I set about transforming our barren plot into a garden paradise. It wasn't all plain sailing and dealing with Spanish bureaucracy proved difficult. As time drifted by we started to enjoy a *Life Beyond Imagination*.

For the first time in a long time, I had the freedom to take up some hobbies. Little did I know that writing and viniculture would become my pastimes of choice. With help from our neighbour, Meli, I took my first tentative steps on the road to winemaking. The success of my fledgling hobby was left in the hands of Mother Nature. Initial results were encouraging. My love of winemaking had begun.

As with viniculture, my efforts at writing took time to develop. Under the tutorage of Peter Hinchliffe, former editor in chief of Huddersfield's daily newspaper and founder of an online magazine, my writing slowly improved.

Hobbies are one thing but the financial requirements of day to day living were never far from our thoughts. After successfully buying, renovating, and selling a second property, we decided to look for another. Eventually, we found the ideal project, a romantic ruined farmhouse with *Endless Possibilities*.

Events have a way of keeping our lives in perspective, and this was particularly so when Melanie's dad was diagnosed with terminal cancer. A surprise fortieth birthday party turned into an emotional, but happy, final family reunion.

Later that year we offered to help our friends, Bob and Janet, convert their unloved house into a luxury holiday rental. Weeks before the first guests were due to arrive, the builder had a serious on-site accident. We had no alternative but to roll up our sleeves and finish the job. A season that could have turned into a disaster ended in success and satisfied customers. The question was, could we duplicate that success and build our own holiday rental property?

Finding the perfect place was challenging; buying it proved far more difficult. The lack of official paperwork led to lengthy delays. Thirteen months after agreeing the purchase, we finally took possession. That's when the problems really began. The wisdom of buying a house without water or electricity was put to the test. By the time we'd resolved those issues another twelve months had passed. The time had come to put the frustrations of the past behind us and concentrate on the *Opportunities Ahead*.

Throughout the wait we'd kept ourselves busy. There can't be many people who can add moonshine distillation to their curriculum vitae. Our second year in property management presented an unexpected opportunity, a house swap to the far side of the world. All we had to do was make the arrangements. After all, how difficult could it be to organise the trip of a lifetime?

We soon discovered that restoring a Spanish ruin requires a unique skill set. The two most important are a vivid imagination and a great sense of humour. Above all, be prepared to sacrifice your sanity: if you're not crazy when you start, you will be by the time it's finished.

Keeping the costs down came at a price. The work was hard and the hours long. Suppliers and subcontractors tested our patience but throughout it all we managed to maintain a healthy work-life balance.

During our house swap holiday to Australia I realised a *Driving Ambition*. The trip of a lifetime took us from rural Galicia to Wollongong in Australia via Shanghai in China. A forty-nine-day tour to six countries on three continents, flying 27,000 miles and driving over 13,000 kilometres. On our return, the house restoration had moved on apace but there was plenty still to do before we could welcome paying guests to our holiday rental home.

By the end of May the main contractor had finished his work. The gardens and grounds would take a little longer to complete, but Melanie and I could finally make a start on designing the interior. Our mission was to provide quality accommodation for *The Discerning Traveller*.

Hard work and quality fittings helped transform our blank canvas into a cosy home. Choosing a name is never easy but after much consideration we settled on *Campo Verde*. A luxury farmhouse in the Galician countryside with a name that rolled off the tongue in any language. We'd put our hearts and souls into creating this romantic hideaway, and invested a large part of our savings. Only time would tell if we'd made the right decision.

Speaking of time, Melanie gave up on her vegetable patch and handed responsibilities for its upkeep to me. I suggested an alternative use, a vineyard, and Melanie agreed. Making it a reality provided a much-needed distraction from work at the house. As for harvesting the grapes, that would take between three and four years to realise.

Our first year of holiday lettings became *A Season To Remember*. Within months of starting to advertise, the number of reservations far outstripped our expectations. In an effort to gain repeat business, guests were treated to an evening of free wine and tapas and a complimentary souvenir to take away. Every client was different and *Campo Verde* hosted characters from around the globe, but not everyone played by the rules.

As for the vineyard, that got off to the worst possible start when a well-intentioned neighbour gave us some questionable pruning advice. Thankfully, no long-term damage was done and all the grapevines survived.

Spring, summer and autumn were dedicated to our fledgling enterprise, but winter belonged to us. Our destination of choice was the Costa del Sol. It's often referred to as the Costa del Crime. We were to find out first hand, why.

Back home in Galicia, our efforts to establish a new vineyard suffered another setback when Celso's sheep took an interest. My attempts to remedy the situation almost ended in disaster. To ensure *An*

Excellent Vintage we decided to adopt another vineyard. Upscaling production came at quite a cost.

A month before the harvest, Jazz lost her battle with cancer. Melanie and I were heartbroken. We'd vowed never to have another dog but the pain was more than we could bear. Some pledges are meant to be broken and within days of losing her, we'd rescued Slawit: a Portuguese *podenco* with a strong will and a stubborn nature. The two dogs couldn't have been more different, which was probably a good thing.

Who would have thought that Slawit's aversion to travel would have caused us so many problems, and worse was to come? From the day she entered our lives, Slawit ran us ragged, testing our patience and our resolve.

Life in the Galician countryside is rarely dull and often educational. Over the years we've added some unusual activities to our CVs. Thanks to our neighbour, Meli, we became honorary chicken-sitters. Melanie took to the role like a duck to water, no pun intended. As for me, I doubt anyone will be offering me a job.

My skills lie elsewhere. Six years after putting pen to paper, I joined the ranks of published authors. The end of that story became the beginning of another. Reviews were mixed. Undeterred I threw myself into marketing. I opened a Facebook account, used my creative skills to build a website and, in an effort to reach a wider audience, started penning a weekly blog.

There's rarely a dull moment with *Life In A Foreign Land*. After years of producing mediocre wine, we finally achieved our goal of making wine we'd be happy to pay for. Success in one activity underlined our failure in another.

Slawit's recall training had gone from bad to worse, and her separation anxiety disorder resulted in an attempt to eat her way out of house and home. Unfortunately, it wasn't our home. We made good the repairs and an understanding landlord allowed us to return, but her behaviour would have lasting consequences.

In a year that marked my half a century one event stood head and shoulders above the rest. Imagine my surprise when the Spanish manufacturer of my orthopaedic footwear produced the most comfortable boots I'd ever owned. For me, they were the cobbling equivalent of walking on air. This unexpected and much appreciated gift offered a level of mobility I could only dream of, and an opportunity not to be missed.

The new year began with a flurry of excursions to old haunts and new destinations. Neither Melanie nor I are ones for following travel guides. We're more *The Accidental Explorer* types. The magic of Málaga and the charm of Estepona's old town left lasting impressions. As for Ronda, questions remained over its links to literary greats.

Writing a weekly blog gave Melanie and I the opportunity to uncover secrets of our local area. From Napoleonic war crimes to prehistoric burial sites, and a Civil War aviator to the Camino de Santiago. When friends introduced us to the captivating melodies of Portuguese fado music, we were instantly hooked.

A new neighbourhood committee resulted in some excellent village fiestas including a communal summer paella and, my personal favourite, *magosto*: an autumn feast in honour of the humble chestnut.

After four years of wintering in Elviria we felt a change was in order. Making the reservation proved problematic but we got there in the end and couldn't have been happier with our choice. Our move along the coast to Sitio de Calahonda proved to be a winner.

Whether it's winter, spring, summer or autumn, they're all *Seasons To Be Cheerful*. Having changed the destination of our winter getaway, the last thing we expected to stumble across was a property we could afford to buy. In the end, it wasn't to be, but knowledge gained is never wasted.

Attending four wine fiestas in four months was quite a feat, but visiting two in two different countries in under twenty-four hours was potentially record-breaking. Months of work culminated in the publication of my second book, but neither of us had expected an autograph hunter to turn up on the doorstep unannounced.

Helping travellers in distress is an occupational hazard when you are the owners of a holiday rental property. When sisters from Canada got into trouble with their hire car, we were happy to step in and become their tour guides.

Towards the end of the year, a demand from the Spanish tax authority caused quite a stir, but cool heads and sound advice put the matter on hold. Only time would tell if we made the right choice.

The new year sent shockwaves rippling through our peaceful lives when two earthquakes in quick succession caused panic on the Costa del Sol. That was nothing compared to the seismic political events unfolding in the UK. Lies, misinformation, and catchy slogans resulted in a vote to leave the EU and brought our future in Spain into question.

A special wedding anniversary and a milestone birthday tested my planning skills to the limit. In the space of three days, we went from *Here To There And Back Again* taking in the sights of the Douro valley in Portugal. Two weeks later, Melanie's birthday surprise involved flights from Santiago de Compostela to Málaga and a two-night break in a boutique hotel in Estepona.

When Melanie's aunty came to stay, problems with the car caused quite a panic but my home mechanics saw us through. When the dust from the referendum had settled, we decided to take back control of our own future. After all, how difficult could it be to become Spanish citizens? We were about to find out.

1

Found without Trace

As any long-suffering sports fan will tell you, supporting your hometown team is never easy. Take Huddersfield Town Football Club for example. It was over forty-six years since they had last graced the top flight of English football. During that time, they'd had their ups and downs: long periods of disappointment punctuated by fleeting moments of elation but, after wallowing in the lower echelons of the Football League for what seemed like an eternity, the club had its sights set firmly on the promised land of the Premier League. Admittedly, we were only halfway through the season, but never before had they been within touching distance of the leaders at this point in the season.

Town were currently fourth in the Championship with the same number of points as third-placed Reading. At the end of the season, the top two teams would gain automatic promotion; the four clubs below them would fight it out in the playoffs to see which one would join them. Even at this stage, automatic promotion looked unlikely but, if their current form continued, there was every chance they'd reach the playoffs, and from there anything was possible.

On a less positive note, our efforts to gain Spanish citizenship had flatlined of late, and our initial enthusiasm had started to wane. We'd completed the easy parts of the process by securing copies of our birth certificates and marriage certificate, and having them translated and notarised. We'd also applied for our criminal record certificates. Melanie's came back without a hitch; mine was a little more complicated.

The online form required applicants to list any previous convictions. To my knowledge I didn't have any and replied as such. Unfortunately, the Criminal Records Office didn't agree and asked for clarification. I was mortified and racked my brain for an explanation; having a criminal conviction was hardly something I'd forget in a hurry. Unlike a quiz show, I wasn't able to phone a friend or ask the audience, and for the life of me I couldn't think of anything I'd done that would merit a criminal record. I'd collected a few motoring offences over the years, who hasn't; but surely those weren't criminal convictions, were they?

With no other action available to me, I decided to come clean and list every traffic offence I'd ever been sanctioned for dating back to my first speeding ticket, aged seventeen. Whatever I'd said did the trick and, without explanation or rebuttal, they forwarded my certificate. On closer inspection there was a slight difference between Melanie's and mine. Hers stated "No Trace" while mine said "No Live Trace". We could only hope both would satisfy the Spanish authorities. Despite that minor setback, obtaining those documents had been relatively straightforward and, by the time we'd secured them, we'd both reached the qualifying residency term of ten years even though we'd lived in Spain for much longer. It was the remaining two requirements we were struggling with.

Obtaining a Spanish language qualification to the level DELE A2 and sitting the CCSE Spanish citizenship exam would be by far and away the most challenging parts of the application process, both of which we were hoping to sit later in the year. My failure to secure the services of a one-to-one Spanish tutor hadn't helped but, if truth be known, it was a more deep-seated problem that was dogging my progress.

Some people take to studying like a duck to water; in my case it's more like a lead weight. To date, I'd used every excuse in the book to avoid knuckling down to some studies. Like writing one, for example. Which wasn't to say I hadn't been working hard because I had. So much so that by the 1st of January I'd begun editing the fourth book in The Journey series but, if I was serious about passing these exams, time was of the essence.

Once again, we'd welcomed in the New Year on the Costa del Sol and would be here for a further two months before heading back to Galicia. The reason we choose to winter in this part of Spain can be found in the name: the Sunshine Coast. This year, however, it hadn't always lived up to its billing. As well as warm sunny days we'd also experienced everything from torrential rain and menacing clouds to high winds and thunderstorms. Since the turn of the year, overcast skies and cool temperatures had been the order of the day.

'What are we going to do if it's like this while Richard and Yvonne are here?' asked Melanie.

'I've no idea. How long are they here for?'

'Three nights, four days, but I think they've got an early flight on their final day.'

This trip marked a milestone for them; it would be the first time they'd visited us without bringing their kids. It was difficult to believe that their eldest, Mason, who was four on their first visit, was now at college, and their daughter Erren, who'd turned one that same year, was old enough to be left alone under the watchful eye of her gran.

On the 17th of January, we left the apartment shortly after 10:00 am to collect our guests from Málaga Airport. As usual, we were cutting it fine. Thankfully, the travelator between the short stay carpark and the terminal building was working. Getting Slawit to step on was easy; the problem was getting her off.

'Come on,' said Melanie, pulling her lead.

As we raced into the arrivals hall, Richard and Yvonne were entering from the opposite direction.

'Have you been waiting long?' asked Yvonne.

'Ages,' I replied.

'Don't listen to him; we've only just got here,' said Melanie.

When we'd left the apartment, the weather hadn't quite made up its mind. By the time we got back, we couldn't have wished for a better day. The earlier clouds had disappeared, the breeze had dropped, and the sun had come out to play.

'These are for you,' said Yvonne, handing me half a dozen pork pies.

I couldn't have been happier.

'Thank you. You can come again. Look what I've got.'

Melanie was in the kitchen preparing lunch.

'Lucky you.'

'I might share them with you if you're good.'

'You might, might you?'

We ate lunch on the terrace staring out across the Mediterranean Sea. On a cloudless, still day, bright sunlight reflected off the cool blue water like shards of polished steel. When we'd finished eating, we relaxed in the afternoon sunshine and caught up on news from the UK.

That evening, we dined at Miel y Nata, our favourite Italian bistro along this part of the coast, and ended the day sipping shots of caramel vodka while teetotal Yvonne kept an eye on us.

When we rose the next morning, the weather had taken a turn for the worse. The open market in La Cala de Mijas provided the perfect distraction, or so we'd hoped. On such a dull and overcast day, the Mediterranean looked more like the North Sea as we made our way east along the coast road. When we arrived in La Cala, we'd never seen the market so quiet, and we hadn't been there five minutes when it began to rain. Hoping it might pass, we huddled together under cover at one of the stalls.

'I thought you said it was always sunny on the Costa del Sol.'

Yvonne's tongue-in-cheek remark left Melanie and me feeling a little guilty.

'We told you not to bring the weather with you,' replied Melanie.

Wandering around an open market in the rain was no one's idea of fun so we hot-footed it back to the car in favour of an early lunch. An hour later it was still grey and overcast, but at least it had stopped raining.

'Let's go for a stroll around the old town in Marbella,' I suggested.

'Why not?' replied Melanie.

Marbella's old town is one of the few remaining jewels in this overdeveloped stretch of coastline and, in spite of its popularity, has managed to maintain much of its old-world charm. So much so that if you listen carefully, you can still hear vestiges of its past echoing through the narrow streets and alleyways. Of course nothing on this stretch of the Med is sacred, and the area is now a hive of small independent retailers, bars, restaurants, boutique hotels, and tacky gift shops.

'I can't believe this weather,' said Melanie, as we drove west towards Marbella.

I'd flicked on the windscreen wipers, but it didn't last long.

When driving into Marbella, I always follow the same route. I'm sure there must be easier ways, but if it ain't broken why fix it? Besides which, if I'm unable to find street parking on the way in, I can always use the multi-storey carpark on Avenida Mercado.

'There's a space,' said Melanie.

We were in luck.

One of the things I like most about parking in this part of town is the element of surprise. For all the world we could have been slap-bang in the middle of this modern and very exclusive resort, but we were actually less than twenty metres from the narrow, cobbled streets of the old town. Richard and Yvonne were as surprised as we'd hoped they would be, and suitably impressed that we knew where we were going.

To the uninitiated, the maze of narrow streets and tight alleyways can feel quite intimidating, but you're never far from a familiar landmark. Our destination was the centre of this historic old town, Plaza de los Naranjos or Orange Square. En route, I couldn't resist taking them down a few crab alleyways, so called because if you meet someone coming in the opposite direction you have to shuffle past them sideways.

It hadn't crossed my mind that, due to the weather, all the bars surrounding the square would be closed. We were devastated. There's something uniquely Spanish about sipping freshly squeezed orange juice in the shade of a leafy orange tree. Admittedly, it wouldn't have been quite as appealing in these conditions; nevertheless, it was one of those location-specific experiences we'd wanted to share with them.

'Aw that's a pity. Do you think they'll open later?' asked Melanie.

I looked to the heavens.

'I wouldn't count on it,' I replied.

'Let's walk a bit further. You never know, we might find somewhere else.'

From Plaza de los Naranjos we exited west along Calle Estación. A number of shopkeepers were starting to reopen after lunch, an indication that the time had moved on to four o'clock. During the summer months, I doubt they get the opportunity to enjoy a proper two-and-a-half-hour Spanish lunch break.

'Is that what Richard had at your fiesta?' asked Yvonne.

Although not directed at me, her question caught my attention. I knew exactly what she was referring to: churros. When they'd visited us in the summer, Richard had bought some from a street vendor at the fiesta in Monforte de Lemos. When I turned around, they were staring at a poster in the window of Churrería Marbella, a tiny establishment on the corner of Calle Estación and Plaza de la Victoria.

'It is. Shall we stop?'

I think Melanie knew the answer before she'd asked.

Churros are traditionally accompanied with a cup of hot chocolate, and Yvonne is nothing if not a chocoholic.

Her answer was a resounding yes. Sitting inside was out of the question; the place was far too small. Outside in the square, there were half a dozen tables, two of which had been wiped dry of rainwater. We took a seat and waited to be served.

'What would you like?' asked the waitress.

'Chocolate and churros.'

'For four?'

'Yes please.'

Richard had been in two minds whether to order a hot chocolate, but Yvonne offered to finish what he couldn't. Most churros are served as six-inch fingers of deep-fried choux pastry. What the waitress returned with was something completely different and totally unexpected. The single churro had been fried in a tight swirl which measured roughly forty centimetre in diameter, and the cups of chocolate sauce were so decadently rich we could literally stand our teaspoons up in it. Accompanying this gigantic swirl of deep-fried choux pastry were half a dozen sachets of sugar. Yvonne and I couldn't wait. We ripped open the sachets and sprinkled the sugar across the top. Melanie was first to dive. Using the tips of her fingers, she tore off a piece and dunked it into her warm chocolate sauce.

'That is absolutely delicious,' she said, licking sugar crystals off her lips.

Yvonne was next followed by Richard and then me.

For those of us with a sweet tooth, the combination of deep-fried pastry, sugar, and rich chocolate sauce was utterly irresistible. We tore off piece after piece, dipping, dunking, and devouring. Richard was first to concede defeat. Even Melanie gave up in the end. As for Yvonne and I, we could have carried on eating until we'd exploded.

If you ever find yourself between showers in Marbella and searching for something to do, look no further than Churrería Marbella. It might have been our first visit, but it definitely wouldn't be our last.

That evening we decided to dine at our favourite Chinese restaurant, the Hong Kong in Sitio de Calahonda. The lift from the apartment took us directly into the underground parking area. From there we headed down the hillside towards the sea.

'Have you seen the temperature?'

Richard's astonishment was mirrored by our own. The digital display read two degrees centigrade.

'Is that snow?' he added.

It couldn't be, could it?

Quickly, I flicked on the wipers and a line of melting sludge confirmed his suspicion.

'I think it's sleet,' I remarked.

We can't control the weather, but we do feel responsible when it lets us down. To make matters worse, we'd been telling them for years how fabulous it was over winter.

'It's warmer than this at home,' remarked Yvonne.

They couldn't resist having a dig, but we all saw the funny side.

On their final full day, the weather was almost as bad: cold and overcast, but at least it didn't rain.

'If you think the weather is bad here, take a look at this,' said Melanie, handing me her tablet.

She'd been reading an article in *La Voz de Galicia*, Galicia's regional newspaper. In it, they'd reported that the river Cabe, which runs through the centre of Monforte de Lemos, had frozen over and people were able to walk from one side of the river to the other.

'There's always someone worse off,' I replied.

West of Marbella is the resort of Puerto Banús which, even on a good day, is not everyone's cup of tea. It's built around an exclusive marina and gives ordinary folk like us the opportunity to see how the other half live. It's nothing if not interesting and, with little else on the agenda, it was the perfect place to while away a few hours.

The marina is home to a flotilla of floating palaces, and the quayside is a veritable showroom of exclusive marks: Ferrari, Maserati, Bentley, and Rolls Royce to name but a few. The backdrop to this manmade harbour is the stunning La Concha mountain but, on a day like today, with the summit enveloped in thick grey clouds, even that lacked its usual appeal.

'I bet it's raining up there,' remarked Melanie.

Despite the unusually bad weather, Richard and Yvonne had enjoyed their short break but, as if to rub salt in the wound, the following morning the clouds parted and the sun came out to bid them farewell. Proof if needed that the sun does shine on the Costa del Sol.

From that day until the end of January, we were treated to some of the best weather of the entire trip. Cool in the shade, but comfortably warm in the sunshine. If only we could order it on demand.

'Can we stop to let Slawit out?' asked Melanie.

We were heading back to the apartment from a shopping trip to Fuengirola. We'd been to a British supermarket to stock up on a few essentials for home: packets of Coleman's chilli con carne seasoning and Aquafresh toothpaste. After that we went to Dunnes department store where I'd bought a shirt and Melanie picked up a few pairs of her favourite leggings. We'd rounded off our shopping extravaganza with a trip to Primark in the Miramar shopping centre. You can never have too many pairs of seven-euro jeans.

On the approach road to the apartment, there's a dirt track which leads up into the mountains. I pulled off the road and we hopped out. Before opening the back, I took a deep breath. On multi-stop trips like this, the probability of Slawit throwing up increases exponentially. Slowly I lifted the tailgate and Slawit poked her nose out.

'Just wait,' I told her.

Any higher and she'd be off, and neither of us was in the mood for a cross-country chase. Carefully, I opened it a little further and then grabbed her collar. On this occasion she'd managed to keep the contents of her stomach to herself. I clipped on her lead and she leapt to the ground, delighted to be back on terra firma. A short walk and a call of nature, and I lifted her back into the car for the two-minute drive to the apartment.

'Oh!'

'What?'

'Look.'

Melanie was sitting in the passenger seat with the door pull in her hand.

'What did you do?'

'Nothing, it just came off in my hand. I didn't mean to do it.'

'I know you didn't, but it hasn't come off on its own.'

'Well it did, so how am I supposed to close the door?'

Her tone suggested it was all my fault.

'Wait there.'

I ran around and closed it for her.

By the time we got back to the apartment, apportioning blame took a back seat to finding a replacement.

'Do you know what they're called?' I asked.

'Is it a *tirador?*'

'I thought that was a door handle.'

'Isn't that what it is?'

'Not really, it's more of a door pull than a handle.'

'Well, I don't know then.'

Until we knew any different, I'd go with *tirador* and hope for the best.

An internet search suggested the industrial estate Poligono Guadalhorce on the outskirts of Málaga might be the best place to begin our search.

The next morning, after Melanie had returned from walking the dog, we headed off towards Málaga. When we arrived, I'd never seen so many breakers' yards in one place.

'We might as well start at one end and work our way along,' I suggested.

On a Wednesday morning in February, I couldn't believe how many people were waiting to be served.

'Tuesday must be a popular day for accidents,' I quipped.

We waited our turn, and moved forwards as people were served. I always feel quite nervous in such places. Everyone else always seems to know exactly what they want and, more importantly, what it's called. Clutching the broken door pull I made my enquiry.

'Do you have a handle? It's for a 2003 Renault Megane.'

I'd been eavesdropping on others in an attempt to sound as if I knew what I was talking about.

'*Agarradero*,' said the sales assistant, before heading out into the yard.

I looked at Melanie for any indication she knew what was going on.

'What did he say?' I asked.

'I don't know.'

Regional accents or local colloquialisms can often result in misunderstandings or confusion; add to that a one-word response and he could have said anything. We decided to step to one side and allow others to be served. As time ticked by, I began to wonder if his reply was the kind of language reserved for the nine o'clock watershed. We were just about to give up hope when he returned.

'*No tenemos* (We haven't got one),' he said.

Not the response we were hoping for but at least we'd understood him. I thanked him, as Brits tend to do, and we left.

'Well, that was a waste of time.'

I sensed that Melanie had already had enough. I ignored her comment.

'We might as well walk to the next one.'

Moving the car would only upset Slawit and besides which, the second establishment was right next door, and there was a third one after that. We joined another long queue and waited our turn.

'Do you have a handle? It's for a 2003 Renault Megane,' I asked.

'*Agarradero.*'

My blank expression prompted an explanation.

'*No es un tirador es un agarradero* (It's not a door handle it's a door pull),' he added, before wandering off into the yard.

That cleared that up.

Several minutes later he returned with an entire door card. Not exactly what we were looking for, but beggars can't be choosers.

'How much is it?' I asked.

'Thirty-five.'

At that price it wasn't such a bad deal. I was about to get my wallet out when I spotted a problem. Our door pull was coated with a rubberised finish; the one on the card was completely smooth.

'What do you think?' I asked Melanie.

'We might as well see if we can get the right one. We can always come back if we can't.'

She was right. I thanked him for his efforts but declined his offer.

Would it be third time lucky?

'What did he say it was called?' I whispered to Melanie while we were waiting in the queue.

'*Tsk! Agarradero.*'

If I couldn't remember one word from two minutes ago, what chance did I have of passing the Spanish language exam?

'Do you have a door pull? It's for a 2003 Renault Megane,' I asked, showing him the *agarradero*.

'We should have. Come with me,' he said, gesturing us to join him.

Melanie and I walked around the counter and followed him into the yard. The place was full of vehicles stacked three high in orderly rows. They weren't in any particular order, but he seemed to know where all the Renaults were. Having drawn a blank with the first three vehicles, he had one left to show us. He pulled open the front door and peered inside.

'This is it,' he said, gesturing for me to take a look.

The car might have seen better days, but the interior was in much better condition than ours.

'That's the one, and can I have that as well?'

The door release handle looked almost brand new.

'*La manija?*'

Seemingly none of the handles were *tiradors*.

'That's the one.'

'*Algo más* (Anything else)?' he asked, with a cheeky smile.

'*Nada más* (Nothing else),' I replied.

The two handles or should I say *agarradero* and *manija* came to twenty euro. Time and money well spent, to say nothing of the educational value.

When we got back to the car, Slawit seemed none the worse for her ordeal and, by the end of the day, I'd fitted the new handles and the car looked almost as good as new. At least on the passenger side.

2

You Know Who

One of the things we really look forward to during our winter getaway is an authentic Indian meal. On this trip, we'd discovered the Spice Lounge, one of the best Indian restaurants in the area.

On Saturday evening, we drove down the hill towards the coast for a weekend treat. Unlike UK curry houses of the late 70s, this was a proper restaurant with linen tablecloths, gleaming cutlery, sparkling glasses, and impeccable service. Every dish was cooked to order and prepared in full view of the customers.

We started with poppadoms and pickles before sharing onion bhajis and chicken pakora. For mains, I couldn't resist lamb dopiaza and Melanie had one of her favourites, chicken tikka masala. To accompany the main courses, we shared a Peshwari naan and pilau rice.

Land of Rivers and Trees

'That was delicious,' said Melanie, as we strolled back to the car.

We'd parked on the opposite side of the A-7 to the restaurant and crossed the busy coast road via a footbridge.

'I don't remember the ramp being this steep,' I said, gulping in mouthfuls of night air.

'You weren't as heavy when we arrived.'

She had a point.

On the drive back to the apartment we stopped to let Slawit out to spend a penny and then continued on. A remote control gave us access to the *urbanización* and then into the underground parking area.

'Don't tell me the lift is out of order,' said Melanie.

We'd been waiting for what felt like an eternity, and Slawit was getting restless.

'Stop it!'

With such big ears you'd think she'd be a bit more responsive.

The last thing anyone needs when living in an apartment block is the lift being out of order, more so when you're staying on the top floor and have just eaten an enormous meal.

'Are you sure you pressed the button?' I asked.

'Of course I did.'

I pushed it again to make doubly sure.

'I bet someone has wedged the door open,' I said.

People often cover the light sensor when they're unloading their shopping. We do it ourselves.

'At this time of night?'

Come to think of it, it did sound unlikely.

'Just be patient,' I replied.

We waited and waited, and waited some more.

'It's not coming. You stay here and I'll see if someone has left the door open,' said Melanie.

As appealing as her offer sounded, how would I know if she couldn't find a fault? The last thing either of us wanted was to be climbing up and down stairs.

'I might as well come with you,' I replied.

Melanie unclipped Slawit's lead and she raced off up the stairs. We followed at a more sedate pace. The higher we climbed, the more I regretted eating that last piece of Peshwari naan. Anyone who tells you that oxygen is only required above 8000 feet has never tried climbing eight flights of stairs after a hearty Indian meal, but it could have been worse. On the third floor we bumped into Felipe. Earlier in the evening he'd returned from doing his weekly shopping, half of which was trapped inside the lift. Perhaps next time he'll cover the light sensor.

We never did find out what time the lift was repaired but, the following morning, normal service had been resumed.

On Monday morning I had one thing on my mind.

'I want to get my hair cut today,' I said.

Melanie had returned from walking the dog, and we were sitting on the terrace enjoying breakfast in the sunshine.

'Well, you can do.'

I would have preferred to wait until we got back to Galicia, but it had grown so long it was starting to annoy me.

'If we call at Paco's on our way back from the supermarket will the shopping be OK?' I asked.

We tend to do our weekly shop on a Monday.

'It'll be fine.'

When it comes to getting my hair cut, I'm quite particular. At my age, I guess I should be grateful I've still got some. My stylist in Monforte de Lemos owns a modern unisex salon. It's a clean, bright establishment with a lively buzz. More importantly, she's always done a fabulous job at a great price.

'*Como siempre* (Same as usual)?' she asks, when I take a seat.

It's a very reassuring question that allows me to relax in the sure and certain knowledge she knows exactly how I like it.

While we're away, things are very different. We'd stumbled across Paco's the first time we stayed in Sitio de Calahonda. It's a traditional Spanish barber tucked away in El Zoco, a rather seedy shopping centre in one of the oldest parts of the resort.

It's fair to say that the two establishments couldn't be more different. At Paco's, waiting customers were invited to sit on a threadbare sofa that, if it wasn't salvaged from a skip, should have been, and his one and only barber's chair was so tatty it probably doubled as a dentist's chair at the end of the nineteenth century. Unfiltered fluorescent tubes made the place glaringly bright, and Paco's idea of cleanliness was to sweep hair clippings into a pile in one corner.

However, my biggest concern was Paco's cutting technique. He had a habit of clicking the scissors before, during, and after each cut. It was quite disconcerting and, if I had to guess, I'd say he'd served his apprenticeship under the tutelage of Edward Scissorhands. That aside, he'd always done a reasonable job at a fair price which, in this neck of the woods, couldn't be sniffed at.

That afternoon, we drove along the coast to the Mercadona supermarket in La Cala de Mijas. It's one of the more scenic routes to a supermarket, although we used to enjoy the drive from our home in Huddersfield through the village of Helme to the Safeway supermarket in Meltham. On our way back to the apartment, I parked at the rear of El Zoco and we made our way through the narrow walkways to Paco's. As it turned out, we were in luck; the place was empty.

'*Hola*,' I said, as we entered.

Paco looked up from his phone. I wasn't absolutely certain, but his expression suggested he might have recognised me. This was my third visit, so perhaps that qualified me as a regular. I took a seat in the ripped leather barber's chair and Paco wrapped me in a nylon cape. I'd like to say it was done with all the grace of a seasoned matador, but Paco's demeanour had more in common with a dozing goatherder than a daring bullfighter.

Within seconds of me taking my seat, he'd anointed me with barber's water, and run a comb through my once golden locks. Preparations complete, he commenced. Click, click, click, snip, snip, click, click, click, snip, snip, click, click, click. I forced myself to look in the mirror as tufts of grey hair fell to the floor. Happy with his work, he turned his attention to my eyebrows. The final act of my personal grooming session involved pulling a razor blade from its holder, replacing it with a new one, and removing the fine hairs on the back of my neck. All in all, he'd done a good job. My fringe was slightly longer than I would have liked but, at the risk of being scalped, I decided to keep that to myself. Not exactly who dares wins, but I'd run the gauntlet and survived the ordeal.

'He's done a good job,' said Melanie, but she would say that.

The following evening, we were treated to a magical sunset. The day had started out bright and sunny. We'd enjoyed lunch on the terrace and a stroll along the boardwalk later in the day. On our return, we sat outside to catch the last rays of sunshine.

'Would you like a drink?' I asked.

The time had moved on to 5:00 pm. In a little over an hour, the temperature would start to drop.

'Yes please.'

'White?'

'That would be lovely.'

I pulled the cork on a fruity white wine from the Rueda region. Half an hour later, the sun slipped below the opposite hillside, and lengthening shadows crept across the housing developments below us. Half an hour after that, only the tops of the tallest apartment blocks were still bathed in sunshine. Eventually, even they went dark. At that point, most people would have called it a day and retired inside, but not us. The evening was still young, and we hadn't yet finished the bottle of wine. We zipped up our fleeces and were rewarded with a fabulous display of twilight colours.

As the light faded, tones softened and contrasts intensified. On the distant horizon, bold shapes emerged. Swathed in lilac, the Rif Mountains of Africa began to appear, framed against a graduated backdrop of peaches and pinks. The colours alone were stunning, but staring out across the Mediterranean Sea on a hidden continent felt quite surreal. It was an incredible sight, and one we will forever associate with our winter breaks on the Costa del Sol.

'Philip and Lesley have invited us for drinks and nibbles,' said Melanie.

'Who?'

'Philip and Lesley. You know who they are.'

Why do people assume that if they know who they're talking about, you will?

'Have I seen them?'

'No, but you know who I mean.'

There she goes again.

'Philip's always leaning over his balcony smoking a cigarette,' she added.

If that was a clue, the answer eluded me.

'I've told you about him. He's always there, every time I take Slawit for a walk.'

If I wasn't mistaken, there was a hint of annoyance in Melanie's tone. Failure to acknowledge who she was talking about would imply a previous lack of attention. I concluded that discretion was the better part of valour, and gave my memory the benefit of the doubt.

'Ah – yes, I know who you mean.'

'Well, Lesley is his wife.'

A blank expression prompted another explanation.

'You know, the woman I speak to at the dog park who sometimes gives me a lift back. That's his wife and she's invited us round for drinks and nibbles.'

Piecing together Melanie's ramblings was like finding the answer to a cryptic clue.

'Are they the couple from Newcastle?' I asked.

'That's the ones.'

'Why didn't you say that? Anyway when?'

'When what?'

'When have we been invited round?'

'Tonight.'

It seemed I didn't get a say in the matter.

'Where do they live?'

'Here, in block one. Don't you listen to anything I tell you?'

Talk about a loaded question. I had no intention of shooting myself in the foot.

'What time?'

'About seven.'

I could only hope that their interpretation of drinks and nibbles was better than the last such event we'd attended. On that occasion, the drinks had flowed freely but the nibbles were limited to peanuts, crisps and a large bowl of hummus which instantly became off-limits when one of the hosts turned out to be a double-dipper.

At five minutes to seven, the three of us made the short walk from block three to block one. If that makes the place sound like a WWII prisoner of war camp, nothing could be further from the truth. The security here prevented people from breaking in, not out.

Even though I'd never met her, Lesley greeted me like a long-lost family member, and although Slawit had never been to the apartment before, her nose led her straight into the kitchen.

'Slawit, come here,' called Melanie.

'She's alright. Go through, Philip's on the terrace,' said Lesley.

Philip was equally friendly, which didn't surprise me: northerners have a reputation for being hospitable.

In contrast to our apartment, they'd created a comfortable, contemporary home.

'Daisy, get down,' called Lesley.

Daisy was their adorable, if somewhat lively, fox terrier who had decided to commandeer the sofa.

When it comes to socialising, Slawit is something of a loner but, despite both dogs being bitches and Slawit having just emptied Daisy's food bowl, the two dogs got on like a house on fire.

My reservation about the nibbles proved ill-founded. As a former restaurant owner, Lesley had put on a fabulous spread including: quiche, pork pies, chicken wings, slices of pizza, garlic bread, crisps, chorizo, and a selection of cheeses. There was also a tub of hummus and fingers of pita bread but, unlike the previous event, the correct etiquette was followed at all times.

Philip and Lesley were great hosts, and we could hardly believe it when the clock chimed four in the morning.

'We really must go,' I said.

That's when we realised Philip had already taken himself off to bed.

'Thank you ever so much, and the next time you must come to us,' said Melanie.

That night we slept like logs, but such nocturnal activities rarely go unpunished, and so it proved. The following morning, I felt like my consciousness had been transplanted into a very ill person.

'I've had an email from Tony and Margaret; they want to know if we'd like to meet up before we go home.'

We first met Tony and Margaret when they'd stayed at the rental property we used to manage for our friends Bob and Janet, and then again when they stayed at *Campo Verde*. Over the last three years, they'd spent March and April holidaying on the Costa del Sol, arriving in the area a few days before we leave and, with the exception of last year when the blown cylinder head gasket scuppered our plans, we'd always met up.

'That would be nice. When do they get here?'

'On Thursday the 23rd.'

We were heading back to Galicia three days later.

'I thought about asking them to come here for a drink and then going for lunch in Cabo Pino,' I added.

That was the plan last year before car problems had forced us to cancel.

'When?'

I wanted to leave Saturday free for packing which left Friday. The following day, I heard back from Tony. They would love to meet up.

'I'd better make some biscuits,' said Melanie.

'Biscuits?'

'Don't you remember? Margaret always has a plate of bourbons and custard creams when we go to theirs.'

How could I forget; they were a rare and much appreciated treat.

Late on Friday morning, they arrived as planned.

'This is lovely,' remarked Margaret.

I sensed they were slightly envious of our view.

'We thought we'd go to Cabo Pino for lunch,' I said.

Cabo Pino is a small but exclusive marina located between Sitio de Calahonda and Marbella. It's home to Albert's, an upmarket burger restaurant. Choosing where to eat is a delicate balancing act, especially when you don't know your guests that well. Menu, price, and location are all vital. As far as we knew, neither Tony nor Margaret had any special dietary requirements, which is always a help. The view from Albert's dining area was spectacular and, although it wasn't the cheapest place along the coast, neither was it the most expensive. All we could do was hope for the best. Having caught up on news, we made the short drive along the coast.

When we arrived, they seemed very impressed with the surroundings; the service was great, and the food delicious. In short, it couldn't have gone any better. We later discovered that they'd returned on their own, which told us everything we needed to know.

Two days after that, we were up at the crack of dawn and on the road by 7:05 am. Even at that time of day the A-7 coast road was busy. It's always a little sad to be leaving our winter retreat and, although the weather hadn't been the best, we'd had a fabulous time. With our batteries recharged, we were ready to face the year ahead.

Our biggest concern was the low volume of enquiries we'd had for our holiday rental property,

Campo Verde. Over the year, the holiday letting industry had changed beyond recognition and we didn't like its direction of travel. Traditionally, the majority of our bookings came between Christmas and the end of the first week in January, stimulated in part by the increased number of holiday adverts on TV. So far this year it had been very disappointing. To date, we'd had just three enquiries, none of which had so far resulted in a booking.

'What are we going to do about the house?' I asked.

'I don't know. What can we do?'

'Perhaps we should put it on the market and do something else.'

We'd spoken about it on numerous occasions over the last few years and, now more than ever, delaying a decision could have long-lasting implications.

'Like what?'

'Perhaps we could renovate another house and sell it,' I suggested.

I'd been looking online at what was available. Supply wouldn't be an issue; there were plenty of properties for sale in Galicia. The problem would be finding one we could make money on. In most parts of Spain, purchase tax and sales tax make it very difficult to profit from buying and selling property. The situation hadn't been helped by the UK's decision to leave the European Union, although exactly when that would be was anyone's guess.

In the wake of last year's referendum, the UK parliament had been in a state of paralysis. Strong cross-party opposition had thwarted the government's attempts to leave at any cost, but it was only a matter of time before the lunatics took over the asylum.

When that happened, I suspected sales of Spanish homes to British buyers would fall through the floor. Rumours had been circulating that non-resident owners would only be allowed to remain in the country for a maximum of 90 days in any 180. As for those dreaming of living here, strict visa conditions and increased income requirements would make it nigh on impossible for all but the most wealthy. No one told that to the masses when they were voting to leave.

The conversation had come to a natural conclusion. As with most things, postponing a decision was the easy option but, unless the situation improved, we couldn't put it off forever.

Something we could agree on was the need to get the telephone reconnected. We'd had to jump through all manner of hoops to get it installed, only to find we didn't need it, but a rural property with a working landline would be a major selling point should we decide to sell.

Ten hours and five minutes after leaving Sitio de Calahonda, we were back home in the land of rivers and trees. All in all, we'd had a good run. The morning mist had stayed with us until we'd reached the outskirts of Madrid but, from that point on, the sun came out and we couldn't have wished for better driving conditions. Slawit had been awake for most of the journey, sitting bolt upright on the back seat. As soon as I let her out, she chased around the garden with her nose to the ground and tail in the air, eager to discover who'd been trespassing in her absence.

Once unpacked, we retired to the far end of the garden with a glass of wine to watch the sun setting behind the woody knoll. Perhaps returning home wasn't that bad after all. Within half an hour of it setting, plummeting temperatures forced us inside.

'There's a leak in the laundry room.'

Melanie had been outside to put on a load of washing before we went to bed. If the idea of having a laundry room sounds pretentious, think again. As well as housing a washing machine and dryer, it also has a toilet and wash basin for anyone caught short while swimming. As such, it started life as the outside bog until Melanie mentioned it to her granny. Back in her day, an outside lavvy was the only convenience most homes had. To avoid any confusion we decided to rebrand it.

'What kind of leak?'

'Doh! A water leak.'

I really should try to engage my brain before opening my mouth.

I ignored her sarcasm and went outside to investigate. Melanie followed me out. I'd suspected something like this might happen after reading the newspaper article about the river in Monforte de Lemos freezing over. I'd wondered then if Jack Frost would leave us his calling card. When I opened the door, the floor was covered in water.

'Where do you…'

'Ssh!' I said.

I'd never find the leak if I couldn't hear where it was coming from.

There were three possible causes: the washing machine, the toilet, or the wash basin. I started with the easiest, the basin. It didn't take me long to spot a dribble of water running down the flexible hose connecting the stopcock to the tap.

'Found it. It's either the hose or the tap that's leaking.'

'Can you fix it?'

I could, but it was a bit late to be starting now. Fortunately, most Spanish homes have an independent stopcock for every piece of bathroom furniture or domestic appliance. Personally, I think it's plumbing overkill, but they do come in handy in situations like this. Rather than shutting off the water, I could isolate the offending article.

'I'll shut the stopcock and take a look at it in the morning,' I said.

When I tried to turn the small shut-off handle it wouldn't move.

'What's the matter?' asked Melanie.

'This cock's stuck.'

'I beg your pardon.'

The last thing I needed was a comedian.

'It's nothing a pair of pliers won't shift,' I said, barging past her.

My tools were next door in the shed.

'These should do the trick,' I said, holding them up like an Olympic torchbearer.

I stepped back into the puddle and leant around the back of the wash basin. As I turned the handle, the plastic fixing broke.

'Bugger!'

'What's happened?'

'It's snapped off,' I said, showing her the evidence.

The look on Melanie's face said it all. "These things don't snap off on their own." What had started out as a something-and-nothing job had suddenly become a much more complicated task requiring the services of a plumber.

'What are we going to do now?' asked Melanie.

Ironically, turning the stopcock was much easier without the plastic handle.

That night, when I switched off the bedroom light, I couldn't help thinking how quickly our homecoming welcome had turned into an unwelcome return.

3

Repairs and Renewals

Galicia's weather is nothing if not unpredictable. Within hours of our return, it had changed from bright and sunny to overcast and wet.

'That didn't last long,' remarked Melanie, as she nudged open the bedroom door carrying two mugs of steaming coffee.

'What didn't?'

'The weather.'

Slawit wasn't bothered about that. She ran past Melanie and leapt onto the bed to claim her morning treats, clearly none the worse for yesterday's long drive home. Having drunk our coffees, Melanie took Slawit out for her morning walk, and I made a start in the laundry room.

Over the years, this outside storage facility had become a dumping ground for everything we didn't really want, but were reluctant to throw away. A clear-out was long overdue. Anything worth saving I placed under the porch out of the rain. The rest I dumped on the gravel outside the laundry room. By the time Melanie returned, the garden was littered with junk.

'I'm back,' she called, from the kitchen door.

'Do we need all this stuff?' I said, pointing at the pile of rubbish.

Given the look on her face, anyone would have thought I'd accused her of hoarding.

'What stuff?' she snapped.

The evidence was staring her in the face.

'This, for example.'

'What is it?'

'An inflatable banana that's been burst for at least five years.'

'How do you know it's burst?'

'Look,' I said, showing her an eight-inch gash down the seam.

'*Tsk!* Well, that's no good. It needs throwing out. I hope you're going to clear all that up when you've finished,' she said, before going back into the kitchen and closing the door behind her.

After a thorough inspection, I concluded that the only leak was coming from the wash basin.

'It's just this that's leaking,' I said, showing Melanie the flexible hose.

'I'm not surprised. It must be at least twenty years old.'

During the renovations, we'd bought all new bathroom furniture and fittings but, in an effort to save money, we reused the old toilet and wash basin in the laundry room.

'Can you ring Ramón and see if he can call in?' I asked.

Had I not broken the stopcock, it would have been an easy fix. Now we needed the services of our go-to plumber, Ramón. Melanie made the call.

'He can't come until Wednesday,' she said, holding her hand over the receiver.

'That's fine. We're not in a rush.'

After three months away, there are plenty of jobs to do on our return. Top of the list was the car's annual roadworthy test or ITV (Inspección Técnica de Vehículos).

Before making an appointment at the test centre, the old girl needed two new tyres, and brake discs and pads on the front. We'd always used Neumáticos Novoa in Monforte de Lemos for tyres and the Renault main dealer for mechanical repairs, but we'd come to the conclusion that main dealer servicing was a waste of money. It wasn't that they'd ever done a bad job; we'd actually been very happy with their work, but main dealer servicing came at a price, and our fourteen-year-old car no longer merited that kind of expense.

When I'd first mooted the idea of finding somewhere new, Melanie suggested our neighbour Toño might be able to help. He and his twin brother operate an automotive repair shop on the industrial estate on the outskirts of Monforte de Lemos. I use the term automotive because they'll work on just about anything from high-performance production cars to family saloons and tractors to buses. If it's got an engine, they'll fix it, but it's fair to say I was more than a little apprehensive about switching. Toño's son, Diego, also worked with them as a mechanic, but what tipped the scales in their favour was their willingness to pick up and drop off, a major consideration when you're a one-car family.

In an effort to keep costs down, I'd decided to source the brakes myself and ask Toño to fit them when they serviced the car. Genuine Renault parts would cost a small fortune, but our friend Roy had recommended an online parts stockist called Euro Car Parts. Having browsed their website, I was struck by how many different brakes were available for a Renault Megane. To avoid ordering the wrong parts, I needed to take a closer look at the existing ones.

'I'm just going to check which brakes we need,' I said, before slipping outside.

Try as I might, I couldn't see a thing. The wheel would have to come off. I began by wedging a stone under one of the rear wheels to make sure the car didn't roll off the jack. Having loosened the wheel nuts, I jacked up the car, unscrewed the nuts, and removed the wheel. That gave me unrestricted access to the disc and pads and, more importantly, their serial numbers. I jotted them down before refitting the wheel. The final job was to tighten the wheel nuts. Everything was going fine until the very last one. Using all the force I could muster, I pushed down on the wheel brace only for it to slip off the nut sending me crashing headfirst into the wing. If that wasn't bad enough, I scratched my glasses in the process. I was furious with myself.

'Look what I've done,' I said, holding out my glasses.

'What?'
'I've scratched the lens.'
'How did you do that?'
I explained.

'Are you alright?'

Apart from my wounded pride and a lump on the head, I was fine. As for my glasses, why is it they never fit properly after you've knocked them?

'Did you find what you were looking for?' she asked.

'I hope so.'

Only time would tell if the parts I needed matched the serial numbers I'd found.

'When you get a minute, can you take a look at the kitchen tap?' asked Melanie.

'Why, what's matter with it?'

'It's really stiff.'

When choosing the kitchen, Melanie had gone for a double sink rather than one with a drainer, and a giraffe-neck mixer tap to swivel between the two.

'I'll order these parts and then take a look.'

'OK.'

As luck would have it, the serial numbers matched the parts I needed, and both discs and pads were in stock. Delivery would take up to forty-eight hours. All we needed now were two new tyres. As soon as I'd sorted the tap, we could nip into Monforte de Lemos to get a price.

'Right then, let's take a look at this tap.'

'Did you get everything you needed?'

'I did. They should be here in a couple of days.'

Talk about an unstoppable force meeting an immovable object. The tap was stuck solid. At that point I should have conceded defeat and asked Ramón to take a look at it when he came to replace the stopcock, but I just couldn't help myself. I had to try and fix it.

'I'm going to have to take it off,' I said.

While I gathered some tools, Melanie emptied the cupboards under the sink. When I came back, the kitchen floor was littered with every household chemical known to man. I don't know what it is about Melanie and cleaning products, but she can't resist trying anything new.

Lying on a cold tiled floor with my shoulders resting on the inside of the sink unit and my arms raised above my head was hardly the most comfortable working position. I began by turning off the stopcocks to both hot and cold water but, when I loosened the nuts on the flexible hoses, water dribbled down my arms. Why is it that a thimbleful of liquid feels more like a pint? Disconnecting the hoses and unscrewing the retaining nut allowed me to access the horseshoe-shaped retaining plate. Having removed that, I could finally extricate myself from the sink unit and take a look at the tap but, in a momentary lapse of concentration, I fumbled the retaining plate and watched in horror as it fell down the back of the sink unit. Why oh why hadn't I waited for Ramón?

'I've dropped the plate.'

'What plate?'

'The plate that holds the tap onto the sink.'

'Don't you have another?'

'No, they're specific to this job.'

'Where has it gone?'

'Down the back of the unit.'

I couldn't believe I'd been so careless.

'Does one of these splashboards come off?' I asked.

The splashboards at the base of the kitchen units are made of the same marble as the worktops. From memory, one of them could be removed to provide access to the dishwasher. If I could get underneath the units, I might be able to fish it out.

'It's that one,' said Melanie, pointing at a small length of marble directly below the appliance.

Thank heavens for that.

With the aid of a screwdriver I teased it out, only to find the space for the dishwasher was independent of all the kitchen units. My day was going from bad to worse.

'Do you think Otero's will sell them?'

Why I thought Melanie would know was anyone's guess.

'I don't know.'

'We'll call in when we go to get a price for the tyres.'

'If we're going into town, can you drop me at the supermarket?'

'Of course. If you do that, I'll go to Otero's and then pick you up. We'll call at the tyre place on our way home,' I suggested.

Trying to take anything positive out of this fiasco was stretching it, but at least we could kill three birds with one stone.

'What would you like for lunch?' asked Melanie.

'Is it that time already?'

Choices were limited as we hadn't yet done a weekly shop, but you can't go far wrong with beans on toast. While the beans bubbled and the bread toasted, I dismantled the tap and discovered a worn rubber washer was the most likely cause for its lack of movement. One more item to add to the shopping list.

At four o'clock we headed into town. I dropped Melanie at the supermarket and then drove on to Otero's builder's merchant. The staff couldn't have been more helpful and, although they didn't sell individual retaining plates, an entire replacement kit, including the plate, was only €2.90.

'Do you have one of these?' I asked, showing him the worn rubber washer.

'I'm afraid not.'

That was a shame.

When I collected Melanie, she suggested the *ferretería* in Sober might have one.

'We'll drop in on the way back.'

Our next port of call was Neumáticos Novoa.

'I'll have to order them, but if you call back tomorrow morning, I'll be able to fit them while you wait,' said the owner, Diego.

That was Diego the tyre fitter, not to be confused with Diego the mechanic.

'How much are they?'

'How does ninety euro sound?'

We'd been buying tyres from Diego for over a decade, and in all that time the price for Michelin 205/55R16 tyres hadn't changed. The first time we'd bought them they were the best price in town. I could only imagine they were even better value now.

'We'll take them. What time in the morning?' I asked.

'*A las nueve, más o menos* (Nine o'clock, more or less).'

We agreed to call back first thing in the morning.

'I'm not looking forward to that,' I said, on the drive home.

'What?'

'Hanging around in Diego's while he fits the tyres.'

Diego's workshop was like most tyre fitting places: open to the elements all year round with a windowless waiting room which, at this time of year, was colder than the inside of a fridge.

'There's no point in both of us going. I'll do that and then I can take Slawit for a walk while I'm waiting,' said Melanie.

'Are you sure?'

'Certain.'

I felt a bit guilty but she was right; there was no point in both of us hanging around in a windowless fridge when she could be out walking the dog, and I could stay at home and get some editing done.

Before going home, we called at the *ferretería* in Sober. Melanie's suggestion was spot on: they had exactly what I needed.

'How much?' I asked.

'Five cents.'

Back home I wasted no time reassembling the tap. By the time I'd finished, it twisted and turned like a fairground waltzer. All I had to do then was refit it to the sink without dropping the retaining plate.

'There you go; as good as new,' I said proudly.

'Excellent!'

It might have taken me all day but, at a total cost of €2.95, I couldn't have been happier.

Later that evening, Melanie was in the kitchen preparing dinner, and I was in the lounge setting up the laptop in readiness for an evening of *Inspector Frost* DVDs, all of which we'd seen numerous times before.

'Have you put the sprinklers on?' called Melanie.

My heart sank. Of course I hadn't. At this time of year, Mother Nature provides more than enough water for the lawns.

'No,' I replied.

'Well, they're on.'

The programmer for the sprinklers was housed in a control box mounted on the boundary wall in the front garden. I went outside to investigate. Imagine my horror when I discovered yet another leak, one more victim of Jack Frost's cold snap. A quick inspection revealed that the borehole pressure gauge was to blame and, unlike the wash basin, stopping the leak would mean shutting off the entire water supply. Talk about bad luck.

I glanced at the time: 7:15 pm. Since the plumber's merchant in Monforte de Lemos stopped trading, the only other place that might have a replacement was Otero's and, from memory, they closed at 8:00 pm. I wasn't certain they'd stock them but, if I wanted to find out, there wasn't a moment to lose.

'We've got a leak.'

'Not another, where?'

'The pressure gauge in the control box. I'm going to have to turn the water off.'

'You're joking.'

'I was wondering if Otero's might have one.'

'Will they be open?'

'I'm not sure. I think they close at eight.'

Time was of the essence and standing around discussing the matter wasn't helping. I switched off the electricity supply to the water pump and unscrewed the broken pressure gauge.

'Right then, I'm off.'

'Can I come?'

'If you want.'

'Well, I can't do anything without water.'

'Come on then.'

We made it to Otero's with less than ten minutes to spare. Thankfully, they had exactly what I needed and it was only €2.50.

'Will you need some of that tape?' asked Melanie.

She was referring to PTFE, or plumber's tape. It's one of those items you almost feel obliged to buy whenever you're doing a plumbing job, but I was confident I'd have a few partly used rolls knocking about in the shed, and I knew exactly where to find them.

By the time we got back home, darkness had consumed the earlier twilight. My first job was to locate some PTFE tape. As I'd suspected, tucked away in the shed along with other plumbing related items were five rolls, two of which hadn't even been opened.

Used correctly, plumber's tape provides a watertight seal between threaded joints, or in this case, the pressure gauge and its housing. The secret is to wind the tape anticlockwise around the thread. Failure to do that will cause it to unravel when you tighten up the joint. To avoid making a mistake, I prepared the pressure gauge in the shed. From that point on, I'd be working in the dark.

'Will you hold the torch for me?' I asked.

I handed it to Melanie and she followed me outside.

'Keep it steady.'

'I am doing!'

I bit my lip. Another word out of me and I'd be holding it myself.

In the trembling light of an underpowered torch, I finally managed to screw the gauge into its housing. Then for the moment of truth.

'I think that's it. Can you nip inside and flick the power back on?' I asked.

If it did start to leak, I wanted to be on hand to react. Melanie handed me the torch and went inside. Moments later the front door opened.

'Are you ready?' she called.

'Ready when you are.'

'OK, it's on.'

As the water pressure built, the electronic switching mechanism clicked on and then off.

'It's as dry as a bone,' I called, triumphantly.

Our first day back had been a mixed bag of disasters, from a leaking hose to a broken stopcock, a stiff mixer tap to a lost retaining plate, and a scratched pair of glasses to a leaking pressure gauge. As the saying goes, things could only get better.

4

The Price Is Right

I'm not sure what's worse, a wailing alarm clock or the sound of rainwater gurgling down the drainpipe. By the time we go out of bed, the rain had stopped, but I suspected it would be short-lived.

'Are you sure you don't want me to come with you?' I asked, as Melanie readied Slawit for their trip into town.

'Certain.'

No sooner had she left than it started raining again. I waited for it to stop before checking the pressure gauge for leaks. Thankfully, the control box was as dry as a bone. Perhaps from now on I should do all maintenance jobs in the dead of night by torchlight, but then again...

As a consequence of fighting fires, or in this case repairing leaks, asking Movistar to reconnect the telephone at *Campo Verde* had fallen down our list of priorities. Before starting work on the book, I decided to put that right.

Two and a half hours after setting off, Melanie and Slawit were back home.

'I rang Movistar while you were out,' I said.

'That's good, what did they say?'

'It shouldn't be a problem. Someone will ring us when they can do it. There's something else.'

'What?'

'Have you noticed the pool pump running since we've been back?'

In an effort to stop unwanted algae forming in the swimming pool, we keep the pump running while we're away. It operates on a timer and runs three times a day for a total of five hours in every twenty-four. I hadn't given it much thought since we'd been back, but I couldn't remember hearing it running or seeing the rippling effect on the water.

'Erm no, I can't say I have,' replied Melanie.

I went outside to take a closer look. Switching the pump from automatic to manual had no effect. If I wasn't mistaken, something similar had happened previously, but the harder I tried to recall, the less I could remember. The most likely cause was an electrical gremlin but, for the time being, resolving this issue would have to wait. I'd ask Ramón to take a look tomorrow when he came to replace the stopcock and leaking hose.

Shrove Tuesday is one of those dates I always forget but never tire of. It conjures up childhood memories of warm cosy evenings in Yorkshire sitting at the dining table eating pancakes. After dinner

Melanie made a bowl of batter and heated a frying pan. It doesn't matter how old I get; I can't resist warm pancakes drizzled with Lyle's Golden Syrup. Nowadays, a gentle squeeze dispenses a precise measure of liquid sweetness. Back in the day, we used to dip a tablespoon into that famous green and gold tin, scoop out a dribbling orb of loveliness, and create swirling patterns over the pancakes.

The following morning, we hadn't been awake half an hour when the phone rang. Melanie raced into the lounge just in time to catch the caller.

'That was Ramón. He'll call in at 3:30,' said Melanie.

Five minutes later, he sent a WhatsApp asking for photos of the offending articles. I suspected he wanted to know which parts to order.

'Can we go up to the post office after breakfast?' asked Melanie.

'Of course.'

While we're away, the postlady puts our mail to one side and we collect it on our return. If there's anything to sign for, she takes it to our accountant, Paula. It's one of the many benefits of living in a small community where everyone knows everyone else, and nothing is too much trouble.

After being away for thirteen weeks, the only mail we had was three bills, two Christmas cards, and a marketing mailshot.

Back home, I booted up the computer and checked my inbox. One message caught my eye. It had been sent the previous evening, and the subject line read "visit to Galicia". Curious to know more, I opened the message.

From: Deborah XXXXX
Sent: 28 February 20:17
To: Craig Briggs
Subject: visit to Galicia

Dear Craig

I read all three of your books recently after we decided we were interested in moving to Spain; I visited Galicia once many years ago in the 90s, but I haven't been back since and we are really looking forward to coming next weekend.

My partner and I are booked into the Parador hotel in Monforte de Lemos. Like many who come to Galicia, we are entertaining the idea of a move. Am I right in thinking you are not a real estate agent? I know you have a rental property yourself but I wasn't sure at the end of your last book if you were considering making real estate a broader vocation.

In any case, we wouldn't mind looking around and I wonder if you can recommend any one realtor in particular. I love the idea of living in the Ribeira Sacra because of the microclimate and we'd like to get a feel for the lay of the land when we come this weekend. The websites that look interesting are Galicia Rustica and Galicia Vista but I'm sure you know what's what.

Any advice you can give or thoughts you may have will be much appreciated.

Many thanks!
Deb and Hugo

When it comes to responding to these types of enquiries, I have something of a reputation.

'I've had an email from a reader,' I said.

'A fan?'

Melanie likes to tease.

'That's right, a fan.'

'And what did they have to say?'

'She said that her and her partner are coming to Monforte this weekend, and staying at the Parador.'

'Very nice.'

'They're thinking of moving here and are coming to view some properties.'

'Really.'

'Yes, and she wanted to know if I could recommend an estate agent.'

'Are you going to?'

'I thought I would; it can't do any harm.'

'Why don't you offer them *Campo Verde*?'

'Do you think so?'

'I'm joking.'

Joke or not, Melanie's comment got me thinking. I sauntered back into the office to compose my response.

From: Craig Briggs
Sent: 1 March 12:28
To: xxxxxxxxx@xxxx.com
Subject: re: visit to Galicia

Dear Deborah

It's always nice to hear from readers, particularly those considering a move to the area. When we first moved here, almost fifteen years ago, I briefly considered becoming an estate agent; that idea quickly faded. You will know from my books that we have bought three properties altogether, two from local agents and one directly from the owner. We live in the first one, sold the second, and rent out the third one, but property tycoons we are not.

Giving advice is always difficult. Obviously, I've heard of the two agents you mentioned, but I have no specific knowledge of either. As far as I'm aware, neither specialise in properties within the Ribeira Sacra. The two local agents we have used are Laybe and Monfortina, and I'm happy to recommend them both. Their offices are within walking distance of the Parador. Neither has changed very much since we used them ten years ago, but they are both Spanish speaking. There are also a number of other estate agencies in Monforte de Lemos.

Unfortunately, the weekend is a particularly bad time for viewing property. Most shops and all the agents will be closed from lunchtime Saturday until Monday morning. Sunday trading hasn't yet reached this quiet backwater.

The weather forecast during your stay doesn't look good, but don't let that put you off. At the moment, we are still in the throes of winter but, by the end of this month, the countryside will come alive as everything bursts into bloom.

If you need any help during your stay, to bridge the language barrier or just to get some inside information, please don't hesitate to get in touch. We'd be happy to help.

Wishing you the best of luck.
Craig and Melanie

Before sending it, I asked Melanie to take a look.

'What do you think?' I asked.

'We'd be happy to help, would we?'

She was joking, of course.

'Lunch will be ready when you've sent it,' she added.

I assumed that meant it had her seal of approval.

Isn't it always the case; we'd just sat down for lunch when a blast on a horn signalled a delivery. I went outside to meet the driver.

'*Señor* Bricks?' he asked.

'*Si*,' I replied.

I opened the gate and he handed me a package. The weight took me by surprise and I almost dropped it. If I wasn't mistaken, the new brake discs and pads had arrived.

'What is it?' asked Melanie, when I stepped inside.

'I think it's the brakes.'

'That was quick.'

'We'll nip down to Toño's after lunch and book the car in for a service.'

Melanie glanced at the clock.

'Let's go now; he'll definitely be home, but he might not have started eating.'

We're not keen on interrupting our neighbours at lunchtime. It tends to be their main meal of the day when the whole family get together. Too early and people are eating; too late and they're having a siesta.

'Come on then,' I said.

Pilar, Toño's wife, answered the door and called him. It was clear that they'd already started eating.

'Sorry to interrupt your lunch, but we were wondering if you could service the car for us,' I said.

'No problem. Bring it down tomorrow at 2:30,' he replied.

Toño would take it to work with him and drop it off that evening on his way home. Now that's what I call service.

We hadn't been home long when the phone rang.

'That was Ramón. He's going to be late,' said Melanie.

'How late?'

'About 4:30.'

When he arrived, he wasted no time replacing the stopcock. Watching him work, I was glad I'd left it to him. Using plumber's tape is one thing, but I draw the line at horse hair. Ten minutes after arriving, he'd changed the stopcock and replaced the leaking hose. Once again, the wash basin was leak-free and watertight.

'Could you take a look at the pool pump while you're here?' I asked.

'What's wrong with it?'

'It won't switch on.'

A few minutes later, he'd diagnosed the problem as a faulty condenser.

'I'll have to order one. I'll give you a call when I've got it.'

On that note he packed up his tools and headed back to his van.

'What about a bill?' I asked.

'Pay me when I come back.'

Whether it's plumbers, builders, decorators, or electricians, when it comes to paying tradesmen, they're all the same. No one wants to take your money.

The next morning, when I opened my inbox, Deborah had replied to my email. She thanked me for the information and our offer to help, but I got the impression they wanted to go it alone, an admirable quality for anyone hoping to make a new life abroad.

At 2:30 pm we dropped the car off at Toño's.

'If you need a car, you can use mine,' he said.

We graciously declined, but his neighbourly gesture went above and beyond. In all the years we'd been taking the car to Renault, they'd never offered us a courtesy car. Shortly after nine, he dropped it off.

'How much do I owe you?' I asked, pulling out my wallet.

'I'm not sure. I'll get Diego to call you.'

I guess I should add motor mechanics to that list of reluctant tradesmen.

Later that evening Melanie's phone pinged.

'This is from Diego.'

She paused to read the message.

'How much were you expecting it to be?' she asked.

If we'd taken the car to Renault, a full service would have cost somewhere in the region of 350 euro. Add to that new brake discs, pads, and the outrageously expensive labour cost and I doubt we would have had much change from 500 euro. Surely it would be less than that.

'I don't know, how much is it?'

'Guess.'

I suspected Melanie was teasing so went low.

'Two hundred and fifty.'

'Less.'

'Two hundred.'

'Less.'

'One hundred and fifty.'

'Less.'

'Less than one hundred and fifty euro. I don't know then; how much is it?'

'Thirty euro.'

If Melanie was yanking my chain, she was doing a good job of hiding it. Even taking into account the cost of the parts, we'd saved ourselves an absolute fortune.

Within twenty-four hours of collecting our mail, the postlady was outside the house tooting her horn. Melanie was walking the dog, so I went out to meet her. We do have a mailbox mounted on the gatepost, but she prefers the personal touch. Either that or she can't be bothered to get out of the car.

'*Hola, buenos días* (Good morning),' I said.

'*Para ti* (For you),' she said, handing me two envelopes through the open window.

'*Gracias* (Thank you).'

I recognised the sender immediately; only the council could apply self-adhesive labels so badly. Before I'd walked back to the house, I opened one of them. My suspicion proved correct. This weekend the council were hosting a free-to-attend concert in the *casa de cultura*. For reasons known only to them, every time they host such an event, both Melanie and I receive exactly the same notification.

'There's a letter for you on the table,' I said, on Melanie's return.

'Yes, I saw it.'

'Aren't you going to open it?'

'Don't tell me, there's a concert at the *casa de cultura*.'

The envelope was unmistakable.

'That's right.'

'Who's playing?'

'It's a pianist from Madrid. Would you like to go?'

'Would you?'

'Why not. Let's ask Roy and Maria if they'd like to join us.'

'OK. It's a pity Parada Dos has closed down; we could have made a night of it.'

Last year, one of our favourite restaurants, and the only eatery in Sober, closed down when the owners retired.

'What about going to Bar Ribeira Sacra for tapas?' I suggested.

Bar Ribeira Sacra sits in the heart of the village, a short walk from the auditorium.

'That's an excellent idea. I'll ring Maria after breakfast.'

Maria seemed keen to meet up. After a long Galician winter, even a piano recital sounds exciting.

'Are we going down to Toño's this lunchtime?' asked Melanie.

'What for?'

'To pay the bill.'

'That's a good idea, but I want to go for a quick test drive first.'

As lunchtime approached, we drove up to Sober.

'How does it feel?' asked Melanie.

'The brakes are fine, but look,' I said, pointing at the dashboard.

Melanie leant across. The fuel injection service light had lit up. I doubted it had anything to do with the service, but we needed to get it sorted before the ITV test.

When I showed Toño he wasn't sure what was causing it, but he said he'd get Diego to call at the house and take a look. It wasn't until we got home that I realised we'd forgotten to pay him. Shortly after lunch, Diego called in.

'It's probably something and nothing, but I'll have to hook it up to the laptop. Can you bring it to the workshop on Monday?' he asked.

'No problem. There's one more thing, I forgot to pay your dad earlier,' I said, reaching for my wallet.

'Give it to me on Monday,' he said.

Foiled again.

That afternoon I booked the car in for its ITV: 2:30 pm on Tuesday. Time was short and we had no idea what the consequences of missing the test might be.

The weekend marked a change in the weather from damp and overcast to frosty and clear. With a bit of luck, I'd soon be able to prune the grapevines. It's the main reason we return at this time of year, but I prefer not to do it in the rain. Once finished, I'd be able to spray them with pesticide to prevent beetles from eating the new buds.

'I'm going to nip up to the wine shop and get some more of this,' I said, holding out an empty pesticide bottle.

'What is it?'

'That stuff to stop the beetles eating the vine buds.'

'Don't you prune them first?'

'Yes, but I'm hoping to make a start next week.'

'OK, will you need me?'

'No, I'll be fine.'

EnoGalicia specialises in products and services for the winemaking industry, and is housed in a former pharmacy close to the town hall in Sober. If you didn't know it was there, you'd probably walk straight past it. I pushed open the door and stepped inside. The owner was working in the stockroom at the rear.

'*Hola,*' I called.

He looked up and came into the shop.

'Have you got some of this?' I asked, showing him the empty container.

'Do you have a card?'

'A card?'

'*Una tarjeta de productos fitosanitarios,*' he said, pulling a plastic card out of his wallet and sliding it across the counter.

I shook my head; I'd never seen one before. In an effort to comply with EU regulations, the government had introduced a registration scheme for anyone wishing to purchase or handle agricultural products such as pesticides and herbicides. Without the card, only small quantities of a limited number of products could be purchased. Fortunately, the minimum quantity for this particular product would allow me to treat the vines this year but, with an eye on the future, I would definitely need to get my hands on *una tarjeta de productos fitosanitarios.*

'How do I get one?' I asked.

'You have to take a course at the agricultural college in Monforte de Lemos. Do you know where it is?'

I didn't, but his instructions seemed clear enough. I made my purchase and thanked him for his insight. Back home I explained my findings to Melanie and then checked online to ensure I'd understood him correctly, which I had. The implications of these new regulations were stark. Without a card I would struggle to get the essential supplies I needed to produce wine. There was no alternative but to take the course. When I suggested as much to Melanie, she was not impressed.

'Why do I have to do it as well?' she asked.

'Come on, it'll be fun.'

I doubted it would be, but without her moral support I feared I might not survive.

'I'll tell you what, we'll drive to the college on Monday and get some more information. What do you say?' I added.

'I thought we were taking the car in on Monday.'

'We can go to the college afterwards. It's not that far from the workshop.'

'Go on then. It can't do any harm to ask.'

That evening we left home at 7:30 pm for the five-minute drive to the village of Sober. We'd arranged to meet Roy and Maria in the Ribeira Sacra bar for preconcert drinks.

'It's coming on,' I said, tipping my head towards the Plaza del Ayuntamiento.

Before we'd left for our winter break, the council had started renovating the main square and work was nearing completion.

'They'll have to get a wiggle on if they're going to finish in time.'

'In time for what?'

'The wine fiesta.'

'Of course. When is it?'

'I'm not sure. I think it starts on the 8th of April.'

The highlight of the village social calendar is the annual Amandi wine fiesta.

When we got to the bar, Roy and Maria were already sipping their drinks. I ordered a glass of white for Melanie and I had a beer. Maria was keen to hear how our winter break had gone.

'It's been really cold here. Even the river Cabe froze over,' admitted Roy.

'We read about it in the newspaper.'

Time passes quickly when you're catching up on news. We downed our drinks and wandered across the square to the *casa de cultura*.

Tonight's performer was Esperanza Martin, a talented twenty-four-year-old pianist from Madrid.

'How does Luis manage to entice such accomplished musicians to Sober?' I asked.

Luis Fernández Guitián is our local mayor.

'I think his wife arranges them,' said Maria.

Which begged the question, how did she manage to entice them? Before I had a chance to ask, Esperanza stepped onto the stage to muted applause. Once again, the auditorium was less than a quarter full. Given the weather, a low turnout seemed inevitable.

Esperanza's playing didn't disappoint. The first half of the concert featured music by Debussy, Scriabin, and Albéniz with the second half dedicated entirely to Chopin's Sonata No 3. Her reward for such a flawless performance was a complimentary bottle of wine presented by Luis. I guess it's the thought that counts, but he wasn't finished there.

In common with most politicians, Luis is not one to miss an opportunity to endear himself to the electorate. Before we could get to our feet, he invited everyone to share a glass of wine with him in the reception. His offer coincided with the start of the *mes do* Amandi (month of Amandi).

A few years ago, Luis decided to extend the two-day wine fiesta into a month-long celebration. Given that the actual fiesta wasn't for another five weeks, it seemed he was keen to extend it even further. Not ones to refuse a free glass of wine, or anything else for that matter, we were happy to join him. Before heading home, we couldn't resist a return visit to the bar for a nightcap and tapas. All in all, a great evening.

5

Acronyms Rule OK

Back in the mid-80s, when I worked as an insurance salesman, industrial estates were one of my favourite hunting grounds. These centres of innovation were home to fledgling enterprises taking their first tentative steps on the slippery slope to success. The industrial estate in Monforte de Lemos couldn't be more different. It's a quiet, sparsely populated area, built on the outskirts of town on a piece of unloved scrubland.

'I think that's it,' said Melanie.

This was our first visit to Talleres Hijos Vásquez Piñeiro, where Toño and his brother, and Toño's son Diego, plied their trade. I pulled up outside a large industrial unit and we made our way towards the entrance. First impressions weren't great. The place was a tip with vehicles and components scattered everywhere. There were several family cars, one of which was high on a lift, a tractor in one corner with a minibus alongside, and two small delivery vans.

'*Hola!*'

Diego had spotted us standing at the doorway.

'*Un momento* (One moment),' he said, before dropping what he was doing and walking into an office.

Seconds later, he reappeared with a laptop under his arm. Given the state of the place, it was difficult to believe that computer diagnostics had reached this neck of the woods, but nothing could have been further from the truth. Diego knew exactly what he was doing and, without saying another word, plugged the laptop into the car's ECU and tapped away on its filthy keyboard. Within seconds he'd diagnosed the problem as a faulty preheater.

'I'll have to order one, but it shouldn't be long if you'd like to wait,' he said.

I glanced at the time. Our trip to the agricultural college would have to wait. Recambios Roberto is the only motor factors business in Monforte de Lemos and, within ten minutes, their liveried van pulled up outside. Diego wasted no time fitting the new part and formatting the error code. Not only were we good to go, but I even managed to pay them. Next stop, the agricultural college.

'It should be around here somewhere,' I said.

'I thought you knew where it was.'

'I do, it's around here somewhere.'

'What's that?' said Melanie, pointing at a sign.

'Told you.'

'*Tsk!*'

A long access road took us through orchards and vineyards. I guess it pays to practise what you preach. After 400 metres it opened out into a parking area and beyond that the college.

'Who knew this was here?' remarked Melanie.

From the main road, the place was completely hidden. I drove past the carpark and stopped outside the main building. An unassuming entrance led into a large lobby. We looked for signs of life, but the place was abandoned.

'What now?' whispered Melanie.

'I guess we'll have to wait.'

A few minutes later a woman entered from one of the internal corridors and asked if she could help us. We explained why we were there.

'The man you want to speak to won't be long. Take a seat and he'll be with you shortly,' she said.

It turned out we'd arrived during their morning break. True to her word, a few minutes later a man entered through the same door. Once again, we explained why we were there.

'Come into my office,' he said, holding the door open for us.

We took a seat and he thumbed through a desk diary.

'The next course starts on Thursday the 30th.'

What began as an enquiry had turned into an enrolment. Melanie said nothing. I suspected she knew this might happen. The course was spread over six days ending with an exam on the final day, and lessons would run from nine in the morning until one. I had no idea that obtaining a *tarjeta de productos fitosanitarios* would be so involved and, by the look on Melanie's face, neither did she.

'Do you speak galego?' he asked.

'A few words,' said Melanie.

'Oh.'

A long pause did little to ease our anxiety.

'It's just that the course is organised and funded by the Galician government.'

He paused again. If he was hoping we might reconsider, he was mistaken.

'Don't worry, I'm sure we can sort something out,' he said.

If he couldn't, a difficult task would become nigh on impossible.

'It's 8.92€ each,' he said.

I couldn't imagine how they'd arrived at such a figure, but at least we didn't have much to lose.

We registered our intent and agreed to return on the 30th of the month at 9:00 am.

'Where did you park?' he asked.

After everything we'd discussed, his question caught us off-guard. Was he planning to escort us off the premises?

'We're right outside the door,' I replied.

'That's for staff only. You'll need to park in the public carpark during the course.'

We hadn't yet put pen to paper and we were already in bother. We assured him we wouldn't make the same mistake again and left.

'What have we done?' said Melanie, as we stepped outside.

'It'll be fine.'

Even I didn't believe that but, as the saying goes, nothing ventured, nothing gained.

'Let's see if Paula is in,' I said, as we pulled away.

'What for?'

'To find out how to register for the citizenship exams.'

Paula was our accountant and go-to person for all administrative matters.

'Shouldn't we make an appointment?'

Melanie wasn't as keen, but we were on a roll so why stop now?

'We can do if she's not there.'

'Go on then.'

We were in luck. Paula was in the office, and she had time to see us. Unfortunately, she couldn't help with our enquiry, but promised to find out and let us know.

'I'll email you,' she said.

We thanked her for her time and headed home for lunch.

Later that day, I was in the office editing the next book when I heard the phone ring. I was about to get up when Melanie answered it. Shortly afterwards she pushed open the office door.

'That was Ramón, he wants to meet us at Vilatán,' she said.

Why on earth would Ramón the plumber want to meet us at the rental property?

'What for?' I asked.

'To reconnect the phone.'

It took a few seconds for my brain to catch up.

'Oh, that Ramón. I thought you meant the plumber.'

'Why would the plumber want to meet us at Vilatán?'

'Exactly. Anyway, when?'

'When what?'

'When does he want to meet us?'

'Now!'

We'd known Ramón for years. He'd installed the phone line at home and the one at *Campo Verde*. The guy was a workaholic and something of a frustrated comedian, although much of his routine was lost on us.

'What did you say?'

'I said we'd be there in twenty minutes.'

'We'd better get a move on then.'

By the time we arrived, the clock had moved around to 3:30 pm. An hour later he'd reconnected the phone, and our chances of selling the house had improved immeasurably.

Within twenty-four hours of talking to Paula, she'd responded with an email. Online admissions were handled through the Instituto Cervantes website, an institution set up by the government in 1991 to promote Spanish language and culture. Once registered, we could sign up to sit the CCSE citizenship exam and the DELE A2 language exam.

'I've heard from Paula,' I said, when Melanie returned from walking Slawit.

'That's good. What did she say?'

'We need to apply online. I thought we could take a look after breakfast.'

Two heads are always better than one in these situations.

After breakfast we ambled into the office and I opened the Cervantes website. The registration process was fairly straightforward, and we quickly found what we were looking for. The earliest we could sit the Spanish language exam would be the 14th of July, but the citizenship exams were held every month.

'What about June?' I suggested.

'Why June?'

'Why not? We definitely won't want to do both exams in the same month, and June would give us plenty of time to prepare.'

Melanie could see the logic.

'How much is it?' she asked.

'Eighty-five euro.'

'Each?'

'Each.'

'And what about the other?'

'That's a hundred and twenty-four.'

'Crikey! This is costing us a fortune.'

'Why don't we sign up for the citizenship exam today, and the other one next month?'

'That's a good idea.'

The wheels were now in motion. In a little over three months, we would be sitting the most important exams of our lives.

'What time are we setting off for the ITV?' asked Melanie, over lunch.

'Two o'clock should give us ample time.'

We'd done everything we could to ensure the car would pass. All we had to do now was get there on time, cross our fingers, and hope for the best. What I hadn't counted on was getting stuck behind a tractor en route to the test centre. As if the ordeal wasn't stressful enough.

'We're going to be late,' I said.

Melanie didn't say a word. She knew we had plenty of time.

A shortened wait did little to reduce my anxiety but, once again, she passed with flying colours.

'You haven't forgotten that I'm going to *gimnasio* tonight, have you?' asked Melanie.

She was referring to the council-run keep fit classes which take place once a week in the *local social* or village hall. In her absence, I was charged with switching on the oven twenty minutes before her return. Failure to do so would delay dinner.

'Of course not. What time does it start?' I asked.

'Six.'

That evening at 5:50, Melanie made her way down into the village. A little over an hour later, she crawled back home.

'How was it?'

'Hard going.'

After a three-month absence, it was going to take her some time to get back into the swing of things.

After a depressingly slow start to the holiday season, we finally got off the mark with our first two bookings. Despite that, I couldn't shake the idea of offering the house to Deborah and Hugo. We didn't hear from them during their short stay, but I was keen not to let this opportunity pass without mentioning it. At the very least, it would force us to confront an issue we'd been reluctant to address.

'I've been thinking,' I said, over breakfast.

'What about?'

'About what you said.'

'What did I say?'

'About offering *Campo Verde* to Deborah.'

'I was joking.'

'I know, but perhaps we should.'

Melanie was acutely aware of the number of bookings we had.

'If we did sell it, what would we do then?'

I didn't say as much, but I thought she was getting a bit ahead of herself.

'I don't know, but we can't go on like this. Perhaps we could use the money to buy an apartment in Monforte de Lemos and let it out long term.'

'If we did offer it to them, how much would we want for it?'

'I'm not sure. I thought we could tell them we were selling and see what their response was.'

'I guess we could try for nothing.'

'In that case I'll send her an email and we'll take it from there.'

Later that morning, I composed my offer.

Dear Deborah

Since I last wrote, Melanie and I have decided to sell our rental property. As yet, we haven't advertised it and would appreciate your discretion.

Everything you might want to know about the place is on our rental website. The property will be offered fully furnished.

If you are interested, or would like more information, please don't hesitate to ask.

Kindest regards
Craig and Mel

'Will you take a look at this?'

Melanie was sitting in the lounge reading. She followed me into the office and took a seat in front of the computer.

'That's fine,' she said.

'You don't think it's too short?'

'No. If they're interested, they'll ask how much it is.'

'That's what I thought.'

It's fair to say our expectations were low. We'd never met Deborah and Hugo and didn't know how serious they were about moving to Galicia or what they were looking to buy, but at least we'd made a start.

Kicking off the day with bright sunshine and a cloudless sky made a pleasant change. It had only been eight days since we last saw the sun, but it felt like months. After coffee in bed, Melanie took Slawit out and I checked my inbox; Deborah had replied.

'I'm home,' called Melanie.

I waltzed into the kitchen to give her the news, but she beat me to it.

'There's free pancetta at the bar in Rosende this evening,' she said.

'How do you know?'

'There are flyers pinned up in the village.'

'What time?'

'Eight o'clock.'

'Do you want to go?'

'I'm not sure; do you?'

'Let's think about it. Anyway, I've got some news.' I paused for effect. 'We've had an email from Deborah.'

'That was quick. What did she say?'
'Come and take a look.'

From: Deborah XXXX
Sent: 9 March 20:17
To: Craig Briggs
Subject: re: visit to Galicia

Dear Craig

I'm so surprised to hear it—from what we can see from the photos, it's an absolutely beautiful house and we liked the whole area very much. Your virtual tour is not working, by the way.

I see the house has two bedrooms, does it also have two bathrooms? To be able to see more photos, if you have any, would be great—kitchen and inside dining areas would be good to see as well as bathroom/s.

As the house is in a village, I take it there is not much land with it; it would be good to know how close the neighbours are. What's the square footage of the house?

And last but not least, what kind of price are you looking to achieve for the property?

All the best
Deborah & Hugo

'What do you think?' asked Melanie.
'Well, it's not a no.'
'What are we going to do?'
'Answer her questions, but don't build up your hopes. It can't be this easy to sell a house, even one as nice as ours.'
'Why isn't the virtual tour working?'

To give people a taste of where they'd be staying, I'd put together a virtual tour of the house and grounds, and uploaded it to our website.

'I don't know, but I'll take a look.'

'And what about the price?'

Valuing properties in this area is tricky. Demand is in short supply, and no two properties are alike. During the restoration, we'd kept a tight grip on the purse strings and, in most instances, we'd bought really well. Anything over 90,000 euro would show us a profit, to say nothing of the income we'd enjoyed over the last nine years. That said, we didn't want to give the place away. Taking everything into account, we settled on a price of offers over 100,000.

As for the virtual tour, when I checked the website, I discovered the host, a company called Weebly, had changed their subscription options. Features that were once free now had to be paid for. Not to be outmanoeuvred by a greedy US tech company, I uploaded the video to YouTube and added a link from the website to there. Where there's a will there's a way.

Armed with this new information, I fashioned a reply.

From: Craig Briggs
Sent: 10 March 14:30
To: xxxxxxxxx@xxxx.com
Subject: re: visit to Galicia

Dear Deborah

We have been thinking about selling the house (*Campo Verde*) for a year or so. Over the last thirteen years the holiday letting industry has changed beyond recognition.

The shortness of the letting season in Galicia, coupled with the number of properties available, has made it increasingly difficult to make a living.

Thanks for letting me know about the virtual tour on our website. This YouTube link has the same video.

https://www.youtube.com/watch?v=5jeFidyfduM&t=21s

To answer your specific questions, the house has two bathrooms; the master bedroom is en suite and the other bathroom is right outside the second bedroom.

As you are aware, *Campo Verde* is situated in the village of Vilatán. The accommodation is split over two floors each being 1,270 square feet, a total of 2,540. All the living space is currently on the first floor, leaving plenty of opportunity downstairs for future expansion. The property deeds would also allow for the construction of a second building (garage possibly) of 450 square feet.

The outside space covers 600 square metres (6,450 square feet). As a rental property, we've avoided adding to this but there is the possibility of buying the field directly in front of the house which I estimate to be about 2,000 square metres (215,250 square feet).

As for the price, we're looking for offers over 100,000 euro. When we instruct an agent, the asking price will be slightly higher to take into account their fees and give us room to manoeuvre. For anyone looking for this type of property in a village location within the Ribeira Sacra, we believe it represents excellent value for money. Unfortunately, this corner of Spain is not for everyone.

I hope this helps and, if you need to ask any more questions, please feel free to get back in touch. If you are interested, we would consider delaying appointing an estate agent.

Best wishes
Craig and Mel

For the time being, we could do no more. I didn't think for one minute we'd sell the place at the first time of asking but, having gone this far, it was time to consider offering the house to a wider audience. It was a real shame. We'd loved being hosts to our guests and ensuring everyone left *Campo Verde* with cherished memories. In the main, we'd managed to achieve that, but it was time to move on. What that would look like was anyone's guess, but we'd face the future with optimism and enthusiasm.

'I'm going to start pruning the vines,' I said.

Melanie was in the kitchen preparing tonight's dinner.

'Will you need me?'

'If you wouldn't mind. Give me half an hour, and then you can start collecting the clippings?'

'No problem. I'm nearly finished.'

A few hours later, we called it a day. We'd pruned all the vines at the front of the house and those down the side. One more session would finish it off.

We really couldn't have asked for better weather at this time of year. It had been one of those perfect spring days that you never want to end. Having changed out of our work clothes, we retired to the far end of the garden with a glass of wine to watch the setting sun.

'What time did you say the free pancetta started in Rosende?' I asked.

'Eight, why?'

'Shall we go?'

If you don't want the day to end, why should it?

'We can if you want.'

'What about dinner?'

'It'll keep. It's only goulanoff.'

Goulanoff is one of Melanie's culinary creations, so called because it's a cross between goulash and stroganoff.

'Are you sure?'

'Certain. Come on, let's go.'

During the summer months, the bar in the village of Rosende is one of our favourite haunts. The owner, Miguel, does an excellent selection of tapas and they serve Estrella Galicia 1906 on draft.

His offer of free food had brought the locals out in force. For Miguel, it was an inexpensive way to promote the bar in what would otherwise be a quiet time of year. For his customers, it provided them with a few free rashers of deliciously fatty and mouthwateringly salty pancetta.

When we arrived, Martin and Barbara were at the bar. They'd moved to the area a few years after us. Originally from Germany, they'd spent quite some time working in the UK before moving to Spain. They're a very enterprising couple who operate a number of businesses including a small horticultural company. Martin was leant against the counter talking to Miguel and Barbara was sitting on a bar stool next to him. They invited us to join them, and we were happy to oblige. We'd bumped into them before at different events, but didn't really know them that well.

An hour later than advertised, attendees started gathering outside. There's no waiting on ceremony at these events. It's every person for themselves. Miguel and his staff had been hard at work. We joined the Spanish equivalent of a queue and waited in line to pick up a clean serviette and chunk of crusty bread. As those in front were served, we shuffled forwards. Ahead of us, rashers of pancetta were spitting and smoking on a large hotplate. We offered up our bread, and Miguel did the honours. The meat had been cooked to perfection. Oozing fat soaked into the bread, adding to the moreish flavour. No sooner had we finished than we were back for a second rasher. By the time we headed home, the clock had slipped past one in the morning. The day hadn't so much ended as passed seamlessly into a new one.

There's always a price to pay for such night-time shenanigans, and a lie-in failed to clean the slate. To make matter worse, we'd heard nothing from Deborah, but we'd made up our minds. Come what may, we would put the house on the market. All I had to do then was identify the most effective and least expensive way of doing that.

Given our fragile condition, we decided to delay pruning the rest of the grapevines in favour of less strenuous activities. Melanie spent most of the day with her nose in a book, and I started researching our selling options.

The house had been designed and furnished with foreign holidaymakers in mind. Those same features would appeal to an international market. It seemed reasonable to concentrate our efforts on securing a foreign buyer. Besides which, Spaniards would be more likely to value the house based on the cost of restoring a similar property than its turnkey appeal.

One online estate agency caught my eye: micheliaproperty.co.uk. They weren't so much agents as an online property portal for independent sellers. They charged a flat fee for a listing and no commission on sales. What appealed to me most was the lack of reliance on anyone else. We already had professionally taken photos and an appealing description that could easily be amended to target buyers rather than renters.

In addition to a listing on their dedicated website, the advert would also be placed on ten of the top selling property portals across Europe including Hoopla in the UK. This was exactly what we were looking for.

'I think I've found a place to advertise the house,' I said.

'Where?'

I explained what I'd found and how it worked.

'And how much does it cost?'

'They've got four options: twenty quid a month, thirty-six quid for three months, forty-eight for six, or ninety-six forever.'

'Forever?'

'Yeah. If you pay them ninety-six quid, they'll list the house until it's sold.'

'That sounds alright, and what about other fees?'

'There aren't any. We really can't lose.'

'And what do we have to do?'

'Input the details and upload the photos. They even put the ad on Hoopla, and all the top European sites.'

'It sounds too good to be true.'

'That's what I thought, but I've looked through some of their listings and it's all legit.'

'In that case, what are you waiting for?'

My idea had certainly got Melanie's seal of approval, but it couldn't harm to wait a few days to see if Deborah would reply.

Unlike the weather, we felt much livelier the following day, and breaks in the showers provided enough opportunities to finish pruning the grapevines.

The day after that, Deborah emailed. As we'd suspected, her response wasn't what we'd hoped for, but at least she'd had the courtesy to reply.

From: Deborah
Sent: 12 March 20:34
To: Craig Briggs
Subject: re: visit to Galicia

Dear Craig

Thank you very much indeed for sending all these marvellous pictures of your house—it's even better than I imagined it was.

Your email gave us a great deal of food for thought, and one of the things we were thinking about was a long-term rental in Monforte or even Leon (not Galicia, I know) so that we could take some time to look around and orientate ourselves. We've spent days scouring the maps and looking at all the logistics and options—I'm sure you know how that goes!—and I suspect that, at the end of the day, a place a little further south may offer us better transport and connection options for the things we want and need to do.

Our next trip will probably centre around Segovia and we'll see if we will like the area as much as we do Galicia—it's a completely different atmosphere I imagine. I must admit though to spending several hours dreaming about living in your house and imagined the view across the fields, eating outdoors and cooking in that kitchen. We thought your projected price was pretty good, considering the level to which you have brought the house, and I can imagine upgrading the downstairs and having the front field too.

Thanks too for giving us the heads-up on your plans, and I hope you'll find the right buyer quickly. Looking forward to seeing where Book 4 takes you both!

All the best
Deborah

The final paragraph was the most telling. It was nice to hear they could have imagined living there and that the price was fair, but it was obvious that this house wasn't for them. I guess we were both a little disappointed, but if at first you don't succeed…

6

The Mind Boggles

At this time of year, frosty starts produce a unique landscape. Silken threads of finely woven webs sparkle in the morning sunshine, and the frozen tears of freshly pruned grapevines create slender icicles.

'If you see José María while you're out, can you ask him if I can borrow his grafting tool?'

Melanie was getting ready to take Slawit out for her morning walk.

'OK, but I don't always see him.'

Our friend José María owns the village winery. Last year he'd lent me a tool used to graft one grape variety onto another. After a shaky start, I'd finally got the hang of it only for a late frost to kill all the grafts. I was keen to give it another go although I'd have to wait for the weather to improve.

On her return, Melanie was excited to share some news. She'd bumped into our neighbour Marisa, and found out that someone had taken over the restaurant in Sober. This was great news. We'd really missed eating at Parada Dos since the owners retired.

'They've renamed it,' she said.

'What?'

'O Xugo. They used to have a bar called that in Monforte.'

'We'll have to give it a go before the wine fiesta. If it's any good we can book a table.'

'That's a great idea.'

'By the way, did you see José María?'

'I did. Here you go,' she said, pulling the tool out of her pocket.

'Fantastic!'

'He said you should wait until it warms up before doing it.'

'I was going to.'

While Melanie had been walking the dog, I'd been surfing the internet to see if any of the local estate agents had anything to offer in the way of apartments.

'I thought we might go into Monforte this morning,' I said.

'What for?'

'To see if we can have a word with Pilar at Laybe.'

In partnership with her brother Jaime, Pilar owned Laybe estate agency in the centre of town. When we first moved to the area, she'd been instrumental in ensuring our dream became a reality.

'What about?'

'To ask her advice on the pros and cons of long-term letting.'

If anyone would know about the local rental market, she would. If it wasn't a feasible option, the sooner we knew the better.

'We ought to wait until this afternoon.'

'Why?'

'You know how busy the office is in a morning. She's more likely to have some free time later in the day.'

Melanie had a point.

At 4:30 pm, we left home and drove into Monforte de Lemos. We parked in the public carpark adjacent to the town's most iconic landmark, the sixteenth century Jesuit college known locally as the Escolapios. From there we strolled into the centre of town along the riverbank footpath.

Whenever we meet Pilar, she greets us like long-lost family.

'How can I help you?' she asked.

We explained the shortcomings of our current business model and how we'd like to change it. Going forward, we'd prefer to be less hands-on with a more regular income.

'Come with me. I have something to show you,' she said, getting to her feet.

This was typical of Pilar. Why waste time talking about something when she could show us?

We followed her out to her car. To look at it, you wouldn't think she had two ha'pennies to rub together; the Rolex on her wrist indicated otherwise.

'It was a gift,' she once told us.

Pilar's driving style could best be described as passive aggressive. As a passenger I never felt in danger, but neither did I feel safe. We hadn't been driving five minutes when she stopped in Rúa Carude.

'This is for sale,' she said.

We were looking a relatively small terraced property with a cute wooden balcony but, apart from it being less than 300 metres from the town centre, I couldn't imagine why she'd brought us to see it.

'There are four units here, three one-bedroom studios and a two-bedroom apartment on the ground floor, but I can only show you one because the others are occupied.'

We were lost for words. How on earth had anyone managed to squeeze all that living accommodation into such a small building?

My idea of apartment living was based around a high-rise block, not studios that had been shoehorned into a traditional town house. We couldn't wait to see how they'd managed to do it.

Pilar unlocked the front door and we followed her into a small lobby. The two-bedroom apartment was on the ground floor. Directly in front, a staircase led to the first floor. Compared to the narrow façade, the building seemed to go back forever. A corridor connected two studios, one at the front and the other at the back, and a second, central staircase led up to a third studio in the loft.

The standard of workmanship was top drawer, and the fixtures and fittings were of the highest quality. Pilar showed us one of the studios which had recently been vacated by a supply teacher from the nearby college. We knew from our friend Silvia that transient professionals are a relatively lucrative and well-established market in Galicia, particularly in the teaching profession.

The apartments were currently grossing a modest 12,000 euro per annum, and the place was on the market, with a sitting tenant, for 130,000. Given the figures, this wasn't the project for us, but it had opened our eyes to a whole new sector of the letting market and a property type we would never have considered.

'Do you have time to take a look at *Campo Verde*?' I asked, as we walked back to the car.

It seemed only fair to let her take a look, and it couldn't harm to get an independent valuation based on selling it locally even though we'd set our sights on a wider audience.

'Of course,' she said.

Pilar hadn't seen the house before but, when it comes to local properties, nothing much gets past her and her brother. She thought we'd done a great job. There were a few things she would have done differently and, if we'd been targeting the local market, we probably would have done them, but we weren't. As for her valuation, that was roughly in line with our own.

The next day, I couldn't get the viewing out of my head. If we did sell *Campo Verde* and reinvest the proceeds in another property, any return would have to provide us with the income we needed, otherwise what was the point?

'I saw Meli while I was out,' said Melanie, who'd just returned from walking the dog.

Meli is our nearest neighbour.

'How is she?' I asked.

'She's fine. She's going on holiday on the 8th of April.'

'Don't tell me, a spa break?'

'That's right.'

Since Meli's husband had died, she'd been taking at least two holidays a year. Her favourite destination was the Aguas Santas spa and golf resort in Pantón, seven kilometres from home.

'She's asked if I'll look after the chickens again,' she added.

A few years ago, Meli asked us to feed her chickens while she was away in exchange for their eggs. It turned out to be a great deal and we'd been doing it ever since.

'Is that the first day of the wine fiesta?' I asked.

'Yes, I think it is.'

After breakfast, I spent the rest of the morning working on the next book. For me, editing is the most enjoyable part of the process. It's also the most taxing, and by lunchtime I was ready for a break.

'I'm going to mow the lawns after lunch,' I said.

At this time of year, it's important to make the most of the weather; you never know how long it will last. While I did that, Melanie worked her way through a mountain of ironing. When we finally called it a day and retired to the far end of the garden with a glass of wine, Ramón the plumber turned up unannounced to replace the faulty condenser.

'It's the wrong size,' he said.

It didn't matter which way he fitted it; the cover of the control panel wouldn't close.

'I'll leave this one with you and order a new one,' he added.

At least that way the pump would work.

'How much do we owe you?' I asked, as he readied to leave.

'Pay me next time.'

We still hadn't paid him for fixing the leak in the laundry room. Would we ever get to settle the bill?

More bad news followed. Later that evening, Huddersfield Town lost 4–0 away to third from bottom Bristol City. They were still in the playoff places, but couldn't afford many more results like that one.

Continued good weather allowed us to get more gardening done. I began by spraying the grapevines to make sure beetles wouldn't eat the new buds. After that I emptied the compost heap onto the tomato bed and worked the contents into the soil. My final job was to rake the chickweed off the vineyard in preparation for rotovating. It's a thankless job, but without doing it the rotovator gets clogged up in no time. For the second consecutive evening, we were able to sit outside with a glass of wine and watch the sun setting behind the woody knoll.

'What's for dinner?' I asked.

'Stew and dumplings.'

Even cold evenings have their compensations.

Come rain or shine, Slawit needs her morning walk. When we woke on the 21st of March, it was absolutely chucking it down. Fortunately, both Melanie and Slawit have wet weather gear, but it's not always enough. When they returned, Melanie's offshore sailing jacket had done its job, but from the waist down she was soaked to the skin. It was a similar story with Slawit. Her coat had kept her body dry but everywhere else was dripping wet.

'Craig!' called Melanie.

On days like this, it's my job to dry Slawit, but for her it's just a game. I held out the towel and she rushed into it headfirst, wriggling and writhing as I tried to rub her dry.

'Stand still!' I said, but she didn't pay a blind bit of notice.

We spent the rest of the day confined to quarters. I worked on the advert for Michelia Property, but couldn't bring myself to publish it.

Within twenty-four hours the rain had moved on to pastures new, and fine weather afforded us the opportunity to get out and about. The property we'd seen with Pilar had opened our eyes to a range of different possibilities. If we could find the right place at the right price, I was convinced we could achieve the level of income we were aiming for. To that end, we spent the next few days viewing properties in Monforte de Lemos. Most were at the lower end of the market, but all had the potential to be converted into multiple units. The cheapest place we looked at was an enormous attic, on the market for under 22,000 euro. That said, it needed an awful lot spending on it. The problem was, so did every other property we viewed, and the more we delved into the mechanics of buying, refurbishing, and renting the less attractive it looked.

Before we knew it, we were setting the clock for a 7:45 am alarm call. How quickly the 30th of the month had come around. The only benefit of getting up at such an ungodly hour was the beautiful sunrise. Intense reds and glowing oranges lit up the distant horizon. An hour later, when we left for the agricultural college, we were more than a little apprehensive.

'Remind me again, whose idea was this?' I asked.

'Yours, and don't forget to park in the public carpark,' said Melanie, as we made our way along the long driveway.

How could I forget?

When we entered the college, there were roughly twenty others waiting in the lobby, and small cliques had already started to form. There were a number of different courses depending on individual responsibility. We'd enrolled on the basic course which would allow us to purchase and use chemicals, but not supervise others. Attendees ranged from farmers with smallholdings to men and women with an allotment or kitchen garden. Basically, if you wanted to use herbicides and pesticides you had to take the course and pass an exam. I thought it excessive but, given how dangerous and harmful these products can be to the environment, I guess it wasn't such a bad idea after all.

Nine o'clock came and went as did five past, ten past, and quarter past. At twenty past a tutor invited us into a classroom. We took a seat and she introduced herself as Lourdes. First things first, the paperwork. She handed out a folder which included a registration form and payment details. As was usual in these situations, payment could only be made through a high street bank. She was at pains to stress that only candidates who had handed in the supplementary paperwork and could prove payment would be allowed to sit the final exam.

On the plus side, those who failed to achieve the required pass mark could resit the exam at no extra cost, although they wouldn't be allowed to attend the course again. It seemed they'd thought of everything. By the time all the i's had been dotted and the t's crossed, Lourdes invited everyone to take a coffee break. All very civilised, but we hadn't learnt anything about handling chemicals.

On our return, work began in earnest. Unfortunately, no one had told Lourdes about our linguistic shortcomings. Melanie and I looked at each other and we weren't alone. When she finally noticed our blank expressions, she paused.

'Does everyone understand galego?' she asked.

Melane and I, along with one other person, admitted our ignorance.

'Oh, that's unfortunate,' she said.

Sympathy was in short supply.

'Does anyone mind if I continue in Spanish?' she asked.

Thankfully, no one did, although some were more reluctant than others. Galician pride runs deep.

Her compromise had little effect on my understanding. The speed of her narrative and use of words I'd never heard before left me none the wiser and, on the numerous occasions she slipped back into her native galego, there seemed little point in mentioning it.

Those who say that pictures speak a thousand words have never sat through an illustrated ecotoxicological training course narrated in galego. By the time the first of the five half-day tutorials had come to an end, my head was spinning.

'So, how much of that did you understand?' asked Melanie, as we strolled back to the car in a state of semi-consciousness.

'What was that?'

For a moment I thought someone was speaking English to me.

'I said, how much of that did you understand?'

Someone was speaking English to me.

'I think she said something about it costing eight euro ninety-two.'

The cost of the course was one of the things I'd remembered. Do numerals count?

'Is there any point in carrying on? There's no way we're going to pass an exam.'

'You worry too much. Of course we will.'

The folder we'd been given contained this morning's course notes along with a general outline of what we could expect over the remaining four days. When time allowed, I'd translate the notes and we could take it from there.

After lunch we headed into town to visit Fincas Saviñao, another local estate agent. I'd seen a number of interesting properties on their website which were worth taking a look at. Annoyingly, they'd all been sold. It's not uncommon in this part of the world for agents to leave properties on their website to lure prospective buyers through the door, but our time hadn't been wasted. We found out from the agent that local developers often get advance warning of properties about to come to market. I wasn't surprised. If it was easy to break into this marketplace everyone would be at it, but it did put us at a disadvantage. The more we unearthed the less attractive this idea became.

Back home, I set about translating the course notes. It's amazing how pictures, graphs, and tables come to life when accompanied by written explanations.

'This is not as complicated as I thought,' I said, handing Melanie a copy of the translation.

It wasn't called a basic course for no reason.

If anything, the following day's tutor was worse than the first one. By the time we'd finished, our brains were scrambled.

'I haven't a clue what's going on, and I don't know why I'm here.'

Melanie was clearly in need of a pick-me-up.

'I'll tell you what, let's try the new restaurant in Sober this lunchtime,' I suggested, as we walked back to the car.

'Now that's a good idea.'

With the exception of a *xugo* or yoke hanging above the door to the dining room, nothing had changed since the previous owners retired. Even the pictures hanging in the restaurant were the same. What had changed was the number of diners, but these things take time to get off the ground.

Service was swift. We ordered a bottle of white wine and, after taking our orders, the waitress brought a basket of thickly cut, crusty bread. I chose spaghetti bolognaise for starters. When it came, the portion was enormous. For my main course I went for something a little different, a roasted pork chop, chips, and a fried egg. An unusual combination, but everything was cooked to perfection.

'*Postre?*' asked the waitress.

Had it not been included in the price, I might have given it a miss but, as it was, I couldn't resist.

'*Qué hay* (What is there)?' I asked.

Like the first two courses, the pudding menu was delivered orally. One item caught my attention: death by chocolate. After such a large meal, I'm surprised it wasn't. All in all, we'd had a very good *menú del día*, for only ten euro a head.

'Shall we book for the fiesta?' I asked.

'I don't see why not.'

Unfortunately, they weren't taking bookings. We couldn't blame them; it would probably be their busiest night of the year.

'We'll have to make sure we eat in good time,' I said.

'I suppose so.'

If previous years were anything to go by, we'd be among the first to take our seats.

After two difficult mornings, the weekend would give us the opportunity to collect our thoughts and ready ourselves for the coming week.

7

The Final Act

First thing on Saturday morning, I translated Friday's course notes and gave a copy to Melanie.

'Is this it?' she asked.

'That's it. I bet we could do the whole course in a day, two at the most.'

'I don't know about that, but there isn't much here.'

After lunch, I decided to rotovate the vineyard. It's one of those jobs I love to hate. There's a real sense of achievement once it's done, but it doesn't matter how often I do it, it never gets any easier. By the time I'd finished, my arms felt like lead weights and my knees and ankles were killing me.

The next day I felt as stiff as a board, but at least the sun was shining. At this time of year, the weather has a habit of tricking us into believing that summer is just around the corner, but we know different.

'Let's have breakfast outside,' I suggested.

This was the first time it had been warm enough to sit out since we'd returned from Andalucía, and I was determined to make the most of it.

Later in the day we went to *Campo Verde*. Before the start of every holiday season, we always clean the wooden ceilings and internal stone walls. It keeps the place looking as good as new and, with the first guests due to arrive at Easter, there was no time to lose.

Before we knew it, the weekend had slipped by and we were heading back to college for another mind-numbing session of *fitosanitario*. Our new tutor, a chap called Manolo, was so dull he could have put a roomful of insomniacs to sleep. Could things get any worse?

'That was the worst yet,' said Melanie, as we walked back to the car.

'Don't worry, this time next week it'll all be over.'

'Have you *any* idea what that was about?'

'I think it was something to do with spraying near a water course.'

'What did he say about the police?'

'Police?'

'I'm sure he mentioned the police.'

If he had, it had been lost on me, which was hardly surprising.

'Let's call at the bank on the way back and pay the course fees,' I said, as we drove home.

'Do we have to?'

She was joking. At least I hoped she was.

That afternoon, we decided to publish the advert for the house on the Michelia Property website. For better or worse, *Campo Verde* was now officially for sale.

The next morning, we arrived early at college to hand in our proofs of payment at the admin office. As for the lesson, Monologue Manolo was first up. Fortunately, we only had to endure his tedious tones until the coffee break. After that, things picked up. A different tutor and a change of subject made the final lesson almost tolerable. Calculating the correct dosage is one of the most important aspects of using chemicals. The maths was straightforward, although not everyone thought so, and for the first time since we'd started the course, I actually felt as if I'd learnt something.

Before we left, the tutor had an announcement. Due to his busy schedule, the final lesson would be postponed until Thursday with the exam being held on Friday morning.

'That wasn't too bad,' I said, as we headed home.

'I suppose not.'

Yesterday's trip to the bank reminded me that we hadn't yet registered for the DELE A2 Spanish language exam. After lunch, we made a start.

It took us the best part of an hour to complete the enrolment process and make the online payment. At a cost of 248 euro, failure was not an option. If we were serious about becoming Spanish citizens, the time had come to knuckle down to some serious studying.

The fifth, and final, day of the course reminded me of the last day of term. We began with a formal lesson but, after the mid-morning coffee break, went outside to look at different types of equipment. Protective workwear, such as face masks, gloves, and overalls, is graded according to the level of protection it affords.

'These are the type of *luvas* you should wear,' said the tutor, pointing at a reference number printed on the outside of a pair of rubber gloves.

As soon as he'd said the word *luvas*, Melanie and I looked at each other. It had cropped up a number of times in the course notes but, thinking it was a typographical error, I'd substituted it for *uvas,* the Spanish word for grapes. Imagine our surprise finding out that *luvas* were actually *guantes*, the Spanish word for gloves. If anyone tells you galego and Spanish are similar, think again. On reflection, it was a miracle we'd got this far.

The tutor caught us smiling and realised why.

'That's right, *luvas* are *guantes*,' he said.

Everyone joined in the joke.

On a serious note, it's easy to underestimate the value of these types of courses. Until now, the only protective equipment I'd ever worn was a baseball cap, and only then to keep insects out of my hair. If nothing else, this experience had given me a healthy respect for the products I'd been using, and an appreciation of the environment I'd been using them in, which I guess was the point of holding such courses.

As the lesson drew to a close, the only thing standing between us and our *tarjeta de productos fitosanitarios* was the small matter of passing an exam. On a positive note, we were told that our papers would be presented in Spanish.

'Can we use a dictionary?' I asked.

'I don't see why not,' replied the tutor.

What a relief!

Despite the sword of Damocles hanging over our heads, we were sound asleep when the alarm clock thrust us into a new day. An hour later, and armed with my trusty Spanish/English dictionary, we headed off to college for what we hoped would be our final time.

Lourdes was back in charge for the first session. She began by introducing us to the six unsuccessful students from the previous course. If confidence was an ice cube, mine had just melted.

She explained that the exam was made up of twenty multiple-choice questions. Each correct answer was worth one point, and the pass mark was ten, but that wasn't all. Every incorrect answer incurred a penalty of minus half a point. A pantomime groan echoed around the classroom, but she hadn't finished yet. Unanswered questions were penalty-free. A bemused silence descended on the room. Only the Spanish could make such a simple marking system this complicated.

In short, answering ten questions correctly would result in a pass but answer an eleventh and get it wrong, and the candidate would fail. Somehow, that didn't seem fair, and I wasn't the only one seeking clarification. By the time Lourdes had finished her explanation, we were left in no doubt. Guessing was not an option. If we were uncertain of an answer, we should leave it blank. The room fell silent again. My mind was racing with possible permutations. Best-case scenario was ten correct answers from ten questions. Worst-case scenario was answering all twenty questions, getting seven wrong, and failing. On reflection, the odds were still stacked in our favour.

From then until the morning break, Lourdes gave what can only be described as an extremely detailed coaching session. She stopped short of reading the actual questions, but left us in no doubt what we were facing. How six people had managed to fail the previous course was beyond me.

During the coffee break, all the chatter was about possible questions. There's just no helping some folk.

On our return we took our seats and the invigilator handed out the exam papers. There was no mention of a time limit but I suspected if we hadn't finished by one, we'd get thrown out. Nothing gets in the way of lunch.

When instructed, we turned over our papers and began. I started by reading every question and the available answers. By the time I'd translated the bits I was unsure of, one person had finished. They got to their feet, handed in their paper, and left. That initiated an exodus as one person after another handed in their paper and walked out. Eventually, only three of us remained: Melanie, me, and one of the returning candidates.

By that time, I'd answered seventeen questions and was fairly confident of the remaining three but, with nothing to gain by answering them, I decided not to bother. When Melanie stood up and handed in her paper, I followed. Outside in the lobby, I couldn't wait to find out how many questions she'd answered.

'Eighteen. What about you?' she asked.

'Seventeen, but I was fairly sure of the others.'

Confidence was high that we'd passed. The Spanish exams we were due to sit in June and July would pose a much stiffer test, but given how long it had been since either of us had sat an exam, passing this one would give our confidence a much-needed boost. For the time being, we would have to wait until next Tuesday for the results.

After lunch we went back to *Campo Verde* to erect the gazebo and take the garden furniture out of storage. Our first guests would be arriving tomorrow.

'What's happened there?'

Melanie was pointing at a series of holes in the lawn running along the line of the boundary wall. My first thought was a leak from the borehole. Some years ago, a fractured copper valve resulted in a cavernous sinkhole appearing in the middle of the lawn. On closer inspection, I suspected something less dramatic.

'If I had to guess, I'd say rainwater has washed the soil through the wall.'

Drystone walls look the part, but they do have their drawbacks.

'What can we do?'

Filling them with sand was the obvious solution, but these jobs are never straightforward. For the time being it would have to wait until the guests had departed.

The next morning, we drove back to *Campo Verde* to ready the house and gardens for their arrival. By the time we'd finished, the place looked as good as it did nine years ago when we first opened to the public. Looking at it now, it was such a shame we couldn't make it pay.

We took it easy for the rest of the day. We needed all the stamina we could muster for tonight's wine fiesta.

'What time are we going to set off?' asked Melanie.

'I don't know. What do you think, half past seven?'

'That sounds about right.'

The two-day wine fiesta is an all-day affair. Every so often, loud explosions shatter the silence of the countryside as fireworks are launched to mark the start and end of different events. Poor Slawit was terrified and would dash into the house every time one went off.

That evening we made our way to the village of Sober. We couldn't have wished for better weather: warm and still. En route we paused to take in the outstanding views across the Valle de Lemos. Lush forests and green pastures stretched out into the distance as far as the eye could see.

When we arrived, the square in front of the town hall, Plaza del Ayuntamiento, was busy with partygoers. The builders had managed to get most of the remodelling finished but, for one year only, the council had swapped the familiar tunnel-shaped marquee for a longer, narrower one.

The fiesta attracts a host of street traders and roadside attractions, and all the usual suspects were present. Amongst my favourites are those displaying winemaking equipment and artisan bread sellers. By far the most popular are those selling clothes, leather goods, or fake designer wear.

'Let's have a drink at the bar before we start tasting the wine,' I suggested.

The Bar Ribeira Sacra on Rúa do Comercio would give us the opportunity to indulge in one of our favourite pastimes, people watching. We took a seat outside and waited to be served. Two mobile eateries had set up on either side of the bar. I guess nowadays they'd be called popups, but travelling restaurants have been around for as long as there have been local markets. To our right, a *churrascaria* or grill was cooking pork sausages and cuts of beef and pork on a huge barbecue, and to the left, a *pulpería* was boiling octopus in a large copper caldron.

'What time do you think we should eat?' asked Melanie.

Every so often, fatty aromas drifted down the street from the *churrascaria*, igniting our tastebuds. In previous years we'd booked a table for nine o'clock and always been one of the first to dine. I saw no reason to change. When I glanced at my watch there was just enough time to try a few glasses of wine before dinner.

Gone were the days of buying a commemorative earthenware vessel to taste the wine. Nowadays, the price of participation was the purchase of a two-euro wine glass available from the council. We started with last year's winner, and our personal favourite, a fine red from the Val de Lenda winery. Comparing one year to another is virtually impossible, but I suspected they'd be in with a shout of picking up this year's prize. Our second choice came from Adega Naz, a small winery two and a half kilometres from the centre of Sober. The two wines, although very different, were both excellent.

'What time is it?' asked Melanie.

'Time we were making a move.'

The restaurant O Xugo was less than a hundred metres from the square. We slalomed our way through the busy bar and into the restaurant at the rear. As I'd suspected, we were amongst the first to eat. Since our last visit, a week ago, the new management had added a splash of colour to the walls with large-scale photographs of some of the area's most iconic scenes: the view from the Miradoiro de Pena do Castelo and the Santuario da Nosa Señora de Cadeiras.

'These are nice,' remarked Melanie.

For starters, we couldn't resist sharing a *tabla de embutidos* (platter of locally produced cured meats and a selection of cheeses). Melanie went for a burger and chips for her main course, and I ordered an *entrecote* steak, medium rare, served with grilled green peppers, mixed salad, and proper chips. Once again, everything was excellent and, for fifteen euro a head including a bottle of wine and coffee, we couldn't complain.

Having settled the bill, we wandered back to Plaza del Ayuntamiento passing one of my favourite fairground attractions en route: *camas elasticas* or trampolines. Seeing them always reminds me of the first fiesta we ever attended in Galicia.

Back in the square we made a beeline for the marquee, and tasted another two wines before buying a bottle from Adega Naz.

'Let's take it over there,' I said, pointing at one of the benches in front of the town hall.

From our elevated position we watched the night's proceedings unfold. On the run-up to midnight, a crowd gathered in front of a temporary stage adjacent to the town hall. Tonight's entertainers were a local rock band called Gin Toni's. They have something of a cult following in the area and a good-sized fan base who follow them from gig to gig. Thankfully, everything was good natured, as it always is at these events.

Unbeknown to us, band members were using the town hall as a dressing room. Imagine our surprise when, one after another, they filed out of the front door. Last to appear was their charismatic frontman. Dressed in a black-and-white checked suit and sporting thick curly hair and a bushy beard, he was a giant of a man. Out of sight of the audience, he staggered down the town hall steps but, the moment the crowd clapped eyes on him, his whole demeanour changed. He leapt on the stage, strapped a guitar around his neck, and belted out one of the fans' favourite hits like a man possessed. The sound was deafening. Half an hour was more than enough for a couple of old codgers like us. By the time we got home it was two in the morning and my ears were still ringing.

Given the lateness of the hour and amount we'd had to drink, I felt surprisingly lively the following morning.

'I'm going to start grafting the vines this afternoon,' I said, over lunch.

'Will you need me?'

'I don't think so.'

Ideally, grafting should be done before the new buds have opened and after the risk of frost has passed but, as last year proved, that's not always possible.

Even though this was my second attempt, I would hardly describe myself as experienced. Using the tool was relatively straightforward. They're similar to wire cutters except a single cut creates two different impressions like the interlocking shapes of a jigsaw puzzle: one male and the other female. Having said that, it took me all afternoon to create twenty-seven grafts. All I could do then was cross my fingers and hope Jack Frost didn't return.

On the 8th of the month, our neighbour Meli left for her spa break and we began ten days of chicken-sitting. I say we, but it's Melanie who does most of the work except if things go wrong. In that scenario, it's a joint enterprise.

'We seem to have lost a chicken.'

Melanie had just returned from walking the dog. On her way through the village, she'd let the chickens out of the hen hut and into the run.

'Excuse me?'

'Including the cockerel, there were five when I put them to bed, and now there are only four.'

'How on earth have you managed to lose a chicken?'

We'd only been looking after them for two days.

'I don't know, but I didn't do it on purpose.'

'Are you sure you put them all away last night?'

'I thought I had.'

Meli's hen hut looked more like a garden shed than something you'd keep chickens in, but breeze-block walls and a corrugated tin roof were more than adequate to keep a hungry fox at bay. The structure's Achilles heel was its repurposed wooden door which was ill fitting, rotten at the bottom, and held closed with a stone but, for all its flaws, the chickens couldn't have opened it. That left two possibilities: either it hadn't gone to bed or the door hadn't been secured properly.

'So, what do you think happened?' I asked.

'I don't know, maybe there's a chicken rustler in the village.'

I guess that was a third possibility.

'What do you want to do?' I asked.

'What can we do? We'll just have to wait for it to come back.'

'And if it doesn't?'

'We'll cross that bridge when we come to it.'

That evening, when it was time to put the chickens to bed, we strolled down the lane together. If there was a chicken rustler about, she might need protecting; if there wasn't, two sets of eyes would be better than one.

At this time of year, the grass in Meli's chicken run is quite short. In the middle of summer, you never know what might be lurking in the long grass.

'How many can you see?' I asked, as we made our way slowly down the run towards the hut.

'There's the cockerel,' said Melanie, pointing into the opposite corner.

'I can only see three chickens.'

'One of them might have gone to bed.'

Melanie marched off towards the cockerel leaving me to look inside the hut. It took a while for my eyes to adjust to the windowless interior. When they had, there wasn't a chicken in sight.

'There's nothing in here,' I called.

Melanie had adopted her cockerel driving pose: back arched and arms wide apart. While she did that, I scoured the perimeter for any signs of life or holes in the fence, but found nothing. I turned my attention to the interior and that's when I saw it: a cluster of chicken feathers in the middle of a patch of dead weeds.

'I think I've found it,' I called.

Having secured the rest of the brood in the hut, Melanie made her way towards me.

'Oh dear.'

Oh dear indeed.

Sitting in the middle of a cushion of feathers was a perfectly formed egg. One final act before shuffling off its mortal coil. How the chicken had managed to escape from the hut would remain a mystery but, once free, it had met an untimely end. As for the egg, I can only imagine what was going through its mind when that one popped out.

'What are you going to tell Meli?' I asked.

'The truth.'

'Can't we just buy another?'

'I think she might notice.'

She had a point.

'Let's wait until she gets back and then offer to buy her one,' she added.

Other than the cushion of feathers and freshly laid egg, there was no sign of how it had met its untimely end.

'Good chicken-sitters we turned out to be,' I remarked.

'It wasn't my fault.'

I left it at that. Melanie was upset enough but, if it wasn't our fault, whose fault was it?

'Do you think it'll be alright to eat?' I asked, as we walked up the lane.

Given the ordeal it had gone through to lay it, it seemed a shame not to.

8

Two-Minute Updates

I really shouldn't have but, when Melanie and Slawit returned from their morning dog walk, I couldn't resist having a dig.

'How many have we got this morning?' I asked.
'How many what?'
'Chickens.'
'That's not funny.'
I left it at that and moved on.
'Guess who I've had an email from?'
While Melanie was out with Slawit, I'd been in the office checking my inbox and catching up on world events via the BBC website.
'I don't know, who?'
'Martin.'
'Martin who?'
'Barbara's husband.'

'Oh. What did he want?'

'To invite us to their open garden on Saturday.'

'What's an open garden when it's at home?'

I had wondered that myself.

'I guess it's a garden, that's open.'

'Open to who?'

'The public, I suppose.'

'Why would anyone want to do that?'

'I don't know. It's probably a marketing gimmick.'

'And what did you say?'

'I didn't say anything. I thought I'd ask you.'

'Do you want to go?'

'It might be interesting.'

On the evening we'd bumped into them at the bar in Rosende, I was surprised to hear that Barbara had read all my books and really enjoyed them. It seemed only fair to reciprocate their support.

'You do know we've got a bedding change on Saturday morning?'

Guests who stay for longer than a week at *Campo Verde* are treated to a change of bedding and towels at the weekend.

'I know, but I thought we could pop in for half an hour in the afternoon. They're open from twelve until eight.'

'I suppose so. Anyway, what time are we going to the college?'

'As soon as you're ready.'

Today was results day and, despite confidence being high, you never know until it's confirmed. Within the hour we were pulling up outside the college. As we entered the lobby, we bumped into a couple who had also been on the course, Mario and Henrietta.

'We passed,' said Mario, waving a certificate in the air.

'Congratulations.'

'Don't worry, everyone has,' he said.

We smiled and continued on to the administration office for official confirmation.

'Congratulations,' said the college administrator, handing us both an envelope.

The enclosed certificates confirmed our success and, until we received the credit card style *tarjeta de productos fitosanitarios*, would act as proof of our achievement.

'How soon will they be ready?' I asked.

'Six weeks or so but don't worry, you can use those if you need to buy anything. Just call in whenever you're passing.'

We thanked him and stepped outside for a closer look.

The paperwork left more questions than answers. Candidates either passed or failed. There was no indication of how many questions we'd answered correctly or which, if any, we'd got wrong. Apart from that, this achievement could not be underestimated. We'd sat through a course in a language we could neither speak nor understand and triumphed. Sterner tests awaited us but, for the time being, we would bask in our glory.

Buoyed by our success, I turned my attention to the next exams we'd be facing, and in particular the Spanish language exam. To have any chance of success, I would definitely need professional help. Last year, I'd tried unsuccessfully to employ the services of Belen, a local Spanish teacher. At the time, events conspired against us and the proposed lessons didn't go ahead. With no other options on the table, I was hoping for better luck this time around.

'I'm going to email Belen again,' I said over lunch.

The citizenship exam was a different matter. I was confident that with a little more work our chances of passing were very good. After lunch, I retired to the office to continue my studies.

'Those look nice.'

I'd wandered through into the kitchen for a much-needed break.

'Well, you can't have one.'

That told me. While I'd been wading through Spanish culture, history, and the constitution Melanie had been busy baking hot cross buns.

'Aw go on, they're much nicer when they're warm.'

'They've just this minute come out of the oven. You'll have to wait.'

Later that evening we decamped to the far end of the garden to watch the setting sun with a glass of wine and a hot cross bun.

Easter in the UK provides football fans with two matches in quick succession, one on Good Friday and a second on Easter Monday. Depending on results elsewhere, if Huddersfield Town won both these games, a place in the playoffs was virtually assured.

Tonight's opponents were Preston North End, one of the twelve founding members of the football league. Broadcasting restrictions meant that the only way I could follow the game was through live updates every two minutes on the BBC Sport website. I settled down for a nail-biting evening in front of the laptop.

On twenty-three minutes, Preston took the lead only for Town to equalise two minutes before halftime. In the second half, both sides had chances, but it wasn't until the seventieth minute that Town scored a second. Could they hang on for an historic victory?

In a word, no. Nine minutes later Preston scored again. As the clock ticked down, a draw seemed inevitable. On ninety minutes the fourth official indicated six minutes of stoppage time. From that point on, seconds felt like minutes and minutes like hours, but with ninety-five minutes on the clock, Town were awarded a penalty for a foul inside the box. Preston players were furious but the ref was not for turning.

Up stepped Aaron Mooy, Town's star player, to take the spot kick. Waiting for the next update was the most nerve-racking two minutes of my life. As it turned out, Mooy's penalty was blocked by the keeper, but the loose ball rebounded into the path of substitute Collin Quaner who slotted home for his first goal of the season and Town ran out 3–2 winners. Unfortunately, results elsewhere meant they would have to wait to secure their place in the playoffs. Next up, Derby County away on Easter Monday.

On Saturday morning we were back at *Campo Verde* to change the bedding and towels. As usual, the guests were at home when we called. People like to say hello and often have a few queries after their first week.

Half an hour later, we were heading home with the dirty laundry.

'Do you want to go to this open garden?' I asked, over lunch.

'If you do.'

'Yeah, let's go.'

Martin and Barbara live in Mer, a small hamlet ten minutes from home. We weren't exactly sure how to get there, but Martin's directions ensured we found it without any problems. As we walked towards their house, the time had moved on to four in the afternoon. Despite that, we were among the first to arrive. Our hosts greeted us warmly and invited us to wander around the gardens at our leisure. A number of local artisans had also been invited and had set up stalls in the adjacent field. The gardens themselves were very interesting. Contemporary sculptures sat comfortably amongst more traditional garden features.

'Let's take a look at that,' I said.

Melanie looked at me as if I'd gone mad. In a garden packed with unusual curiosities and beautiful flowers, it was a collection of scaffolding poles used to construct an arbour that had caught my attention.

'This would be ideal for the vines to grow over in the front garden,' I said.

'Do you like it?'

Martin had seen me studying it.

'I do. Something like this would be ideal for my vines,' I replied.

'I got the poles from Hierros La Vid on the outskirts of Monforte de Lemos.'

I'd never used the place, but I had a good idea where it was.

'And the clamps?' I asked.

'I bought them online from a company in Germany; you can probably get them in the UK.'

I made a mental note to find out.

An hour or so after arriving we decided to make a move. They'd done a great job creating an interesting and quirky garden, but it wasn't really our thing.

On Easter Monday, I settled down for another anxiety-filled afternoon of two-minute updates from the BBC and didn't have long to wait for a goal. On nine minutes, which was actually ten by the time I saw the update, Town took the lead. For a second game in succession big Collin Quaner had found the back of the net. In hindsight, that was probably the worst thing that could have happened. From that moment on, Derby dominated the game and Town were hanging on for dear life. Halftime came and went, and then fifty minutes, fifty-five, and sixty. Could we do it; could we hang on?

The game passed the seventy-minute mark and then seventy-five, eighty, and eighty-five. Victory here would guarantee them a place in the playoffs. Everything was going to plan until two minutes from time when Jacob Butterfield, a former Town player, equalised for the home side. Disappointed didn't come close. The game ended 1–1 but I couldn't help thinking we'd blown our chances.

Next up was a home game against in-form Fulham. I wasn't sure if my heart could take any more. Before that, we had a confession to make. Meli was returning from her spa break in the morning, and neither of us was looking forward to that.

'Will you come with me?' asked Melanie, as she readied to leave.

'Where to?'

'Meli's, to tell her about the chicken.'

How this was my fault was anyone's guess, but a bit of moral support wouldn't go amiss.

'Of course.'

Meli was watering her *huerta* (kitchen garden) when we arrived. She greeted us warmly with a kiss on both cheeks, and we asked about her holiday. She'd had a wonderful time.

'We have something to tell you,' admitted Melanie.

What did I tell you about joint enterprise?

'One of the chickens has gone, but we'll get you another,' she added.

Melanie made it sound as if the chicken was also on a spa break.

'Don't worry about that, one of them is always going missing,' said Meli, very matter-of-fact.

I could almost hear Melanie's sigh of relief. She'd been dreading this moment.

'Anyway, would you like a lettuce?' she added.

Meli's easy-going approach to life was in stark contrast to the day's other news. Frustrated by the political impasse created by the referendum result, Prime Minister Theresa May had decided to call a snap general election. An increased parliamentary majority would give her the ability to railroad her version of Brexit through parliament.

Since moving to Spain, we'd chosen not to vote in UK elections. Rightly or wrongly, we believed it was the responsibility of those living there to decide their own fate, but this was different. The result of the referendum had left us feeling abandoned by those in power, and it was our duty as UK citizens living in Europe to do everything we could to maintain our rights and freedoms.

The choice was simple: vote for a group of self-serving, right-wing ideologists who would throw everyone under a bus as soon as look at them, or vote for moderation. Reversing the referendum looked nigh on impossible. The best we could hope for was a change in government and a more pragmatic approach.

'We're going to have to register to vote again,' I said.

'What for?'

'Theresa May has just called a snap election.'

'A general election?'

'That's right. On the 8th of June.'

'You're joking. Why don't they just forget about Brexit and get back to running the country?'

I was sure that Melanie's annoyance would be mirrored by millions of people across the UK. The question was, would that frustration translate into votes?

'I'll get in touch with Kirklees Council again, and see if we can get a postal vote.'

Regardless of what happened in the UK, we were committed to becoming Spanish citizens but the help I needed was proving difficult to secure. Frustrated by Belen's lack of urgency, I emailed her again.

After lunch I retired to the office to continue working on the next book. By five o'clock, my mind was ready for a break.

'I'm going to mow the lawns,' I said, as I walked through the lounge.

It felt good to be out in the fresh air. I pulled the mower out of the shed, rolled it onto the lawn, and yanked the starter cord. As usual, it started first time. Rotary mowers aren't renowned for striping, but I do my best. Everything was going fine until all of a sudden, the mower felt as if it was dragging an anchor. Instinctively, I lifted the drive wheels off the grass. For whatever reason, they'd stopped working.

'What's matter?'

Melanie had seen me from the kitchen window and come to the door to find out what was going on.

'The drive wheels aren't working.'

'Oh dear, can you fix it?'

'I'm not sure.'

The underside of the mower was caked in debris. After clearing it away, I found a loose spring. Stretching it back onto its retaining pin was a devil of a job, but I got there in the end. My quick fix was short-lived. Two minutes later, it broke again. On closer inspection, the hooked end of the spring had snapped which was why it had been so difficult to reattach. For the time being, I had no choice but to push.

Why is it that mowers designed to power themselves are twice as difficult to push as manual mowers?

'I see you managed to fix it,' said Melanie, when I stepped inside.

'Actually, I didn't. I had to push it most of the way.'

'What's wrong with it?'

'I think it's just a spring that's broken.'

'Can you get another?'

'I'm not sure. I'll have a look online.'

The problem with buying inexpensive brands is the lack of available spares. The company did have a website but spare parts were in short supply, and replacement springs were not something they stocked.

'They don't sell them.'

'What are you going to do now?' asked Melanie.

'We might have to take it to that place in Escairón.'

The village of Escairón is home to Maquinaria J. Varela, a specialist garden machinery retailer and service centre. Small engineering companies are few and far between in Galicia but, if you want to get your mower, brush cutter, chainsaw, hedge trimmers, or any other piece of garden machinery repaired, there are plenty of outlets. Many will only work on brands they're familiar with, but the chap in Escairón will tackle just about anything. Admittedly, after he's had his hands on something it never quite works the same again, but he does his best.

The next morning I'd had a change of heart.

'I'm going to take another look at the mower before we do anything,' I said over breakfast.

'OK.'

On closer inspection, years of neglect had left its mark, and it wasn't just the spring that had failed.

'Any luck?'

Melanie had brought me a cuppa.

'Possibly. I think the accelerator cable might have snapped. Do you think Meli would let me take a look at hers?'

A few years after we got ours, Meli bought exactly the same model.

'I'm sure she would.'

'Come on then.'

We walked down the lane together, and Melanie explained what I wanted to do.

'It's under the house,' said Meli.

In common with most properties in the area, Meli's living accommodation was on the first floor and she used the ground floor for storage. I pulled the mower outside and tipped it upside down. If I'd thought the underside of mine was dirty, Meli's looked like it had been rendered with wattle and daub. When I finally managed to chip off enough to see what was going on, my suspicion proved correct. The accelerator cable on mine had snapped. Replacing it wouldn't guarantee it would work, but without one I'd never know. We thanked Meli for her help and returned home.

Fortunately, one of the few spares available online was a replacement cable. Only time would tell if that would solve the problem.

On the 21st of April, my worst fears were realised when Jack Frost made an untimely return. Weeks earlier the grapevines had burst into leaf. Some of the canes were over six inches long, and even the grafts had started to leaf. The question was, would any of them survive?

Melanie had other things on her mind.

'Oh no. I forgot to bring the tomatoes in last night.'

We used to grow our own tomato plants from seed but nowadays we prefer to buy seedlings instead.

It's less work, and they fruit much earlier in the season. We keep them in pots until it's warm enough to plant them outside and bring them in at night.

'How are the tommies?' I asked, when Melanie returned with our morning cuppas.

'I think I've got away with it. They were close to the house.'

Melanie and Slawit wrapped up warm before setting off on their morning walk and, as soon as I was up and about, I checked the vines for damage. Some leaves were already showing signs of frostbite, but it was a little early to know how many would be affected.

On their return, I had some news.

'We've had an email from HomeAway,' I said.

HomeAway was one of the internet platforms we used to market *Campo Verde*, and accounted for over eighty percent of all our bookings.

'Oh yes, what did they have to say?'

'Apparently, there's a new regulation coming out which requires anyone letting property in Spain to register with the authorities. If they don't, HomeAway are going to remove their listing.'

'Can they do that?'

'They must be able to.'

'Well, I haven't heard of any new regulation, have you?'

'No, but I've emailed Paula to find out what's going on.'

By lunchtime, the full extent of the frost damage was clear. None of the grafts had survived and a good quarter of all the new growth was affected. Eventually, the tiny leaves would curl up and die, and the young canes would turn black and become spongy. It was such a shame, but at least the tomatoes had survived.

The following morning, we woke to an even heavier frost. For a second year running it looked like we'd have little if any grapes to harvest. It sometimes feels as if the world is against you, and it wasn't just the grapes.

One of the things we love about living in Spain is the laidback approach to life. It's also one of the things we hate. Take Belen for example; eleven days and two emails after first contacting her, she still hadn't responded. I ask you, how difficult would it have been to drop me a line and let me know what was going on?

'I still haven't heard from Belen,' I said at breakfast.

'What are you going to do?'

'I don't know. What can I do?'

'What about Andrea?'

'Andrea who?'

'Gerry's niece.'

We'd bumped into Gerry and his partner Carol during our first summer in Galicia. Melanie's mum, Jennifer, was staying with us at the time and, on overhearing them speaking English, struck up a conversation with them. The next thing you know, we'd invited them round for lunch, and we've remained friends ever since.

Gerry's niece, Andrea, had moved here in the 70s. She was eight at the time and her parents, Diane and Brian, had been true pioneers to this little-known corner of Spain. We never met Brian, but Diane had told us some wonderful stories of those early days. At the time, the main road from Quiroga to Monforte de

Lemos was nothing more than a dirt track. I particularly remember a washing day story when all the village women would congregate on the banks of the river Cabe and how they'd laughed when Diane's knickers went floating off down the river.

As an adult, Andrea became a freelance teacher, helping local children pass their English exams and, over the last few years, she'd added Spanish lessons to her curriculum to help Brits who had recently moved here.

'I'd forgotten she teaches Spanish. I'll email her and see if she can fit me in.'

Within the hour, she'd replied. Not only could she accommodate another student but she'd sent her timetable for me to choose a slot. Given the problems I'd had trying to contact Belen, I couldn't have been happier. My first lesson would commence this coming Thursday, the 27th of April. By that point, I'd have eleven weeks to prepare for the most important exam of my life.

Organising lessons had taken my mind off an equally important issue: Huddersfield Town's push for the playoffs. Today's opponent was Fulham, another team with aspirations of promotion. On paper, it looked like an evenly matched contest. In reality it turned into a rout with Fulham running out 4–0 winners. That loss represented a major setback. Town's next match was on Tuesday evening away to Wolverhampton Wanderers. All I could do was cross my fingers and hope for the best.

Frosty mornings at this time of year are a consequence of bright sunny days and a cloudless night sky. At the same time as we were mourning the demise of our grapevines, we were able to breakfast outside, enjoy lunch in the garden, and sit out until nine in the evening.

On Sunday, temperatures topped 38°C and, while I trimmed the hedge around the vineyard, Melanie dusted off her inflatable recliner and spent the afternoon floating in the pool with her nose in a book.

That evening, as we watched the sun setting behind the woody knoll, we noticed a plume of thick grey smoke on the horizon. A few minutes later, firefighting planes, from the Marroxo airfield, passed overhead. Forest fires at this time of year were rare, and reflected the unseasonably good weather we'd been enjoying. Even more surprising was that it had come on the back of one of the worst winters we'd ever experienced. Perhaps the world's climate was changing.

By the time we retired inside, fading light had grounded the aircraft. Responsibility for taming the flames shifted to firefighters on the ground. They would undoubtedly do their best, but it was unlikely to be good enough. We could only hope no one was in its path.

'Do you think we'll be alright?' asked Melanie.

'I think so.'

We hadn't smelt any burning and there was no sign of ash on the ground. That suggested it was some way off and the wind was blowing it away from us but, before turning in, I packed the passports and laptop just in case. Better safe than sorry.

9

First Impressions

As we slept, firefighters fought the blaze. At first light, waterbombers rejoined the fray.

'That fire is still burning, but it looks a long way off,' said Melanie, when she returned with our morning coffees.

Reassuring for us, but not so for others.

'I thought we could go to Otero's this morning and get some sand to repair the lawn at *Campo Verde*,' I said.

The guests had left, and it looked like being another clear day.

'How much will we need?'

'Two hundred kilos should be more than enough, and whatever's left over we can use here.'

It was better to get too much than not have enough.

By 10:30, I'd hitched the trailer to the back of the car and we were on our way to Otero's builder's merchant on the outskirts of Monforte de Lemos. Fifteen minutes later we were pulling up outside.

'Can I have 200 kilos of sand?' I asked.

Without saying a word, the sales assistant tapped my request into the computer.

'*Algo más* (Anything else)?' he asked.

'*Nada más* (Nothing else),' I replied.

'*Cuatro* (Four euro).'

I knew it would be cheap, but that hardly merited opening my wallet.

'Drive around the back and someone will load it for you,' he said, handing me a slip.

The bulk materials yard was at the rear of the premises.

I'm always slightly nervous in these situations. Despite owning the trailer for the best part of ten years, I'd never quite mastered the art of reversing. It's embarrassing to say the least. Thankfully, the only person in the yard was the lad charged with loading the sand. After several failed attempts to back up to the storage bay, I jumped out, unhitched the trailer, and pushed it into position. The lad took one look at the slip and, instead of shovelling the sand into the trailer, he hopped onto the forklift and, with all the skill of a seasoned pro, lifted a part-full Big Bag off the ground. I guess it was Monday morning after all.

A full Big Bag contains a metric ton and, by the look of it, this one was nearly half-full. As he lowered it into the trailer, the chassis creaked under the strain.

'Will you be alright with that?' he asked.

Not one to look a gift horse in the mouth, I

promptly agreed and, on that note, he went back inside.

'There's more than 200 kilos there,' said Melanie.

Even she'd noticed.

My attempts to push the trailer back to the car met with stiff resistance.

'Give me a hand?' I asked.

We braced ourselves against the back of the trailer and pushed. An uneven surface and excess load combined to thwart our efforts. Thank heavens no one was watching us.

'It's too heavy,' moaned Melanie.

She had a point.

'I'll tell you what, I'll reverse the car up, but make sure I don't drive into the trailer.'

The phrase "work smarter not harder" sprang to mind.

Melanie failed to realise that all the arm waving in the world counts for naught if the driver can't see it. Eventually, I managed to get within a foot of the coupler. All I had to do then was lift it onto the towbar.

'Crikey! That weighs a ton.'

Not quite, but it was a deadlift too much for me. I hadn't realised at the time, but that gift horse was actually laughing at us.

'What now?'

As is often the case, taking a step backwards led to a way forwards.

'I know.'

'What?'

'I'll lift it with the jockey wheel.'

The jockey wheel sits behind the coupler and, although I'd never used it for such, was specifically designed for just that purpose. Rotating a handle on top of the wheel raises and lowers the height of the coupler, but even that was hard work. Eventually I managed to clear the top of the towbar and we pushed the trailer into position. Turning the handle anticlockwise lowered it onto the towbar. As it did, the car's suspension sank lower and lower and lower. We'd had some weight in the trailer before, but nothing like this.

'Are you sure it's safe?' asked Melanie.

I hadn't a clue. According to the log book, the trailer's unladen weight, i.e. how much it weighed when empty, was 185 kilos, and its maximum capacity was 450 kilos. What I'd never quite figured out was if the maximum capacity included the unladen weight. Whatever the answer, the question remained the same: would the car pull this heavy load from the lowlands of Monforte de Lemos to the highlands of Escairón?

'It'll be fine,' I replied.

Forever the optimist but, then again, what choice did we have.

As soon as I drove away, I could feel the weight pulling on the car. I didn't say a word, but suspected Melanie knew exactly what was going on. Thankfully, the roads were virtually traffic-free allowing us to travel in a low gear at a modest speed. The journey passed in silence, which is often the case when you're holding your breath. Twenty minutes after leaving Otero's, we arrived at the house.

'See, I told you it would be fine,' I said.

Filling the holes took more sand than expected but, if I had to guess, there was more left over than I'd actually ordered. Before leaving, I filled two buckets just in case, and we took the rest home.

That evening Huddersfield Town were back in action. Their visit to Wolverhampton Wanderers was billed as their most important game since gaining promotion to the Championship five years ago. As things turned out, one goal decided the outcome, a twenty-five-yard screamer from Izzy Brown. At the final whistle I was over the moon. Huddersfield Town had guaranteed their place in the playoffs with two games to spare.

My sense of elation was short-lived, but I guess that's the lot of sports fans. Winning is a double-edged sword; on the one hand we dare to dream, and on the other we fear the worst. Four clubs would qualify for the playoffs, but only one would emerge victorious.

'I've had a reply from Paula,' I said.

While Melanie had been out with Slawit, I'd checked my inbox.

'A reply?'

'About those new regulations for the house.'

'That was ages ago.'

It was actually five days, but she had a point. Paula usually responds much quicker than that.

'What did she say?'

'She said it would be easier to explain if we called in.'

'When?'

'This morning.'

By eleven o'clock we were driving to the offices of Asesoría Eiriz in Monforte de Lemos. We hadn't been waiting long when Paula poked her head around the waiting room door and invited us into her office.

According to her, the new regulations were a direct result of hoteliers lobbying the government. They'd claimed that unregulated rental properties were having a detrimental effect on the hospitality sector, and successfully argued that, to remedy the situation, all holiday rental properties should be licensed and subject to the same regulations as they were. As a consequence, owners would be obliged to register their property with the local authority who would issue them with a certificate of compliance. Only then could the owner apply for the necessary licence. Furthermore, it would be incumbent on owners to provide the local Guardia Civil (Civil Guard) with details of all guests within twenty-four hours of their arrival.

It all sounded very involved, especially as we were hoping to sell the place but, if we wanted to continue renting, we had no choice but to comply. The first step was to register the house with the town hall in Escairón.

'They might want to inspect it,' said Paula.

'What for?'

'To make sure it complies with all the regulations.'

'What regulations?'

'Don't worry. They might not.'

I sometimes wonder if Paula tells us not to worry so that we will.

'And how much is all this going to cost?' I asked.

'The licence is sixty euro, but I can't apply for that until you have the certificate.'

One more expense we could have done without, to say nothing of the extra workload, but we had no choice. Without a licence we wouldn't be able to operate. We thanked her for her insight and headed home.

The next morning, when I flung open the bedroom window shutters, another heavy frost had blanketed the landscape. Any hope that some of the new growth on the grapevines would survive was well and truly lost.

'Did you bring the tomatoes in last night?' I asked.
'I did.'

I guess we should be grateful for small mercies.

Today marked the start of my Spanish lessons with Andrea. She worked from home and lived in A Pingula, an *urbanización* on the outskirts of Monforte de Lemos consisting of three apartment blocks and a communal parking area. I had a good idea where she lived but, as this was my first visit, I left home in good time. On arrival, I found a parking space, and made my way to the apartment block. Andrea lived on the second floor. I would have taken the lift, but I couldn't get the touchscreen call pad to work. I ask you, what's wrong with buttons? After several failed attempts, I threw in the towel and climbed the stairs.

Each landing serviced four apartments. I found the correct number, rang the doorbell, and waited. When I didn't get a response, doubts began to surface. I checked the door number and then the time. I was definitely in the right place at the right time, so why wasn't anyone answering? Perhaps the doorbell was broken.

I was about to knock when I had second thoughts. Apartment blocks are notorious for transmitting sound and three o'clock was siesta time. If only I'd brought my phone, but I hadn't. I never do. I must have the most immobile mobile on the planet. I checked the time again. If I waited any longer, I was going to be late. I had no choice but to knock. Four quick raps should do the trick. Within seconds, the sound of movement suggested someone had heard. Suddenly, the door opened and a bleary-eyed man in his thirties glared at me.

'*Que* (What)?' he demanded.

Talk about a bear with a sore head.

'Andrea?' I enquired.

'No,' he replied, before closing the door behind him.

My first Spanish lesson wasn't exactly going to plan.

Having gathered my thoughts, I went back downstairs and sat on a bench in the courtyard. Thankfully, I'd brought my laptop. I booted it up and checked Andrea's email. My error was staring me in the face. The flat number was correct, but I'd entered the wrong block. I glanced at my watch. Five minutes late was not a great start.

I closed the laptop, ran into the opposite block, and dashed up the stairs to the second floor. This time, when I pushed the doorbell, Andrea's dog, Patas, responded.

'Sorry I'm late,' I said.

'No problem.'

I thought it wise to explain. I didn't want her getting into trouble on my behalf. Other than that, the lesson went much better than I could have expected. Andrea was a fabulous teacher and, despite my shortcomings, I came away believing that I might actually be able to pull this off.

'How did it go?' asked Melanie.

'Very good, once I'd found the place.'

'What do you mean?'

When I explained, Melanie thought it was hilarious.

'It wasn't funny. Anyway, she thinks an hour a week should be enough, but if I need more lessons, I can have them.'

'That's good.'

'That's what I thought.'

Andrea's enthusiasm injected fresh impetus into my studies. Out of the four disciplines, reading, writing, speaking, and listening, the latter was by far my weakest. It's something I've tried hard to correct, especially since moving to Spain, but it's not easy to change the habits of a lifetime. On this occasion, I didn't have a choice. If I wanted to pass the language exam, I would have to listen, understand, and recall. Slowly but surely, I was training my ears to hear the words, but this would be a long process and I was running out of time.

Once again, we woke to a thick layer of frost.

'Let's go to the town hall in Escairón this morning to ask about registering the house,' suggested Melanie.

Neither of us was keen, but it had to be done.

'OK.'

Campo Verde is situated in the village of Vilatán in the municipality of O Saviñao, and administered from the town hall in Escairón. Even though we'd owned the house for the best part of eleven years, we'd rarely visited the town hall. Property taxes and refuse collection were paid directly from the bank, water came from our own borehole, and a septic tank saw to the waste.

'I can't remember the last time we were here, can you?' I asked, as we made our way towards the entrance.

'We came to see the mayor once, but that was ages ago.'

Some public buildings are easy on the eye; the town hall in Escairón is not one of them. Grey and soulless would be a fair description. The reception was on the first floor and the receptionist was already dealing with someone when we arrived. We waited patiently and then asked about registering the house. To our surprise, she knew exactly what we were talking about. Less surprising was that the only person authorised to issue the certificates was only in the office on Tuesdays and Thursdays.

'If you complete this form and leave your phone number, we'll give you a call when it's ready to collect,' said the receptionist.

'Will you need to inspect the house?' asked Melanie.

'I don't think so. Just fill in the form and we'll get back to you,' she replied.

That was a relief. We were confident the house would have passed scrutiny, but you never know.

'That went well,' said Melanie, as we walked back to the car.

Not really, but I knew what she meant. Negotiating Spanish bureaucracy can often be a nightmare.

Saturday morning brought another light frost, and I spent most of it pinching off frost-damaged vine blooms with my thumbnail. It's never a good idea to leave them on. What was pleasing to see were new signs of life hidden between the dead and decaying shoots. They were unlikely to produce anything of value, but at least the vines had survived to fight another day. When it comes to agriculture, there's always next year.

Later that day, while scrolling through my social media feed, a post from Sober Council caught my attention.

'There's a classic car rally in Sober tomorrow morning,' I said.

'Really.'

I guess it didn't hold the same interest for Melanie.

'I wouldn't mind going if it's fine,' I said.

'Well, we can do.'

I'd often dreamt of owning a classic car. The idea of driving around the countryside in an open top sports car was very appealing. I suspect the reality would be very different. Compared to modern cars, most classics weren't that good when they were brand new and, unlike a fine wine, they don't get any better with age. It's alright for some blokes; they like nothing more than tinkering under the bonnet, but that's not me. I love driving and the most comfortable, safest, and economical way to do that is in a modern vehicle.

The only advantage to frosty starts is the bright sunshine that follows but, on the one occasion I wanted a clear crisp morning, we woke to the sound of rain bouncing off the roof. By eleven o'clock it had stopped, but it was still dull and overcast.

'Are we going to this car rally?' asked Melanie.

'It's not a very nice day.'

'It's up to you, but it looks to be improving.'

I stared out of the window at a brightening sky.

'OK, let's go. We can soon come back if it starts to rain.'

When we drove into the main square, we could hardly believe our eyes. The Plaza del Ayuntamiento was absolutely chocker with classic cars, as was Plaza Campo de Feria, and the surrounding streets, with more arriving all the time. Not for one minute had we expected it to be this well attended.

Most of the cars were practical classics, not concourse examples that are rarely driven. Although a pristine 1950s Ponton Mercedes did catch my eye. Other than that, these were much-loved useable classics. There was no shortage of Minis and an entire family of Fords. Parked down one street was a web of Alpha Romeo Spiders, and I counted at least five Renault 5s and considerably more Renault 4s. Some of the more exotic marks included a Renault Alpine, Porsche 911, Cadillac Coupe DeVille, and a De Tomaso Longchamp but by far the best represented manufacturer was Seat. Built in Spain under licence from the Italian automotive giant Fiat, there were excellent examples of the tiny Seat 500, 600, and 850, the boxy 124, including the high-performance Abrath model, and an iconic Seat Spider 850 in fire engine red.

What I hadn't expected to see was an example of my dad's first car, an Austin 1100, and mine, a mark II Ford Cortina. Other British classics included an old Austin Cambridge. The list went on and on, and I was in my element. For me, this was exactly what owning a classic car should be about, a fun day out for all, admiring cars of a bygone era, and actually using them. The day had started wet and miserable but finished on a high.

10

Weather or Not

Is it me or does time pass more quickly the older we get? It didn't seem two minutes since we were arriving home from our winter getaway, and here we were at the beginning of May. If I wasn't careful, events were in danger of overtaking me. On the seventeenth, Melanie would be another year older and, after the success of last year's trip to Estepona for her fiftieth, I thought it would be nice to go away again, but where to?

On Monday morning I began my search. Ideally, I wanted to find somewhere of historical interest within a four-hour drive of home. Travelling south seemed the obvious choice which led me to Benavente but, after browsing some online photos, I went off the idea. That's when I spotted Zamora. Admittedly, it was a little further, but well within my four-hour driving radius and, according to Google, the old town was littered with buildings of historic interest. Better still, the city would make an excellent base from which to explore Salamanca and Medina del Campo, both of which were on my list of places to visit.

In short, Zamora would be the perfect location for a two-night stay. We could arrive in time for lunch, without having to get up at the crack of dawn, and spend a day exploring the sights. That would leave the second day free to tour the area south of the city. On the drive home, we could stop at Puebla de Sanabria for lunch.

The next step was to find somewhere to stay. My accommodation portal of choice was booking.com. I typed in the location and the dates: two nights commencing on Tuesday the 16th. One hotel caught my eye, Hotel Alda Mercado de Zamora. It wasn't cheap, but it was slap-bang in the middle of the old town and had its own private parking. Everything was falling into place.

The only cloud on the horizon was the weather. Having checked the forecast, I decided to delay booking until nearer the time. Ten-day forecasts are rarely accurate, but at least I'd have a clearer idea of what to expect.

That left Slawit. I always feel guilty leaving her in kennels; we both do, but we didn't have a choice. She simply couldn't be trusted in a hotel room. Kennel owners Dani and Monica had looked after her last year, and I was sure they would do again. For the time being, I'd keep my plans to myself. If the weather turned against us, Melanie would be none the wiser.

Every so often, I get an itch that I just have to scratch. For reasons I can't really explain, I'd become obsessed with owning a Dimage X1, a compact digital camera produced by Konica Minolta. I'd had a Dimage G600 for over ten years and taken some memorable snaps, but it was a bit bulky to slip in my pocket. When the X1 was launched in 2005, it was very expensive, but prices had fallen to a level I could now afford.

My search took me to a website called cashconverters.es, a platform primarily used to sell secondhand tech. The advert described it as being in nearly new condition and the photos confirmed that. Indeed, the original packaging was in such good condition, I could only conclude it had been an unwanted gift. Their loss was my gain, so I placed the order. On delivery, the camera was exactly as described and looked brand new. Unfortunately, the picture quality didn't live up to expectations, but every cloud has a silver lining.

During my search, I'd stumbled across a Sony digital camera at a ridiculously low price. So low, I simply couldn't resist. Not for me I might add, but for Melanie. I briefly considered gift wrapping it as a birthday present but decided against it. Unlike the X1, the Sony had seen some action. The image quality was excellent, but the body had been in the wars and had more than a few battle scars.

When I presented it to her, she didn't quite know what to make of it.

'I thought you could take it with you when you're out with the dog,' I said.

Its ease of use and compact size made it ideal for shots on the go. To her credit, Melanie took to photography like a duck to water and showed a real talent for framing an image.

Two days later, I was working in the office when I heard the phone ring. Shortly afterwards Melanie poked her head around the door.

'That was the council in Escairón. The certificate is ready to collect.'

'That was quick. Let's go and pick it up.'

'When?'

'Now.'

'Alright, give me two minutes and I'll be with you.'

Melanie's two minutes was an expression of intent rather than an actual timeframe.

Fifteen minutes later, we were heading to Escairón. When we entered the town hall, the receptionist had everything ready for us.

'You'll need to pay this at the bank, and then come back here to collect the certificate,' she said, handing me a payment slip.

We should have guessed.

'I thought Paula said it would cost sixty euro,' I said, as we made our way to the bank.

'She did.'

'Well, this slip is for fifteen.'

'That can't be right.'

'I bet the sixty euro is for the licence not the certificate.'

On the opposite side of the square was a branch of Abanca. Service was painfully slow. Some people are more interested in passing the time of day than conducting financial transactions. Eventually, we reached the head of the queue, made the payment, and went back to the town hall with the receipt. The receptionist was dealing with another customer when we arrived but, after a short wait, we finally got our hands on the certificate.

Completing the first part of the process had been fairly straightforward. Before the next guests arrived at *Campo Verde*, we would have to license the property and find out what information the Guardia Civil required from us.

'Let's drop this off with Paula and call at Hierros La Vid on our way home,' I suggested.

'Where?'

'That steel supplier Martin mentioned when we were at their open garden.'

I'd been meaning to find out what they had to offer, and now seemed as good a time as any. As for the certificate, the sooner Paula had it the sooner she could sort out a licence for us.

We dropped the certificate off first and then continued on to the village of Vid.

'What diameter?' asked the owner.

'About that,' I said, making a circle with my thumb and forefinger.

He smiled and called me over to a storage rack.

'We have this or that.'

One looked way too thin.

'How big is that one?'

'Forty-eight point three millimetres.'

I glanced at Melanie.

'That one should be alright, don't you think?' I asked.

'How should I know?'

Mistaking my question for ignorance, the owner had scribbled down the dimension on a slip of paper and handed it to me.

'How much are they?' I asked.

'Sixteen euro.'

That sounded remarkably cheap.

'And how long are they?'

'Six metres.'

At that cost, building a grapevine arbour was a definite goer. We thanked him for his time and went home to consider our options. By the time we got back, lunch beckoned.

'Can you take a look at the fridge?' asked Melanie.

She was in the kitchen preparing lunch. I wandered through and briefly considered complimenting it on its good looks, but thought better of it.

'What's wrong with it?'

'It feels really warm.'

I opened the door, and stuck my head inside. It didn't just feel warm; it smelt warm too.

'That's way too hot. What about the freezer?'

When choosing the kitchen appliances, we'd opted for an integrated fridge freezer.

'That's fine.'

I checked anyway.

'That's strange,' I said.

'Not really. Don't you remember, they've got separate motors.'

It seemed Melanie knew more about it than I did. My expression prompted a response.

'That's how I'm able to defrost the freezer before we go away and leave the fridge until the last minute.'

Melanie was referring to our winter break. I checked the control knobs which were both in the on position, and then turned down the thermostat for the fridge.

'I've turned it down. Let's see what it's like after lunch.'

Forty minutes later, nothing had changed.

'You'd better call the engineer,' I said.

Monforte de Lemos is home to Manuel Rodríguez, the one and only white goods service engineer in the area. Over the last few years, the owner Manuel had taken a backseat and we weren't really a fan of his apprentice, but beggars can't be choosers.

'He said he'll pop in tomorrow morning,' said Melanie.

For the time being, we'd have to make do. I wandered through into the office to continue editing. When my brain tired of that, I turned my attention to Spanish audio. It was surprising how a change of discipline refreshed the parts editing couldn't reach. An hour or so later, even that became a struggle, and I drifted into browsing white goods retailers.

It quickly became apparent that choosing an integrated appliance had its drawbacks. Our existing model had been discontinued which left us with a very specific space to fill. Sizes varied considerably and many that were wide enough were either too tall or too deep. In short, I found fewer than a dozen that would fit in the existing unit. I could only hope ours could be repaired.

The following morning, we didn't have long to wait to find out. According to the engineer, it would cost more to repair than it would to buy a new one and, even if he did repair it, he couldn't guarantee something else wouldn't fail. Basically, it had reached the end of its useful life. As if to add insult to injury, he charged us twenty euro for the privilege.

'What are we going to do?' asked Melanie.

'We'll have to get a new one.'

I suppose fifteen years wasn't a bad lifespan.

'It's such a shame. There's nothing wrong with the freezer,' said Melanie.

'Perhaps someone else can get some use out of it.'

Melanie scoffed at the idea.

'Rafa and Anna might want it,' I suggested.

Rafa, his wife Anna, and their son Marcos live in the village. Anna moved here from Madrid some years ago to look after her brother. When he died, Rafa and Marcos followed her here. Since then, Rafa had struggled to find employment and, from time to time, they were reliant on the good nature of others to get by. If they could make use of the freezer, we'd be happy to let them have it.

'The next time I see him I'll ask,' said Melanie.

'I had a quick look for a new one yesterday afternoon,' I admitted.

'You did, did you?'

'If we want it to go where the old one is, there aren't that many to choose from, but I did find one that looked alright. Come and take a look.'

Melanie followed me into the office and I booted up the computer. The one in question was a Balay from an online retailer called electromacua.com.

'What do you think?' I asked.

'Which way do the doors open?'

'The wrong way.'

Why do manufacturers only produce fridge freezers with left to right opening doors? It's not as if there's a law against them opening the other way. If car manufacturers can produce right and left-hand drive cars, why can't fridge manufacturers produce right and left opening doors? I wouldn't mind, but they're manufactured with that in mind. Rather than do it themselves, they expect their customers to do it or pay extra for the privilege.

What's worse than that is the number of people prepared to accept the inconvenience. Take the apartment we rent over winter, for example. Overall, it's a good size but a compact kitchen is made even smaller by a fridge door that opens into the room. Every time you take something out you have to walk around the open door to get it. Talk about irritating.

'You'll have to swap it over. I'm not walking around that for the rest of my life.'

That told me.

'So, what do you think?'

'It looks alright, and Balay is a good name. How much is it?'

'Three hundred and twenty-three euros and ninety cents.'

'And ninety cents? Where do they get their prices from?'

That's exactly what I'd thought.

'Go on then, let's get it,' she added.

Without further ado, I placed the order. Delivery was promised within forty-eight hours.

Later that day, when Melanie returned from taking Slawit for a walk, she had some news.

'I've had a word with Rafa.'

'And?'

'He'd be happy to take it off our hands.'

'You did tell him that the fridge isn't working?'

'No, I kept that quiet.'

My look prompted a response.

'Of course I told him,' she added.

That was good; at least someone would get some use out of it.

On Wednesday morning, I was back in the office editing. Midway through the afternoon, I continued my Spanish studies. Some people believe that the only way to learn a foreign language is through conversation, but I'm not one of them. Some things are best explained in English and, with that in mind, I'd been making notes of words and phrases I was unsure of when answering the test questions in the study guide. Many were a direct consequence of the exam's multiple-choice answers. Only one could be correct but, to eliminate the others, they had to be translated. Doing that had thrown up a number of grammatical anomalies which I was hoping Andrea could clarify.

When I tired of that, I turned my attention to sourcing some clamps for the arbour. Martin had bought his from a company in Germany, but he was confident I'd be able to find something similar in the UK. Within half an hour I came across ASG Fabrications, a company specialising in steel fabrication and related products. Coincidentally, their factory was located in Batley, West Yorkshire, less than a mile from where my printing business had been. They do say it's a small world.

Amongst their extensive list of goods and services was a product called FastClamp, a range of safe and simple clamps for use in tubular construction. Moreover, they were exactly what I was looking for. Push-fit clamps that slotted into position and were tightened with an Allen key. The question was, would they deliver to Spain and, if so, how much would it cost? There was only one way to find out. I asked the question using their online enquiry form.

Before calling it a day, I checked the long-range weather forecast. Since I'd last looked, the outlook for Zamora had improved slightly, but it wasn't ideal. At some point I would have to make a decision to book the hotel room or forget the whole idea; for the time being, I would cross my fingers and wait.

I had hoped for a reply from ASG Fabrications when I checked my inbox the following morning, but the only message of interest was from electromacua.com confirming that the fridge freezer would be delivered today. Impatient for news on the clamps, I emailed the sales team directly.

'The fridge should be with us before lunch,' I said, when Melanie returned from her morning dog walk.

'I'll empty it after breakfast.'

'Will everything be alright?'

'It should be. I'll put it in the guest bathroom; it's cold in there.'

'Will you need a hand?'

'No, I'll be fine.'

'Have we got an old duvet?'

'What for?'

'To cover the food.'

Melanie looked confused.

'It'll help keep it cold,' I added.

'Are you sure?'

'Certain. Are you sure you don't want a hand?'

'Positive. I'll give you a shout when it's empty.'

While Melanie did that, I went back into the office to continue editing. Twenty minutes later, she poked her head around the door.

'I've finished if you want to drag it out.'

The fridge freezer was housed in a tall unit next to the dishwasher. As well as being a snug fit, it was raised off the floor to the height of the splashboard. The only way to remove it was to drag it out from the bottom. As soon as the front feet cleared the edge of the unit, it listed forward.

'Do be careful,' cautioned Melanie.

Crushed to death by a fridge freezer was not how I'd envisaged my end.

'Can you hold the top?' I asked.

Melanie leant across and supported it while I dragged it further out.

'The back feet are nearly at the edge,' she warned.

With the appliance at an angle of forty-five degrees, the front legs finally touched the tiles. At that point I was able to drag it from side to side until the back feet cleared the unit, allowing me to lower it to the floor. With Melanie's help, we slid it across the tiles and into the dining room.

When I returned to the office, I'd had a response from ASG Fabrications.

From: Briony
To: Craig Briggs
Subject: FastClamps
Date: Thur, 4 May 2017 10:40 AM

Good morning, Craig

We haven't delivered to Europe before but we have had increased interest over the last few months. I have spoken to our courier service who is going to meet with me on

Wednesday and we will discuss prices for shipping to Europe.

If it is okay with you, can I email you on Wednesday afternoon with further information?

I hope this helps.

Kind regards,

Briony
Sales executive

My grapevine arbour was one step closer to fruition.

'The fridge is here!' called Melanie from the kitchen.

I glanced at the time: 12:50 pm. I should have known they'd turn up at lunchtime.

'Craig!'

'Coming!'

The driver knew exactly what he was doing so I left him to unload.

'Do you want me to install it?' he asked.

'The doors need swapping over,' said Melanie.

He glanced at the paperwork.

'That'll be an extra forty-nine euro,' he said.

'I'm going to do that,' I replied.

'Oh, OK.'

He'd clearly never met a thrifty Yorkshireman before.

While Melanie finished preparing lunch, I read the instructions. Swapping the doors looked easy enough, which begged the question why don't people bother? What I hadn't realised was that before the new appliance could be switched on, it would have to stand undisturbed for a minimum of four hours. Had it not been for that, and a bathroom full of slowly defrosting food, I would have waited until after my Spanish lesson to make a start. By the time I'd eaten lunch, I had a little over an hour and a half before I would have to leave. Given last week's fiasco, I didn't want to be late again.

According to the instructions, the doors could only be removed with the fridge freezer in a prone position, which might explain why some people don't bother, and the only tools needed were a flat-head and a cross-head screwdriver. I began by removing the packaging, which in itself was no mean feat. All the parts were already attached to the fridge; it was simply a case of transferring them from one side of the casing to the other.

Unfortunately, there was nothing simple about it. The screws were easy to remove but much more difficult to reinsert and the plastic fittings were a devil to prise out of the casing. By the time I'd finished, the air was blue and droplets of sweat were oozing from every pore. I splashed some water on my face and changed into something more appropriate before hitting the road. When I mentioned my morning's endeavour to Andrea, she sympathised.

'You couldn't do mine before you go, could you?' she joked.

Apparently, every time Andrea wanted something out of the fridge, she first had to close the kitchen door. I guess the short-term pain would be worth the long-term gain.

As soon as I got home, we squeezed the new fridge freezer into position. All we had to do then was wait four hours.

'Let's drop the old one off at Rafa's,' I suggested.
Melanie agreed.

We loaded it carefully into the trailer and I crept slowly down the lane and into the village. Rafa gave me a hand to unload it and we suggested he wait four hours before switching it on.

Somewhat surprisingly, when we came to restock the freezer, everything was still frozen. All in all, we'd had a difficult day, but we got there in the end.

With only eight days until Melanie's birthday, I felt compelled to make a decision. Neither of us would want to go if the weather was bad, but delaying risked losing the room. After due consideration, I confirmed the reservation.

'I've booked to go away for your birthday,' I announced.

'Where to?'

'It's a surprise, but we'll need to book the kennel for Slawit. Would you mind doing that?'

'No problem. How long are we going for?'

'Two nights. We'll be leaving on Tuesday morning, and should be back sometime on Thursday afternoon.'

I left Melanie to make the arrangements and wandered through into the office. Two minutes later she had some unwanted news.

'They can't take her,' she said.

As well as running the kennel, and holding down full-time jobs, Dani and Monica owned a number of show poodles and, on the days we wanted them to look after Slawit, they were showing them at an event in A Coruña.

'Oh dear, what are we going to do now?' I asked.

'Have you booked the hotel?'

'I did it this morning. Is there nowhere else we can use?'

'I'm not sure. What does Andrea do with Patas when she goes away?'

I wasn't sure Andrea ever went away and, even if she did, one of her daughters was still living at home and she had plenty of family members who could look after her. Melanie wasn't convinced and seemed to remember her mentioning a kennel.

'I'll ask her at my next lesson,' I said.

'Even if she doesn't use a kennel, she might know someone who does.'

On Thursday morning Briony from ASG Fabrications emailed. She'd spoken with their courier and sent prices for delivering the FastClamps to Spain. As expected, costs were based on weight. From one to ten kilos worked out at eighteen pounds which I thought was very reasonable. With that in mind, I limited my arbour design to just six clamps and felt confident they would weigh under ten kilos. As soon as we returned from our two-night break, I would place the order. In the meantime, Briony would confirm the total weight and get back to me with a final cost.

Later that afternoon, I asked Andrea about kennels. It turned out that she did use one and couldn't praise them highly enough.

'Patas likes it so much she literally jumps into the back of their van when they come to collect her,' she said.

I doubted Slawit would be that keen, but it was reassuring to know. The people in question operated

Servican, a veterinary clinic and kennel. When I got back from my Spanish lesson, Melanie gave them a call and, fortunately for us, they had availability and were happy to look after Slawit while we were away. With five days to go, everything had fallen into place.

11

If You See Cid…

On the run-up to Melanie's birthday, I'd been keeping a close eye on the weather. When I opened my eyes on Tuesday morning, the brightness of the bedroom suggested we were in luck and, when I flung open the window shutters, my suspicion was confirmed. At least the first day of our getaway looked like being a good one.

While Melanie took Slawit out for her morning walk, I looked on Google Maps to see where the kennels were and then started packing. It's a job I really enjoy. Left to Melanie, the clothes would be in a right state when we arrived at the hotel.

'Did you find out where the kennel is?' asked Melanie over breakfast.

'I think so. It's on Camiño de Lodairo, close to the open market.'

After breakfast, I checked the car's coolant, oil level, screenwash, and tyre pressures. The coolant was fine but the oil needed topping up along with the screenwash, and I put a bit more air in the front tyres.

'Right then, I'm ready when you are,' I said.

Slawit had been on edge since yesterday afternoon when I took the case out of storage. As I lifted her into the back of the car, she knew for certain that something was going on. I'm sure all dog owners would say the same, but I only had to look into her eyes to know how she was feeling, and she wasn't happy.

'Don't look at me like that. You'll love it once you get there.'

I knew that wasn't true, but we couldn't take her with us. Ten minutes later we were heading towards the *feria* ground in Monforte de Lemos, site of the twice monthly market.

'There should be a turning coming up on the left,' I said.

'There's one.'

Fifty metres after making the turn, we came to a T-junction. A road sign read "Camiño de Lodairo".

'Which way now?'

I wasn't sure, but turning left would have taken us onto a dirt track so I went right. Three hundred metres further along, we rejoined the main carriageway.

'I guess I should have gone left.'

I retraced my route back to the T-junction and this time turned left.

'Keep your eyes peeled.'

'What's it called, again?' asked Melanie.

Talk about the blind leading the blind.

'Servi-something or other.'

Given the condition of the track, I'd slowed to crawling pace. We seemed to have been travelling for ages when Melanie clapped eyes on the place.

'Could it be called Servican?' she asked.

'Something like that, why?'

'Because we're here.'

When I came to a stop, a cloud of dust floated past the car. I pulled into a driveway entrance and we hopped out. Carefully, I lifted the tailgate making sure Slawit didn't do a runner, and then clipped on her lead.

'Come on,' I said.

She didn't need asking twice. After all these years, she still hates travelling in the car.

Beyond the gates was a purpose-built single-storey facility on a fully enclosed plot of approximately 2000 square metres. We rang the bell and the practice nurse led us inside. At the rear of the buildings were ten identical kennels, five either side of a central walkway. Each had a good-sized run with a small house at the rear. In that respect we were really happy: Slawit wasn't one for mixing.

'This is for Slawit,' said the nurse.

We encouraged her inside and closed the gate behind her. Slawit didn't know what to think.

'Aw look,' said Melanie, tipping her head towards the enclosure opposite.

Sitting in the middle of the run was a fluffy brown rabbit.

'It was only meant to be with us for two weeks. That was over two months ago,' said the nurse.

'Has it been abandoned?' I asked.

'No, they're still paying for it.'

Slawit was either too traumatised to care or hadn't yet noticed because *podenco*s were bred specifically to hunt rabbits. Poor dog, I wasn't sure things could get any worse.

By the time we left, a fifteen-minute drop-off had taken the best part of an hour.

The drive to Zamora took us west into Ourense before picking up the A-52 heading southeast. At junction 49, we exited the highway and drove across country along the N-631. In common with many Spanish cities, the outskirts of Zamora were very unappealing. Mile after mile of wide avenues were lined with unimaginatively designed apartment blocks. As we approached the old town, the road narrowed and new builds were replaced with older, more characterful properties.

'This is more like it. Keep your eyes peeled. It should be along here somewhere,' I said.

'Is that it on the left?'

One problem with narrow streets is the lack of on-street parking. Stopping outside the hotel was not an option.

'Where's the carpark?' asked Melanie.

'They didn't say.'

'Where are you going?'

'I can't stop here. We'll have to find somewhere to park and walk back.'

A few metres further along I spotted a vacant loading bay and pulled in.

'Can you go and ask them where to park?'

I couldn't leave the car unattended; someone might want to use the bay.

'If I'm not here when you get back wait here,' I added.

Why is it that the shortest wait feels like an eternity when you're parked where you shouldn't be?

Five minutes later, which felt like an hour and a half, I caught sight of Melanie in the mirror.

'There's a turn-off just before the hotel and the parking is underneath,' she said.

Wouldn't you know it, turning around was not an option. I had no choice but to follow my nose and rely on a sense of direction to reach our destination. After driving uphill and down dale, on medieval streets designed for coach and horses, we finally got back to our starting point.

'It's coming up on the left,' said Melanie.

A short road took us to the rear of the hotel. From the underground parking area, we took a lift to reception.

Hotel Alda Mercado was everything I'd hoped it would be. A magnificent, quarter-landing staircase featuring stained-glass windows and an intricate wrought iron balustrade filled the entrance lobby, and the deluxe double room was much bigger than I'd expected. A sitting area and writing desk gave it the feel of a junior suite. There wasn't a view, but the skylight provided ample natural light.

'This is lovely,' remarked Melanie.

'Let's leave everything for now and take a look around,' I suggested.

The time had moved on to 2:00 pm, and we hadn't yet had lunch.

Stone steps led from the reception down to street level. Zamora lies on the banks of the river Duero which, when it crosses the border into Portugal, becomes the river Douro. I knew from my research that the river was at the rear of the hotel, south of our current location. Most of the city's landmarks were to the west so that's where we headed. Within thirty metres of the hotel, we reached the church Iglesia de San Andrés. Immediately before it, half a dozen stone steps descended into Cuesta del Caño.

'Let's go down here,' I suggested.

I felt confident we'd reach the river at some point. Towards the bottom of the hill, we came across another church, Iglesia de Santo Tomé. I suspected we'd be seeing a lot more of them before the day was out, but storks nesting on the belltower provided a photo opportunity not to be missed.

'That could be it,' I said, pointing down a street.

'That could be what?'

'The river.'

'What river?'

'The river Duero.'

We continued on to the main road, and there it was. A gentle meander limited our view but, as we walked westerly along the riverbank, the panorama opened out and we caught sight of the thirteenth century Puente de Piedra or Stone Bridge. An impressive structure consisting of fifteen arches spanning a distance of 280 metres.

It doesn't matter where you go in Spain, you're never far from the Camino de Santiago and Zamora was no exception. For the past eight hundred years, pilgrims travelling the Vía de la Plata, or Silver Route from the cathedral in Seville to the one in Santiago de Compostela, have entered Zamora across the Puente de Piedra. We strolled to the halfway point to take a few snaps.

'That is stunning,' remarked Melanie.

The temperature had been building throughout the day but, standing above the flowing water, it felt comfortably cool.

'Where next?' she asked.

'Let's make our way towards that church,' I suggested.

Perched on a hilltop overlooking the bridge was the Iglesia de San Pedro y San Ildefonso.

On a warm day, the climb from the river was quite a trek. One side of the church was supported by two stone buttresses spanning the width of the street. The stonework blended well with the original masonry, but I suspected they were much newer, no doubt erected to prevent the church from collapsing. When it came to walking underneath them, we didn't hang around.

By accident rather than design we'd found ourselves in the heart of the old town and the small leafy square of Plaza de Arias Gonzalo. In one corner was the restaurant Meson el Castillo, where a stone-pillared portico provided its customers with some much-needed shade.

'I'm gagging for a drink,' said Melanie.

'Let's stop here. We might be able to get something to eat.'

Lunch was not on the menu so we ordered a *tabla* and two beers. When it came, it was exactly what we were looking for: thinly sliced rounds of chorizo, *jamón,* and *salchichón,* along with two different cheeses. We couldn't have been happier.

'Right then, are you ready to make a move? I think the cathedral and the castle are that way,' I said.

'Ready when you are.'

As far as I could tell, we were heading west.

'Let's take a look down here,' said Melanie.

She was standing at the entrance to a narrow lane, and a sign which read "Mirador del Troncoso". A few metres further along, it opened out into a long viewing platform with spectacular views over the surrounding countryside and the river. Directly below us was the Puente de Piedra in all its glory and the remnants of the old Roman crossing. We took some snaps before continuing on.

Less than 200 metres from the viewing point, we entered a small square at the rear of the cathedral. On one side was the eleventh century Casa del Cid, where the famous military leader Rodrigo Díaz de Vivar, better known as El Cid, is thought to have grown up. Opposite that was the seventeenth century episcopal palace, its scale and opulence serving as a reminder of the power and wealth of the Catholic church at that time. Between the two was the Puerta del Obisco or Bishop's Gate.

All these monuments were dwarfed by the twelfth century cathedral. The rear provided the bishop with his own ornately sculptured private entrance and, given its opulence, it's easy to see how these leaders of the faith could have become consumed by their own earthly importance. Having marvelled at the rear, we made our way to the front where we found an equally dramatic entrance on an even grander scale, but the cathedral's most impressive architectural feature was its stone-built dome. We'd never seen anything like it. Even from ground level the craftsmanship looked exquisite.

Beyond the cathedral, overlooking the river and the town, was the castle of Zamora, the foundations of which can be traced back to Roman times. We briefly thought of going inside, but my feet were starting to feel the pace and the hotel was some way off. We continued on to the Plaza Mayor where we stopped for another refreshing beer.

'That's pretty,' said Melanie.

Adjacent to us was the old town hall, a charming building currently used as a police station.

'I don't know about you, but I could do with a siesta,' I said.

Back at the hotel we downloaded our photos and uploaded the best of them to Facebook before putting our feet up.

That evening, we decided to dine at the hotel. The restaurant was housed in the old wine cellar and bore more than a passing resemblance to the dining room in the Parador hotel in Santiago de Compostela. The setting was excellent and the food great but, as we were the only customers, it lacked atmosphere.

'I think we might try somewhere different tomorrow night,' I whispered.

The next morning, we woke to the pitter patter of rain on the Velux window. Nowadays, we never leave home without packing the kettle. Spanish hotels rarely have tea and coffee making facilities, and I flatly refuse to get out of bed until I've had my morning coffee. As for the weather, we could only hope it would improve.

While I sipped my coffee, Melanie opened her cards and presents and then we readied ourselves for breakfast. On this occasion we weren't alone in the dining room, but it was by no means busy. Breakfast was included in the nightly rate. No full English, but I more than made up for it with a slice of tortilla, a wedge of *empanada* (a flat pie), a ham and cheese sandwich, two cups of coffee, a chocolate muffin, and a bottle of mineral water.

'I'm stuffed,' I said, as we made our way back to the room.

'I'm not surprised.'

'You can talk.'

I suspected we'd be having a light lunch.

'So, what have you got planned for today?' asked Melanie.

'I thought we could take a look at Salamanca and then drive on to Medina del Campo.'

'Salamanca sounds nice. What is there at the other place?'

'That castle we drive past on the A-6 when we go south for winter.'

Melanie's expression suggested she hadn't a clue what I was talking about.

'You know the one I mean. Every time we drive past, I say we'll have to stop there one day.'

'The one that looks brand new?'

'That's it.'

'Oh, OK, but can we have a look at the market before we set off?'

'What market?'

'The one opposite.'

'Of course.'

The air felt damp as we stepped outside, but at least it wasn't raining. Directly opposite was the municipal food market. On the pavement outside were colourful displays of freshly picked fruit and vegetables. We had a quick look before going inside. The place reminded me of Todmorden market hall in the Calder Valley in West Yorkshire. The goods were different, but the atmosphere was very similar. Unfortunately, shoppers were less plentiful but, on a day like today, it was hardly surprising.

'Have you seen enough?' I asked.

'I think so.'

We made our way back to the hotel and took the lift to the underground parking area. Salamanca is less than seventy kilometres from Zamora. Forty-five minutes later, I'd found on-street parking within sight of the city's iconic cathedral. What I hadn't realised was that it can be seen from miles around, a fact my feet were unlikely to forget in a hurry.

The building itself was built on such a scale, it made Zamora's cathedral look like a village church.

'Do you want to go inside?' I asked.

'How much is it?'

Entry into such historic buildings is rarely free and, while we appreciate these marvels of medieval architecture require constant maintenance to preserve them for future generations, the Catholic church isn't exactly poor and nine euro each seemed a high price to pay.

'We're not paying that,' said Melanie, and I agreed.

In comparison, the cathedral in Santiago de Compostela is free to enter. I wonder which Jesus would approve of?

'Let's take a look at the Plaza Mayor instead,' I suggested.

Salamanca's Plaza Mayor is famous for its student buskers. On warm summer evenings they don medieval costumes and serenade tourists for little more than the cost of a drink. Given the weather, and the time of day, we were unlikely to see such nocturnal activities, but we couldn't visit the city without seeing its iconic square.

From the cathedral we walked along Calle Rúa Mayor, a pedestrianised thoroughfare lined with interesting and colourful shops.

'Look at those.'

Melanie had stopped at the window of Mulas, a delicatessen specialising in *hornazo ibérico*. This traditional pasty is made from fluffy bread dough and filled with *jamón ibérico*, *lomo* (cured pork loin), and local chorizo. Before baking it's decorated with a distinctive latticework and glazed. Further along, another shop had legs of *jamón ibérico* hanging from the walls like wallpaper.

What surprised us most about Salamanca was the number of visitors. Surrounding every place of interest were groups of day-trippers or schoolchildren listening to a guide or teacher. I doubt even Santiago de Compostela would be this busy on a miserable day in May. As well as being a World Heritage Centre and home to one of the oldest universities in Europe, Salamanca boasts many outstanding Moorish, Romanesque, Gothic, Renaissance, and baroque monuments.

A signpost guided us through an alleyway and into the Plaza Mayor. The square was on a scale we'd never seen before. A continuous series of arcades and galleries, many of which housed bars and restaurants, enclosed all four sides of the square. Above those were three storeys of apartments built in the Spanish baroque style featuring floor to ceiling windows and narrow balconies with iron railings.

'Let's get a drink,' I suggested.

My feet were feeling the pace. We took a seat under a large parasol. Service was swift, due in part to the onset of rain. It wasn't heavy, but it was persistent. Sunshine or rain, large parasols come in useful. As we sipped our beers, I noticed a curious sculpture in one corner of the square: an eight-metre-tall white elephant, standing on its trunk. Every hour on the hour, this unusual artwork let out a loud farting noise and ejected a puff of white smoke.

It's not every day we find ourselves sitting in the rain in one of Spain's most iconic squares when an eight-metre-tall elephant lets rip. I later discovered that Gran Elefant Dret was the work of Mallorcan artist Miquel Barceló.

As we made our way back to the car, we reflected on our visit. I'm not sure if it was the weather, the number of tourists, or a combination of both but it was fair to say that Salamanca hadn't stolen hearts. That's not to say we won't return some day but, before then, there are many lesser-known places we'd like to visit.

'Where next?' asked Melanie, when we got back to the car.

'Medina del Campo. It's about an hour away.'

'That's good, we should get there in time for lunch.'

'After the breakfast you had!'

'A glass of wine and tapas wouldn't go amiss.'

I couldn't argue with that.

12

Love at First Sight

The drive from Salamanca to Medina del Campo took us along the *autovia* A-62, a road we first travelled on in the summer of 1993. The year prior to that I'd bought my first Rover 827 and thought it would be fun to spend our two-week summer holiday driving 6000 kilometres from Huddersfield in West Yorkshire to Carvoeiro on the Algarve and back again. In those days, the road surface was nothing like it is today, and the drive from Salamanca to the Portuguese border was particularly arduous, or so we thought. Across the border the roads were even worse. With that in mind, we only stayed a week in the Algarve and spent the rest of the holiday driving back along the Mediterranean coast. That trip made such an impression on us that, from then on, we took at least one holiday a year in Spain before moving here permanently in 2002.

Compared to that road trip, today's drive of eighty-seven kilometres was a doddle. Our destination was Castillo de la Mota, so called because the castle is built on a *mota* or hill overlooking the town of Medina del Campo. Up close and personal, it didn't disappoint. These medieval fortresses were built to keep their occupants safe and their enemies at bay. It's strange how structures designed to repel now attract. Unfortunately, we'd arrived at lunchtime and the ticket office was closed. On reflection, taking a look inside didn't seem that important.

'Shall we come back after lunch?' asked Melanie.

The tone of her question suggested not, and I was happy to go along. We'd seen what we came for, and castles are often more interesting from the outside than they are from within. It was time to find out what Medina del Campo could offer us for lunch.

When visiting new places, it's often a good idea to make a beeline for the Plaza Mayor. We found roadside parking nearby and made our way on foot. Unlike some places, the local council had struck the right balance between new and old. Modern porticos blended sympathetically with their medieval counterparts and allowed us to stroll around without getting wet. On one side of the square stood the imposing collegiate church of San Antolín, built on a scale that would dwarf some cathedrals. Along from that was the equally impressive seventeenth century town hall, and the Casa de los Arcos or House of Arches, where the clergy would keep an eye on their parishioners during fiestas, fairs, and suchlike. You could say it was the medieval equivalent of CCTV.

'What about over there?'

Melanie had spotted a row of open parasols opposite the church. The town offered its visitors two choices, Restaurante Mónaco or Gloria. The clock had moved on to four, too late for lunch but a drink and tapas would keep us going until dinner. With that in mind we chose the latter. They had a great selection of nibbles, and we weren't disappointed. By the time we'd eaten, the rain was barely noticeable. Before heading back to the car, we had a quick wander around and took a few snaps. Despite the weather we'd had a good day out and seen some wonderful sights.

When we got back to the hotel, the rain had stopped and it felt quite warm. Our search for an evening eatery began in earnest: Melanie on her Kindle Fire and me on the laptop.

'What about this?'

Melanie had found an Italian, five minutes from the hotel.

'That looks perfect, let's give it a go,' I said.

'Do you think we'll need to book?'

On a damp Wednesday in May it seemed unlikely but, as it was Melanie's birthday, we made the call.

Unlike some restaurants, the moment you walk through the door of an Italian bistro you get a feel for the place and Restaurante Pinocchio felt perfect. Reading the menu confirmed we'd made the right choice. We skipped starters in the hope our appetites would stretch to a pudding, and chose two main courses to share: oven-baked maccheroni gratinati with bechamel, tomatoes, and chorizo, and pizza Trentino, with mozzarella, tomato, minced beef and barbecue sauce. To accompany the food, we chose a bottle of Flor Innata, a fruity white wine from the Rueda region.

'That was delicious,' said Melanie.

'Pudding?'

'Are you having one?'

I couldn't resist, especially as I'd noticed one of my favourites on the menu.

'I think so.'

'I'm too full. Do you know what you want?'

'Profiteroles with hot chocolate sauce.'

'Oh yes, I think I will.'

'I thought you were full,' I replied, with a cheeky wink.

An opulent pudding finished off a terrific birthday dinner.

At this time of year, it's quite remarkable how quickly the weather can change. When we stepped outside, it felt comfortably warm.

'Let's have a nightcap in the Plaza Mayor,' I suggested.

Old buildings and narrow streets look completely different at night. Moody street lighting transported us through a bygone age but, unlike the surrounding streets, the Plaza Mayor was a hive of activity. Spaniards are nomadic drinkers moving from bar to bar throughout the evening. This creates an ever-changing kaleidoscope of people. We took a seat at Cervecería Plaza Mayor. Melanie ordered a glass of white wine and I finished the evening with a gin and tonic, the perfect end to an interesting and enjoyable day.

The next morning, the weather looked encouraging. After breakfast we'd be checking out, but I had another busy day planned.

'Can you pass me the laptop?' I asked.

Melanie was waiting for the kettle to boil.

Yesterday evening, Huddersfield Town had played the second leg of their playoff semi-final against Sheffield Wednesday at Hillsborough. Four nights earlier, the first leg had ended in a goalless draw. One way or another, the second leg would produce a winner. I'd been tempted to check the result last night, but I couldn't bring myself to spoil the moment.

'Here you go.'

Waiting for the computer to boot up was tortuous; it seemed to take forever. Finally, the desktop appeared. I clicked on the browser icon and once again it seemed to take ages to load.

'There you go,' said Melanie, placing a mug of steaming coffee on the bedside table.

'Thanks.'

'How did they get on?'

'It hasn't loaded yet.'

The browser fired into life and I clicked the BBC Sport icon. I waited and waited. When the page finally appeared, victory was ours. We'd done it; we'd reached the playoff final. One more game stood between Huddersfield Town and the promised land of the Premier League. On the 29th of May, at the national stadium in Wembley, Huddersfield Town would take to the field against Reading FC for the richest prize in football.

The match report made great reading. At the final whistle, the two teams couldn't be separated, and, after a period of extra time, the game ended 1–1. In the penalty shootout that followed, Town's on-loan goalkeeper, Danny Ward, became the hero of the night, saving two of the five penalties.

It's amazing how a favourable sports result puts a spring in your step. I could only imagine what effect it would have had on the town as a whole.

In the space of twenty-four hours, we had gone from breakfast novices to old hats. We knew exactly what to expect and what we were going to choose.

'So, what have you got planned for today?' asked Melanie, as we readied to leave.

'I thought we could go to Toro first.'

'What's there?'

'I've no idea, but it's on the way to Tordesillas.'

'Why does that ring a bell?'

'We drive past it every year when we go south.'

'Ah yes.'

'After that, I thought we could call at Puebla de Sanabria for lunch.'

'That's a great idea.'

We'd visited Puebla de Sanabria before but it's such a beautiful village, it was well worth a second look.

Having settled the bill, we set out on the A-11 in search of Toro. Half an hour later, we exited the main road. A stone archway marked the entrance to Calle Corredera, the main approach road to the town centre. Talk about love at first sight. This narrow one-way street lined with olde-worlde retailers, buildings of historic interest, and the obligatory church was absolutely charming. At the end of the street, the Torre de Reloj or Clock Tower dominated the surrounding streets.

'This is lovely,' remarked Melanie.

On such a busy street it was difficult to take it all in, but I had to agree.

'I need to find somewhere to park.'

I turned into a side street and quickly found a roadside parking space.

'I think the main street is this way,' I said.

Even the residential side streets were charming. Many of the older properties had been sympathetically restored while others were showing their age. This created an urban landscape of character. We joined the high street and headed towards the clock tower. Up close, the shops were even more interesting. Toro was a living community not a tourist attraction, and the shops reflected that.

The town is built on a hilltop overlooking the river Duero, and the surrounding area produces some excellent wines, so much so that it has its own *denominación de origen*, a quality standard for a specific geographical region.

'Let's get a bottle of wine,' I said.

At the top of the street, we'd come across a specialist wine retailer.

'OK, but let's buy it on the way back.'

She had a point.

'That's what I meant.'

Her smirk suggested she didn't believe a word of it, and rightly so.

The impressive baroque clock tower was also known as Arco del Reloj or Clock Arch due to it sitting above one of the ancient gates to the old walled town.

'Let's see where that leads,' I said, tipping my head towards the archway.

Architects of the time based their designs around horsedrawn carriages and people on foot. Today's vehicles tend to be that bit wider. We waited for a white van to drive through and then made a dash for it. Passing through the arch was like stepping back in time; we'd never seen anything quite like it. Imagine if you can a heritage museum with exhibitions covering the last two, three, four hundred years and more. Banks housed in beautifully restored period properties are a common sight on many high streets; much less familiar was the row of timber-framed terraced properties. Once plumb lines had succumbed to the passage of time and now tricked the eye into believing they were flowing like the sea. Remove one building and the whole lot would have come crashing down. Opposite those was the Plaza Mayor, dominated by the magnificent eighteenth century town hall with an inscription on the façade which read "Casa Consistorial" (Town Hall).

'Look at that,' said Melanie.

Towering over the tops of the buildings was a spectacular stone-built dome supported by four towers similar in design to the cathedral in Zamora. If anything, this one was even more impressive. We couldn't resist taking a closer look. What we found was the Colegiata de Santa María la Mayor, built on a scale that dwarfed the church in Medina del Campo.

It fascinated me why a town the size of Toro would warrant such a magnificent building. Given its size, it seemed inconceivable that there wasn't more to Toro than met the eye.

'Take a look at this.'

Melanie was standing next to a low wall with her back to the church. I walked across, curious to know what she'd found. As I approached, the panorama opened out. We were standing on the edge of a steep escarpment. Below us, the stone bridge, Puente Mayor, spanned the river Duero which meandered through the flat plain for as far as the eye could see.

'I bet Laurie Lee walked across that bridge.'

'Who?'

'Laurie Lee, you know, the bloke who wrote that book about Spain.'

'What are you on about?'

'That English poet and author who came to Spain for a wander.'

'Do you mean *"As I Walked Out One Midsummer Morning"?*'

'That's the one.'

'How do you know that?'

'I know lots of stuff,' I replied.

I might even get around to reading it one of these days.

'Anyway, shall we make our way back to the car?'

'I think so.'

We retraced our steps, through the archway and into what felt like a different century. At the wine shop, we stopped and bought a bottle of Toro's finest.

'Ooh look!' said Melanie.

While I'd been deciding which wine to buy, Melanie had seen some artisan chocolates. By artisan, I mean expensive.

'We could have another bottle of wine for the price of those.'

Melanie looked decidedly disappointed.

'Oh, go on then.'

By the look on her face, you'd have thought I'd bought her a ten-carat diamond.

'Where next?' she asked, as we pulled away.

'Tordesillas.'

'What's there?'

'I don't know, but we're about to find out.'

Forty minutes later we found ourselves driving along the bank of the river Duero. I guess we shouldn't have been surprised; if it wasn't for the final 200 kilometres flowing through Portugal, the Duero would be Spain's second longest river. A bridge up ahead would have put us on the wrong side so I turned left into a cobbled road which took us up towards the city. As we reached the top, the road narrowed to half its original width and we found ourselves on a street fractionally wider than the car.

'Breathe in,' I said.

On such narrow streets, driving straight ahead was relatively straightforward, although I'm not sure Melanie would see it that way. The problem came when we reached a T-junction. Scars on every corner were a testament to more than close encounters.

'What about there?' asked Melanie.

She'd spotted a very tight parking space outside a church.

'You'd better hop out,' I said.

One of the drawbacks of owing a two-door coupe is the width of the doors. I teased the car into the space and managed to get out without touching the car next to mine. I could only hope the owner of that vehicle would afford me the same courtesy on their return. A short distance from the church we stumbled across one of the smallest crossroads in Spain.

'Which way?' I asked.

'I don't know. This was your idea.'

'In that case, it's this way.'

'What is?'

'The way we're going.'

Tsk!

By accident rather than design, we found ourselves at the entrance to the Plaza Mayor. In comparison to the other places we'd visited, Tordesillas main square looked neglected and unloved. A banner draped from the town hall read "*Si al Toro de la Vega*" (Yes to the Bull of the Meadow). That's when the penny dropped. Since the start of the decade, Tordesillas had been subjected to protests by animal rights activists opposed to the annual bull run or Toro de la Vega. Dating back to 1524, this medieval festival saw a bull chased through the city streets by a group of lancers, and ended with it being corralled in a meadow and slaughtered. In 2016, killing the bull was outlawed and a new fiesta called Toro de la Peña (Bull of the Virgin Mary) was created.

'Are you hungry?' I asked, as we made our way back to the car.

'Not really.'

'That's good.'

'Why?'

'We're an hour and a half away from Puebla de Sanabria.'

'That's OK, but I could do with the loo before we carry on.'

After a quick pit stop, we were back on the road: the A-6 to Benavente and then the A-52 heading towards Ourense.

The last few days had left the windscreen covered with dead insects. In an effort to clean it, I flicked on the screenwash.

'Oh no!'

'What's wrong?'

'The screenwash isn't working.'

'Perhaps it's run out.'

'It can't have done; I topped it up before we set off.'

'I don't know then.'

'Neither do I.'

I'm sure it's true of all car manufacturers, but Renault owners seem to have more than their fair share of problems. The good thing about that is the number of helpful tips available online. I could only hope the same would be true of the screenwash.

At junction 79, we exited the A-52 and continued on into Puebla de Sanabria. Spain is blessed with many beautiful settlements from the whitewashed villages of Andalucía to the stone-built hamlets of Girona. Puebla de Sanabria is up there with the best of them. The first thing to catch our eye was the fifteenth century castle perched on top of a wedge-shaped hill. From there, houses cascade down the hillside to the floodplain below. To reach the village we crossed the river Tera.

On a previous visit, I'd parked at the top of the hill close to the castle. This time I found a space further down and we walked to the top. If anything, the village was prettier than we'd remembered. Almost every property has been beautifully restored. At the top of the hill was the Plaza Mayor. It's smaller than most but no less beautiful and, on a warm sunny day in May, we couldn't resist photographing everything.

'Right then, shall we find somewhere to eat?' I asked.

The time had moved on to 2:30 pm and, if we weren't careful, we risked missing lunch service again.

'That's a good idea,' replied Melanie.

The walk up to the square had given us the opportunity to check out the available eateries. On the way back down, we made our choice.

'This place looks alright,' said Melanie.

She'd stopped outside Restaurant Sidrería roughly halfway up the main street. A chalkboard suggested they were still serving.

'Can we sit outside?' asked Melanie.

'Of course,' said the owner.

The terrace at the back provided fabulous views over the surrounding area. Below us, the river Tera meandered around the side of the hill and out of sight. To our left were the castle ramparts and, on the right, a footpath flowed down the hillside at the rear of the buildings. We took a seat, ordered a drink, and flicked through the menu.

'What are you going to have?' I asked.

'I think I'll have burger and chips.'

I decided to join her.

Sitting in the warm sunshine, staring out on a landscape of lush meadows, forests, and distant mountains, we couldn't have wished for a better end to what had been a fabulous midweek break.

The clock had ticked round to 4:45 pm by the time we left. Two hours later, we were pulling up outside the kennels. The place was deserted and the gates locked. Melanie called the owner and five minutes later his assistant turned up. Slawit was over the moon to see us but had once again been on hunger strike and flatly refused to eat the food we'd taken for her. Thankfully, she couldn't resist the tinned dog food the staff at the kennel had offered her.

Back home she quickly forgot about being pleased to see us, and spent the rest of the evening sulking. We left her to it; given time she'd come around.

13

Back in the Big Time

On Friday morning I received an email from Briony at ASG Fabrications along with an invoice. Including VAT, the total cost came to £40.44: £18.84 for the six FastClamps and £21.60 delivery. Paying more for delivery than the actual goods always niggles, but I couldn't really complain. Estimated delivery time was four to five working days. I placed the order and made the bank transfer. All I had to do then was wait.

On Saturday morning, bright sunshine encouraged me to investigate why the screenwash wasn't working. I started with the obvious: blockages in the pipework and spray nozzles, and then moved on to the pump. Unfortunately, that was buried deep inside the engine bay and, although I couldn't see it, I could hear the electric motor running. Having drawn a blank with the car, I turned my attention to the internet, and it didn't take me long to discover I wasn't alone. According to the Renault owners' forum, screenwash pump failure was a common fault. Further research led me to a YouTube video detailing the pump's location and how to remove it. The latter appeared to involve dismantling the entire front end of the car. Once removed, the pump could be disassembled, repaired, and replaced without spending a penny.

'I think I've found out why the screenwash isn't working.'

Melanie was in the kitchen emptying the dishwasher.

'That's good. Can you fix it?'

'I think so, but it's a bit more complicated than I thought.'

I should have known it would be. When Renault designed the second generation Megane, their primary focus was on passenger safety. So much so that in their efforts to ensure maximum crash protection, they'd made it virtually impossible to do even the simplest maintenance: like changing a headlight bulb for example. All very reassuring until you needed to replace one.

An hour later, Melanie stepped outside to see how I was getting on. It wasn't until I saw the look of horror on her face that I realised what I'd done.

'What on earth!'

In my effort to remove the screenwash pump, I'd had to unbolt and remove the entire front end of the car.

'It looks worse than it is,' I reassured her.

'I hope you can put it back together again.'

'So do I.'

'You'd better be able to.'

That told me. If I wasn't careful my no-cost fix could end up costing us a small fortune.

With the front end out of the way, removing the pump couldn't have been simpler. Before dismantling it, I rewatched the YouTube video. Ten minutes later I'd made the necessary repair and was ready to test it.

'Can you give me a hand?' I asked.

'That depends.'

'When I give you the word, can you try the screenwash?'

Melanie sat in the driver's seat waiting for my instruction. I restored power to the pump and reattached the inlet and outlet hoses.

'OK, give it a go.'

Melanie flicked the wiper switch and the pump burst into life.

'Nothing's happening,' she called.

'Just be patient.'

Unbeknown to her, I could see the fluid rising up the tube. A few seconds later it sprayed out onto the windscreen.

'OK, you can stop now,' I called.

'Well, it works. All you've got to do now is put it back together again.'

Thankfully, reassembling everything was much easier than taking it apart.

Two days later, when Melanie checked the mailbox, our postal votes for the upcoming general election had arrived. There was no time to lose. We marked our cross next to Thelma Walker, the Labour Party candidate for the Colne Valley constituency, and returned them that same day.

Since returning from Zamora, the weather had been absolutely perfect, so much so that on the 24th of May, the temperature gauge in the car hit 41°C.

'I'd like to nip up to *Campo Verde* this afternoon and mow the lawns,' I said.

I hadn't done it since the last guests left.

'Will you need me?'

'Not for the lawns, but I thought we could bottle the remaining wine.'

We hadn't made any wine last year, but we still had some Garnacha Tinta left over from the year before that. It's not quite as nice as the Mencia and tends to get overlooked, but it was time we started drinking it.

'What's left?'

'Just the Garnacha Tinta.'

'OK.'

At 5:00 pm we left home and headed for the village of Vilatán. When Melanie opened the gate, the lawns were in a right state. I couldn't remember the last time they'd looked this bad. Before starting, I gave Melanie a hand to get everything ready for bottling.

'Fill them to about here,' I said, pointing halfway up the neck of the bottle.

Commercial wineries have automated machinery that injects an exact measure into the bottle. We fill ours manually and rely on a good eye and a steady hand.

'I've done it before, you know.'

I knew she had, but it couldn't harm to remind her. On that note, I rolled the mower outside and left her to it.

The grass was so long I had to cut it twice, first on a high setting and then a lower one. I'd just started the second cut when Melanie came outside.

'Do you want a glass of water?' she asked.

'Yes please.'

She'd read my mind. I was absolutely gagging.

While Melanie went upstairs to fetch us a drink, I took a peep at how she was getting on. Filling bottles directly from the vat is backbreaking work. Melanie had wisely chosen to sit on a garden chair. On one side were the empty bottles and, on the other, neat rows filled with inky-red wine. Talk about organised. A few of the bottles needed topping up but, overall, she'd done a great job. When she came back, she caught me inspecting her work.

'Well?' she asked.

'Very good.'

'But?'

'There are just a few that need topping up.'

'Which ones?'

Anyone would have thought I'd accused her of murder.

'That one, for example.'

I reached across to pick it up and accidentally knocked another one over. Sharp reactions managed to catch it, but not before spilling some wine over the *bodega* floor.

Why is it even a small spillage looks like a flood?

'Craig!'

Melanie was not amused. Quickly she threw a dirty towel over the puddle.

'If it didn't need topping up before, it does now,' she added.

'Have we got a mop?' I asked.

'Just leave it! I'll sort it out.'

In the absence of a naughty step, I drank my water and went outside to finish mowing the lawns. By the time I had, Melanie had emptied the vat.

When it came to corking, I took great care; there'd been enough accidents for one day. All that remained was to clean the vat and then we could go home for dinner. By the time we left, the clock had moved on to ten past eight. That evening we dined outside and didn't come in until twenty past ten. Summer was most definitely in the air.

From time to time, certain events bring into question our decision not to buy a TV. Huddersfield Town's upcoming playoff final being a case in point. That wasn't to say we didn't have access to UK TV channels because we did, but watching them on a fifteen-inch laptop wasn't quite the same. In the main, the streaming service wasn't too bad, but access to major sporting events was patchy to say the least. I could only hope that Huddersfield Town versus Reading FC didn't get the global recognition it so rightly deserved.

On Monday the 29th of May at 3:00 pm BST, the two teams took to the Wembley pitch in front of a crowd of 76,682. The prize: a place in next season's Premier League, and a reported purse of 170 million pounds.

Nervous energy resulted in a hectic start to the game with Town squandering two good chances within the first ten minutes. After that, it settled down to a battle of attrition with both sides more intent on not losing than trying to win. The livestream worked better than I'd expected. There were a few frozen screens and short periods of buffering, all of which seemed to coincide with moments of heightened expectation but, on the whole, it was very good. At the break, the two sides went in all square.

In the second half, Reading started off the brighter of the two without really threatening. At the final whistle, the game remained goalless but, one way or another, someone had to be crowned the winner. The tension was almost unbearable as the teams went into extra time. Reading took the initiative in the first period, fashioning a couple of half-chances but, in the final ten minutes, Town wrestled back control. If anyone was going to win it, Town was.

With four minutes remaining on the clock, Town's charismatic midfielder, Aaron Mooy, fed a ball through to substitute Collin Quaner in the box. With only the goalkeeper to beat, he managed to bundle the ball wide of the post. I couldn't believe it. At the final whistle, the two sides couldn't be separated. The game would now be decided by a penalty shootout.

For the casual observer, penalties are a great way to end a game. They're exciting and quick-fire. For those with a vested interest in the result, they're a nightmare. After forty-six games of the regular season, two playoff semi-finals, and a final, it had all come down to this. Five spot kicks each, with the winner taking all.

Reading won the coin toss and opted to shoot first. Psychologically, they were already in front. Their first player stepped up to the spot and confidently put them one up. Town equalised with their first penalty. Momentary elation was quickly cut short when Reading's second player scored, putting them 2–1 to the good. Next up for Town, their towering German centre back Michael Hefele. He placed the ball on the spot, took a few steps backwards, waited for the referee to blow his whistle, and shot. My heart sank as the Reading goalkeeper guessed correctly and made the save. Was this the end?

As the camera panned away to the next penalty taker the stream froze and the buffering wheel appeared in the centre of the screen. Round and round it went; when it would stop was anyone's guess. Gone are the days when moving the rabbit-eared antenna would restore the picture. All we could do was wait and wait and wait.

Another peculiarity of livestreaming is the delay between transmission and receipt. Events that we were watching had already happened. Throughout the game, Melanie had been in constant WhatsApp communication with her cousin, Sarah. She too was watching the game and, given how long we'd been waiting, I had a suspicion Melanie already knew the result. As much as I wanted to know, I needed to see it for myself. Eventually, the temptation was too much. I was just about to ask her when the picture came back on.

Like a laser-guided missile, my eyes focussed on the top left-hand corner of the screen. The score read 3–3, and one of Town's players was walking towards the penalty spot. My mind was struggling to process the information when the commentator said, 'And this to win the game.' I couldn't quite believe it. In the time it had taken the stream to reconnect, Town had scored twice but, more importantly, Reading had missed twice. Everything now rested on the success of another German centre back, Chris Schindler.

Suddenly, I realised I hadn't taken a breath since normal service had been resumed. I gulped in a mouth of air and held my breath as the referee blew his whistle. Schindler began his run-up, struck the ball and, although the goalkeeper dived the right way, he couldn't prevent it from hitting the back of the net.

We'd done it. After forty-six years of languishing in the lower leagues, we were back in the top flight. Chairman Dean Hoyle and manager David Wagner had done a miraculous job.

That evening we celebrated Town's remarkable achievement with a few glasses of homemade wine. It wasn't every day our hometown team got promoted to the Premier League and, if history was anything to go by, we might never see it happen again.

At some point during the evening, Melanie unearthed an old friend and took a few snaps of him posing by the swimming pool with a bottle of San Miguel. I couldn't resist uploading the image to Facebook. The friend in question was Terry the Terrier, a ten-inch-tall ceramic gnome wearing the Huddersfield Town kit. My sister, Julie, bought me the novelty gnome as a birthday gift many years ago. From that day to this he'd remained in his packaging and out of sight.

'I think it's about time Terry went on tour,' I said.

'What do you mean?'

'Wherever we go, let's take him with us and post pictures of his travels on Facebook.'

'That's a great idea. Terry on Tour, I love it.'

'Something smells good. What are you making?'

I'd spent most of the morning in the office, editing.

'Don't touch them! They're not for you.'

'Who are they for?'

'Gimnasio.'

Today was the final day of Melanie's geriatric gym club, the council-run keep fit classes which begin in September and go through until the end of May. From what I could gather, their final lesson is devoted to eating and drinking. Hardly surprising then that it's the best attended class of the year. Those who turn up are required to take something homemade to share with the group, but they're pretty relaxed about the homemade part. Melanie had made mini-Scotch eggs using quail eggs, and baked some Portuguese tarts.

'They're not going to miss one Scotch egg,' I said.

'If there's any left, I'll bring you one.'

The lady was not for turning.

That evening when Melanie left home, I did some exercises of my own by rotovating the vineyard. By the time she returned, I'd finished and she'd kept her promise. That evening, we sat at the end of the garden nibbling mini-Scotch eggs and drinking homemade wine.

'What else did you have?' I asked.

'Maria brought some buns she'd bought from a bakery in Monforte de Lemos, Marisa came with a bottle of pink Lambrusco, Pilar had made a *bizcocho* (sponge cake), and Manuela and her homecare brought a selection of *pasteles* (pastries).'

'It sounds like you had a right party.'

'We did.'

The only thing getting a workout that evening was their jaws.

'By the way, I put our names down for the *gimnasio* dinner,' said Melanie.

'I don't even go to the classes.'

'That doesn't matter.'

Every year, all the groups in the area gather for an annual dinner. About half a dozen villages qualify to hold their own classes. I joke that it's a self-fulfilling prophecy. They spend all year losing weight so that they can put it back on at the annual dinner.

In previous years, I'd managed to avoid it, but it looked like Melanie had roped me in. Thankfully, I wouldn't be the only non-participating partner to attend; there was at least one other from our village: Pilar's husband Ignacio, and Maria's husband, Roy, would also be attending.

The following day, Wednesday the 30th of May, the clamps arrived from ASG Fabrications. The whole process couldn't have gone much smoother, and the clamps were exactly what I'd hoped for. All that remained was to buy the galvanised steel poles and then work could begin on the arbour.

'Are they what you wanted?'

Melanie seemed somewhat underwhelmed with my purchases. I'd been wittering on about them ever since we'd been to Martin and Barbara's open garden and they weren't exactly exciting.

'They are, so tomorrow afternoon, after my Spanish lesson, we'll go to Hierros La Vid and order the poles. If that's OK with you?'

'I can't wait.'

Don't you just love a smart alec?

14

Terry on Tour

With only six weeks to go until the Spanish exam, I felt I was making good progress. Only time would tell if it was good enough. Andrea had been a godsend. Without her, I couldn't imagine what stage I'd be at.

'How did it go?' asked Melanie.

I'd just got back from my lesson to find Melanie sitting in the sunshine reading her latest chick lit novel.

'Very good. Andrea seems really pleased with me. Anyway, are you ready?'

'Ready for what?'

'To go to Hierros La Vid.'

'Oh yes. Give me two minutes and I'll be with you.'

It was obvious she'd forgotten.

Twenty minutes later we were pulling up outside their warehouse. The chap we'd spoken to previously recognised me straightaway. I guessed they wouldn't get many Englishmen calling in.

'I'd like to order five six-metre lengths of the 48.3 mm diameter galvanised steel poles,' I said.

'Five you say.'

'That's right. Do you deliver?'

'Where to?'

'Canabal.'

'We can do.'

'And how much is it?'

'Fifty euro.'

I glanced at Melanie. Her expression said it all.

'In that case, we'll collect them,' I replied.

Given the FastClamps had only cost eighteen pounds plus VAT to be delivered from the UK, fifty euro sounded an awful lot to take five poles ten kilometres. If only I'd known, we would have brought the trailer with us.

'Can you cut three of them into two-metre lengths?' I asked.

'I can do, but that's extra.'

'How much?'

'Two euro.'

'Per cut or per pole?'

I thought I'd better ask.

'Each pole.'

Even that sounded expensive; after all, how difficult could it be to cut a six-metre pole into three equal lengths?

'We'll take them as they are, but I'll have to go and get the trailer. We'll be back in about half an hour.'

On our return, he hadn't even pulled them off the rack. It wasn't until he did that I began to question the wisdom of our decision. Six metres doesn't seem very long until you see it laid out in front of you. Melanie looked at me as if to say, 'What are we supposed to do with them?' The total cost came to €104.06. I handed him 105 and he gave me a euro change.

If their length posed a problem, carrying them to the trailer highlighted an even greater issue.

'They're a bit floppy,' said Melanie.

That was one way of putting it, but I'd come prepared. Before leaving home I'd picked up a roll of 50 mm brown packaging tape.

'They shouldn't be as bad once I've taped them together.'

At least that was the theory.

'And then what?'

One step at a time.

The trailer was fitted with a set of elevated load rails which allowed us to transport longer items such as a ladder but, unlike the poles, the ladder was half the length and much more rigid.

'If you lift your end into the trailer, I'll lean them up against the load rail.'

'Are you sure?'

I wasn't, but we had to do something.

'Whatever you do, don't let go of them,' I cautioned.

If she did, the whole lot would come crashing down onto the roof of the car.

Once they were in the trailer, it quickly became apparent that the angle of the poles was way too steep. It was impossible to get home without driving under at least one bridge and, even if we managed to sneak under that, I had no idea how many phone lines and electricity cables we'd come across en route.

'That's no good,' I said.

'Can't we leave this end sticking out of the back?'

Melanie had a point. If we shifted the load backwards, the angle would be much shallower.

'That's a good idea; let's give it a go.'

Between us, we lifted them off the bed of the trailer and slid them over the rear gate.

'That's much better,' I said.

'It is, but how are you going to secure them?'

While Melanie held them in position, I used a rope to tether them to the trailer's anchor points. To make doubly sure they stayed where they were supposed to, I secured the rope to the poles with more packaging tape. Heath Robinson, eat your heart out.

'Right then, let's go.'

On a Wednesday afternoon in May, even the main road was quiet, which was just as well. Anxiety levels were at breaking point; they often are when we're hauling a load. Accelerating rapidly risked the poles sliding off the back of the trailer, and an emergency stop would have launched them into the air like six-metre-long javelins.

Whether real or imagined, it's rare we transport anything without hearing one strange noise or another.

'What's that?' I asked.

'What?'

'That noise.'

'I can't hear anything.'

The terror in Melanie's voice was undeniable. We hadn't reached halfway and something was banging that shouldn't be. Fearing the tape had split, I slowly came to a halt and jumped out. After a quick inspection I got back in.

'What was it?' asked Melanie.

'I don't know; everything looks OK.'

Ten minutes into our journey we'd reached the N-120, the main highway to Canabal. Somewhere along this stretch of road was the bridge we had to negotiate. From a distance, I felt confident we'd clear it. As we neared, that certainty ebbed away.

'What do you think?' I asked.

Melanie's eyes widened.

'I don't know.'

'It should fit under.'

'Pull over before you get there and I'll check. Better safe than sorry.'

Twenty metres from the bridge I came to a halt. Melanie hopped out, jogged to the other side, and gestured me to move forwards. Gently, I lifted my foot off the clutch and the car crept slowly forwards, inch by careful inch. With one eye on Melanie and the other on the rearview mirror, I didn't know whether I was coming or going, but her constant signalling suggested I was going to make it. As I reached the bridge I winced, waiting for the sound of disaster. Thankfully, it never came and I glided underneath without so much as a scrape. When we exited the road at Canabal, we realised how lucky we'd been. From the moment we left Hierros La Vid to the time we entered the village, not one vehicle had passed us.

I knew from the outset that the design of the arbour required three of the five poles to be cut into two-metre lengths but it wasn't until we'd unloaded them that I realised the remaining two could also have been cut without compromising the design. Had I known, I would have cut them before we left the warehouse and saved us the stress of transporting them whole. On reflection, I thought it wise to keep that to myself.

Before making any cuts, we laid them out where they would eventually go.

'What do you think?' I asked.

'How high will it be?'

'Two metres.'

I opened the retractable tape measure and held it upright.

'What do you think?' I asked.

'That should be alright. You don't want it too high otherwise you won't be able to reach the grapes.'

'Are you trying to say I'm a short arse?'

I couldn't resist teasing her.

'No, I'm just saying you don't want it to be too high.'

'OK, two metres it is then. If you hold this end, I'll cut them, and try to keep it at this angle.'

Melanie took a firm grip and I prepared to make the first cut.

'Ready?' I asked.

'Ready when you are.'

'There's no turning back once I start.'

'Just get on with it.'

My attempt to add a little drama into the proceeding failed.

Cutting them was much easier than I'd expected, and the push-fit clamps tightened into place with a grub screw. Assembling it couldn't have been simpler. Within an hour, we'd finished, and it looked exactly how I'd imagined it would.

'Are you coming?'

Melanie had laced up her walking boots and was coaxing Slawit's legs through her harness.

'Where are you going?'

'Just around the village.'

On a quiet Sunday afternoon, without a cloud in the sky, how could I resist.

'OK. What are you doing?'

Having sorted out Slawit, she'd picked up Terry and was stuffing him into a tote bag.

'I thought we could introduce him to some of the neighbours.'

For obvious reasons, drink-fuelled ideas rarely survive beyond the evening they're uttered. Melanie seemed intent on making this one a reality.

'Are you sure?'

'Why not?'

'The neighbours might not appreciate the artistic value of posing with a novelty gnome.'

That said, his football kit did bear more than a passing resemblance to that of La Coruña.

'It was your idea.'

That was true, although I don't remember bringing the villagers into it.

Thankfully, the neighbours Melanie had in mind weren't human. First up were Meli's chickens. They weren't in the slightest bit fazed by Terry, unlike Celso's geese. Had it not been for the chain-link fence separating the two, Terry's first tour of Canabal would probably have been his last. Next to enter the fray was Angel's dog, Oddy. Slawit looked at him as if to say, 'Don't look at me, I'm not with them.'

From livestock we moved on to landmarks. The ceramic spaniel cemented to Yolanda's garden wall was an obvious choice. From there we continued on to the freshly painted zebra crossing down Station Street where Terry did a solo impression of The Beatles' *Abbey Road* album cover. After that we wandered on to the thirteenth century village church and, last but by no means least, Canabal's tallest landmark, the chimney of the abandoned brick factory. I particularly liked the shot with it sticking out of the top of his head.

Terry's first tour had been a great success; alas I'm not sure my Facebook friends shared our sense of humour.

At 7:00 am on Thursday the 8th of June, polling stations opened for what would be the most important UK general election in our lifetime. We'd played our parts in trying to oust the Tories, but we wouldn't find out the results until the early hours of the following morning. Between now and then, keeping busy was the most effective way to take our minds off the outcome.

'Do you mind if I come with you this afternoon?' asked Melanie.

I had a Spanish lesson after lunch.

'What for?'

'I thought I could take Slawit for a walk along the river.'

Andrea lived next to the river Cabe on the outskirts of Monforte de Lemos. Over the last few years, the council had developed the riverbank and created footpaths for everyone to enjoy.

'OK.'

'In fact, why don't we set off early and take Terry for a photoshoot in Monforte?'

'Why not?'

Shortly after lunch, having spent the morning dividing my time between editing and revision, we set off to Monforte de Lemos. We couldn't have wished for better weather.

'Look,' said Melanie, pointing at the parking spaces reserved for visiting coaches.

Would you believe it; the only coach parked there was painted in a matching blue to Terry's shirt. If we hadn't known better, it could have been the team bus come to cheer him on. Having taken a few snaps with Terry standing proudly in the foreground, we made a beeline for Parque dos Condes, favoured location of Monforte's wedding photographers. Even without top hat and tails, Terry looked majestic as he performed his trademark knee slide in front of the fountain. From there it was a short walk to the town's most outstanding architectural landmark, the Escolapios.

'We better be making a move,' I said.

It wasn't far to Andrea's, but I didn't want to be late.

While I conjugated Spanish verbs, Melanie, Slawit, and Terry went for a stroll along the riverbank footpath.

That evening, shortly before ten o'clock, we settled down in front of the laptop for what I suspected would be a long night of election results. Even though we no longer lived in the UK, I couldn't ever remember being this engaged in the outcome of a general election.

Twelve months ago, the British public had voted to leave the European Union. Since then, the UK parliament had been in a state of virtual paralysis. The Conservative government were as divided as the rest of the nation on exactly what type of Brexit deal they should be negotiating. There were even those who wanted the UK to leave without a deal.

My greatest fear was not for us but those we'd left behind. In the thirteen years I'd owned my business, I'd lost my biggest customer on three separate occasions and the impact was devastating. The UK was about to throw away its most important trading partner and, even if the country did eventually recover, generations of Brits would have to suffer the consequences.

The Labour Party had promised to negotiate the best deal possible and then hold a second referendum to ensure it was what the people wanted. If they lost this election, the best we could hope for was a smooth transition.

The Tories, under Theresa May, had begun the campaign twenty-one points ahead in the polls but, in the final two weeks of campaigning, the Labour Party, under Jeremy Corbyn's leadership, had started to close the gap. My post-election prediction was for a hung parliament, but it was all to play for.

At 10:00 pm voting closed and news outlets announced the results of the exit poll. If the forecast was correct, the Tories would win the most seats but lose their overall majority. Theresa May's gamble had spectacularly failed.

Shortly after 11:00 pm the first result was declared. By midnight, only a handful of constituencies had declared and Melanie was starting to nod off.

'I'm going to go to bed; I can't keep my eyes open.'

I glanced at the clock. The time had slipped past one in the morning.

'OK, I don't think I'll be long.'

At two o'clock, declarations began to pick up the pace. By three, the two main parties were neck and neck. Four o'clock came and went with Labour marginally in front, but many Conservative constituencies were still to declare. At five o'clock, one result caught my eye and gave me a real lift. The Tories had lost the Colne Valley to Labour's Thelma Walker. For the first time ever, I felt my vote had actually counted for something. It would have been even sweeter had she won by two votes; nevertheless, we'd done our bit to improve the situation. Alas, I feared it wouldn't be enough. By six, it was clear the exit poll had been wrong and the Tories would maintain their overall majority, albeit by a reduced margin. At a quarter past six, I conceded defeat, powered down the laptop, and crept into bed.

Jeremy Corbyn had come within a whisker of victory but failed. As for Brexit, the Tories were so divided I feared the impasse would persist. The question now was, could Theresa May survive such a humiliating underachievement and, if so, for how long?

The next morning, I felt absolutely shattered, physically and emotionally: so close and yet so far.

'What time did you come to bed?'

Melanie had brought me a mug of coffee.

'About quarter past six. What time is it now?'

'Quarter to eleven. So, what happened?'

'We lost, but only just.'

'Oh dear.'

'But we did kick 'em out of the Colne Valley, and the Tory majority has been cut to next to nothing.'

'Well, that's something.'

'I suppose.'

A lack of sleep and a bad result had left me feeling deflated, and I wouldn't be alone.

'You haven't forgotten we're going out tonight, have you?'

'Where to?'

'It's that María do Ceo concert in Ourense. We said we'd take Mitty and Rajan.'

Born in Lisbon, Portugal, María do Ceo moved to Ourense with her parents when she was seven years old. Her isolation from the Lisbon fado scene had given her a very distinctive style, combining the softness of Galicia with the sadness and reflective mood of Portuguese fado.

'Oh yes, I remember. It's not until later though, is it?'

'They're coming here for quarter to eight.'

Thank heavens for that. At least I had the rest of the day to recover.

As was often the case, Mitty and Rajan arrived earlier than expected, but it couldn't harm to get there ahead of the crowd. The concert was being held in the Plaza Mayor, a particularly picturesque part of the city. When we arrived, rows of temporary seating filled the square, and a few people had already taken a seat. Mitty was keen to secure our places. As the start time neared, the square filled to capacity and late arrivals had to stand around the perimeter. Her choice of venue enhanced the overall experience and, once again, her performance was flawless, much to the appreciation of her hometown audience. When the concert came to an end, loud applause and shouts of *bravo* echoed around the square. Such was the acclaim that she had to perform not one, but two encores. As people departed, we ambled back to the car through the narrow, dimly-lit streets. By the time we got home, the clock had moved around to 11:30 pm.

More often than not, June is my favourite month of the year. The weather in September is similar, but in June we have the whole summer to look forward to and the alfresco lifestyle it affords. When the sun slips below the horizon, I pull the cork on a bottle of fine Spanish wine and fire up the barbecue. Nowadays, I prefer gas; it's quick, controllable, and clean, but it does have its drawbacks.

Over time, galvanised steel burners start to rust. Holes in the metal cause the flame to distort resulting in uneven cooking. Ours was in a pretty sorry state and it wasn't just the burner that needed replacing. On closer inspection the bottom of the pan had also rusted through. It was time for a new one and possibly an upgrade. I went into the kitchen to have a word with Melanie but she beat me to it.

'Look what I've got,' she said, tipping her head towards a packet on the kitchen worktop.

The label belonged to Casa da Fonte, an ecological dairy farm located across the valley but owned and run by a former village resident, Xosé (José in Spanish). Indeed, his parents still lived in the village. A few years ago, he started a doorstep delivery and, although the milk was slightly more expensive than the supermarket, we were happy to support him. Since then, he'd added other products to his ecological range such as yoghurts and a deliciously soft, creamy cheese. As for what this was, I hadn't got a clue.

'What is it?' I asked.

'Take a look.'

Carefully, I peeled open the waxed paper package, but I was still none the wiser. If anything, it looked similar to a ball of pastry, but surely it couldn't be that.

'What is it?'

'It's butter.'

I would never have guessed. I'd become so used to seeing a rectangular block wrapped in foil or set in a plastic tub. This was in its natural state, spooned from a churn and moulded by hand into a round.

'Anyway, what did you want?' she asked.

I'd almost forgotten why I'd gone inside.

'Come and take a look at this,' I said, leading her outside.

Melanie took one look at the rust-eaten barbecue and agreed with me; it was time to get a new one. Until then, we'd have to make do with what we'd got.

'Are you sure it'll be safe?' asked Melanie.

'It'll be fine.'

Dinner consisted of strips of chargrilled chicken fillets, and new potatoes smothered in lashings of Xosé's butter. Given its credentials, the taste was rather underwhelming, but better to have tried it and been disappointed than never have tried it at all.

15

Down to This

Having been roped in to attend the annual geriatric gym club dinner, I was pleased to hear that all the villages concerned had chosen the restaurant in Canabal, Parrillada O Regato, to host the event. The term *parrillada* refers to food cooked over an open flame. Basically, it's a great big barbecue. Initial estimates suggested they'd be catering for about eighty. To put that into perspective, the average weekly attendance at the Canabal gym club was four and over double that number, nine, had signed up for the dinner. If nothing else, it demonstrated that people much prefer to eat and drink than exercise.

'They're only complaining,' said Melanie, on returning from her morning dog walk.

'Who are?'

The tone of her remark suggested I should know who and what she was referring to.

'The gym club people.'

Messages had been circulating through their WhatsApp group ever since the mayor of Sober announced a concert on the same evening as the dinner. People were up in arms that they wouldn't be able to go to both. I wouldn't have minded but, given the poor attendance at these admission-free concerts, their bleating seemed somewhat disingenuous. Some folk will complain about anything.

'What time does it start?' I asked.

'What?'

'The concert.'

'Half past seven.'

'And the dinner?'

'Half past eight.'

Talk about a storm in a teacup; performances rarely go past the hour mark.

'Surely they can delay serving dinner for a few minutes,' I replied.

The drive from the *casa de cultura* to the restaurant takes less than five minutes.

'That's what I said.'

'And?'

'They've taken it under advisement.'

Before any decision could be made, every man and his dog would have to have their say. We were later informed that, after due consideration, dinner would be delayed until those attending the concert had arrived.

'We might as well go then,' I suggested.

'I'll give Roy and Maria a call and see if they want to join us.'

On the evening of the 14th of June, we left home a little earlier than usual in anticipation of an increased turnout. It came as no surprise to discover that wasn't the case. Tonight's entertainer, Xoán (Juan) Curiel, was a guitarist and singer songwriter from Santiago de Compostela. His contemporary programme made quite a refreshing change from the mainly classical performers we see at these events. The ladies in particular were especially thrilled; Xoán's dark curly hair, designer stubble, and dashing good looks saw to that. At the end of his set, he gave everyone a free CD prompting some of the senior ladies of the parish to invite him to the gym club dinner, an invitation he gratefully accepted. If nothing else, he'd get a few hearts racing; mind you, given the average age of the attendees, perhaps that wasn't such a good idea.

When we arrived at O Regato the place was heaving. Fortunately, our neighbours had saved us some seats.

'Come sit here,' called Marisa.

Our friend Ignacio was sitting at the head of the table with his wife Pilar on his right and Marisa on his left. I took a seat next to her and Melanie, or Melania as she's referred to, sat next to me. Roy and Maria had followed us down from the concert and sat opposite us. Meli took the chair next to Melanie and Lola sat next to her. Nine members of the Canabal complement present and correct. As for the woman sitting next to Roy, she was something of a mystery, and it wasn't the first time we'd noticed an unknown guest at one of these social events, but no one seemed to mind. Next to her was the dashing guitarist from Santiago de Compostela.

Prior to our arrival, beverages had been brought to the table and, thanks to doctor's orders, Melanie and I would get more than our fair share of wine. Alcohol and medication don't mix, although some were less compliant than others.

The menu had been chosen beforehand and the cost agreed which, on this occasion, worked out at twelve euro per head. By the time they began serving, Melanie and I, along with Ignacio and Pilar, were already on our second glass of wine.

First out of the kitchen were wicker baskets piled high with thick-cut chunks of crusty bread. This was followed by stainless steel platters of *empanada de carne*, a flat pie, the size of a family pizza, made from doughy pastry and filled with onions, peppers, and meat and served cut into triangular-shaped pieces. With more on the way, everyone waited patiently. Service was swift. Next to leave the kitchen were dinner plates piled high with *ensaladilla*, a type of Russian salad, and last but not least, more stainless steel platters laden with *croquetas* (croquettes).

Galicians pride themselves on quantity as well as quality, which was just as well; Ignacio and Pilar are no lightweights. Each platter served roughly five guests which meant two slices of *empanada* each, although Marisa insisted that I have three, an enormous portion of *ensaladilla*, and three if not four *croquetas*, and that was just for starters.

For mains, we were treated to the house speciality: *churrasco*, a selection of barbecued meats including *criollo*, a thick pork sausage, beef steaks, pork ribs, and pork steaks. Accompanying this meat-eater's feast were chips and a fresh mixed salad. The quantity of food was staggering. Platters of grilled meat stacked as high as was practical, mountains of chips, and bowls overflowing with salad. Pudding was a real struggle, but who can resist a slice of Viennetta, and a generous portion of mille-feuille? Certainly not me, and I wasn't alone. We finished the meal with coffee and after-dinner liqueurs which in our case was a generous measure of *licor café* on the rocks.

Having cleared the tables, the presentations began. Each village had bought Dunia, the fitness instructor, a gift which she graciously accepted. By the time we left, the clock had ticked around to midnight. We'd had a fabulous evening with neighbours and friends and, although we'll always be incomers, it was nice to feel part of the local community. As for the geriatric gym club, I could only imagine the calories consumed would guarantee its future.

June's weather had not disappointed. So much so that on the 18th we took our first swim in the pool. Over the years we've become far more selective on the timing of our dips. Call me a fool, but gone are the days I'd go in on the 1st of April. Nowadays, the water temperature dictates our decision. Anything below 26°C and you can forget it, and even then, the idea of taking a dip is often more appealing than the reality.

A couple of days after that, I finally finished editing the fourth book in The Journey series. Melanie still had a few chapters to cast her eagle eyes over before I could pass it on to Louise for a professional edit, but the end was definitely in sight and not a moment too soon. With nine days remaining until we sat the Spanish citizenship exam, I could concentrate all my efforts on passing, but before then we had some entertaining to organise.

Our friends from California, Mitty and Rajan, would soon be heading back to the States. We'd already been to their home for one of Rajan's deliciously authentic Indian curries and now it was our turn. Both are vegetarian, which is always a challenge, but one we relish. Over the years, our repertoire of meatless dishes has certainly expanded. My twice-baked goat's cheese souffle was particularly memorable. Today, Melanie was cooking. It was my job to ready the outside terrace for dining.

'Is there anything you'd like me to do?'

It never harms to ask.

'You can put the kettle on and make us a cuppa if you wouldn't mind.'

'What's for lunch?' I asked, as we sat outside in the sunshine sipping our coffees.

'We're having pea frittata for starters, onion and goat's cheese tarte tatin with tomato salad, green salad, and homemade bread rolls for mains, and lemon curd cheesecake for pudding.'

'Is that all?'

'Ha ha, you're so funny.'

Melanie had pulled out all the stops and everything was delicious. As usual, she'd gone above and beyond but, when guests enjoy their food, it makes all the effort worthwhile.

'What are we doing about the barbecue?' asked Melanie.

Since discovering the rust, I'd been making do. It wasn't ideal, but I knew we'd be getting another at some point.

'I thought we'd decided to replace it.'

'We had, but when?'

'Why, is there a rush?'

'You do realise that Richard and Yvonne will be here in a fortnight?'

Richard, Yvonne, and their two kids Mason and Erren are perennial visitors to *El Sueño*. It's something we both look forward to, but feeding six on a small barbecue was difficult enough without trying to work around an unreliable heat source. Urgent action was required.

'Crikey! We'd better get it sorted,' I replied.

Later that afternoon we drove the forty-plus kilometres to Carrefour in Ourense. The French-owned supermarket is by far the biggest in the area and, during late spring and summer, they stock an extensive range of outdoor furniture and accessories, including barbecues.

'What about this one?' I asked.

A section of the shopfloor had been allocated to showcasing their range of garden products.

'It's up to you. You'll be using it.'

The model I'd been drawn to boasted three burners, two for the grill and a third for a hotplate, and was priced at a very reasonable €125. Unfortunately, when we checked the shelves, they seemed to be out of stock.

'I'll ask at the sales counter,' said Melanie.

The sales assistant confirmed that they were currently out of stock but were expecting another delivery. If we liked, we could order one now and, as soon as they'd been delivered, they would let us know.

'How soon will that be?' I asked.

'They should be here next week.'

That fitted perfectly with our timeframe so we went ahead and ordered one. The only downside was having to pay the full amount there and then.

With only three days to go until the citizenship exam, we stepped up our revision. Entrants are required to answer twenty-five questions from a selection of three hundred and, given that all the possible questions and answers are included in the study manual, you could be forgiven for thinking that passing it would be a piece of cake. In reality, there was very little room for error.

On Monday afternoon we sat down to test ourselves on every single question. Melanie was in the lounge and I went into the office. Having checked my answers, I'd got thirty-six wrong, a vast improvement on my previous best, but by no means good enough. I was particularly weak on questions relating to the government and legislature. I wandered through into the lounge to find out how Melanie had fared.

'How did you get on?' I asked.

'I can't do this.'

She was clearly upset. She'd ended up with a very similar score to me, but Melanie's knowledge of the government was even worse than mine.

'That's not too bad,' I said, trying to reassure her.

'It's terrible.'

'I didn't do very well on that section either, but there's still two days to go.'

'That's what's worrying me.'

'Just forget about the other sections and concentrate on that one.'

I couldn't remember the last time we'd been this stressed.

As well as revising, I was desperate to get the next manuscript off to Louise as soon as possible. Once again, the title had leapt off the pages during the editing process. On Tuesday the 27th of June, I attached *Opportunities Ahead* to an email and clicked send. Later that day, I tested myself again on all three hundred questions. With only two incorrect answers, I was finally ready to sit the exam and Melanie wasn't far behind.

'See, what did I tell you? We're bound to pass.'

We knew it wouldn't be that straightforward; nothing ever is, but even Melanie was feeling confident. We'd worked incredibly hard to give ourselves the best possible chance of success. Only time would tell if we'd done enough.

On the morning of the 29th, we woke early. The exam was scheduled to begin at 6:00 pm in Santiago de Compostela. I'd done all the revision I intended to do, but Melanie couldn't resist going through everything one last time.

Shortly before lunchtime, I received an email from the Instituto Cervantes. Surely they couldn't be changing things at this late date. I clicked the link and read through the message.

'Will you come and take a look at this?' I asked.

'What is it?'

'An email from the Instituto Cervantes.'

Melanie followed me into the office and sat down in front of the laptop.

'Well?' I asked.

'Give me a chance.'

I bit my lip.

'I don't think it's anything to do with today's exam,' she said.

'That's what I thought.'

'It's about the oral part of the language exam. They've moved it to a different day.'

We were originally due to sit all four modules of the Spanish language exam on Friday the 14th of July. The email informed us that the oral part had been rescheduled for Wednesday the 19th. As a consequence, we'd have to make the 280-kilometre round trip to Santiago de Compostela three times instead of two. Not only were the exams costing us a small fortune, but the travel was too.

To complicate matters, both exams were at different venues, neither of which we'd been to before. Today's exam was at the Academia Iria Flavia; the others would be held on the university campus. A search on Google Maps identified both locations, and I felt confident I'd be able to find them. Just in case, we left home at 2:30 pm; the last thing we wanted was to arrive late. It's funny how elusive places are when you're short of time and how easy they are to find when you're not. A little after four o'clock we arrived at the Academia Iria Flavia.

'What are we going to do now?' asked Melanie.

'Let's see if we can find the university.'

It couldn't harm to get ahead of ourselves.

'Do you know the address?'

'It's in that file.'

Melanie reached into the back and flicked through the paperwork. Less than ten minutes later we'd found the place, Cursos Internationales on Avenida das Ciencias and, by the look of it, we wouldn't have a problem parking. That was one less thing to worry about on exam day.

'Right then, let's get back to the academy.'

Unlike earlier, there wasn't a single roadside parking space when we returned. I had no choice but to continue driving until we found one. Eventually, I did.

'I hope you know where we are because I haven't got a clue,' said Melanie.

'It's this way.'

At least I thought it was. Thankfully, my internal compass proved as reliable as ever, and we made it with twenty minutes to spare, ample time to bring my heart rate under control and my blood pressure down to within normal parameters.

On arrival we checked in at reception using our registration form and photo ID, and then waited. One by one, each candidate was called into the examination room and allocated a specific desk. The question paper and separate answer sheet were already there along with a pencil and eraser. When all sixty candidates were seated, the invigilator explained the rules, emphasising that no one would be allowed to leave the room before fifteen minutes had elapsed. At that point, anyone who had finished should place their answer paper face down and leave quietly. Anyone who chose to go would not be allowed to return.

Our goal of becoming Spanish citizens had come down to this, and the spectre of failure weighed heavy on our shoulders. Choosing a path is never easy but, in the end, all you can do is follow your heart. We still had other hoops to jump through and a major hurdle to overcome, but failure today would mean everything had been for nothing.

'Your time starts now.'

I turned over the paper and read the first question. Fifteen minutes later, entrants began to leave, and Melanie wasn't far behind them. I'd also finished and checked and double-checked my answers, but one final run-through couldn't do any harm. I read each question again and, only when I was completely satisfied, turned over my paper and left. Melanie had been waiting in the lobby.

'Well?' she asked, eager to know how I'd found it.

'It was OK, but there weren't any easy ones.'

I appreciate that all questions are difficult unless you know the answer, but I suspect most people living in Spain would know the colours of the Spanish flag are red and yellow.

'Do you think you've passed?' she asked.

'I think so.'

In order to pass, candidates had to correctly answer fifteen of the twenty-five questions.

'What about you?' I asked.

'I've definitely passed.'

She hadn't sounded this confident for months, and it hadn't been that easy.

'What about that question on the judiciary?' I asked.

'I didn't have one on the judiciary.'

'Are you sure?'

'Certain.'

That was strange.

I asked her another, but she hadn't had that one either. After swapping a few more of the questions, it quickly became apparent that we'd had two completely different papers.

'I bet that's to stop people cheating,' said Melanie.

Despite that, confidence was high, but we wouldn't know for certain until the results came out towards the end of next month. Between now and then, we had our most difficult test to overcome, the DELE A2 Spanish language exam.

16

The Art of Being Patient

With the citizenship exam out of the way, and the new manuscript in the hands of Louise, I could concentrate all my efforts on the language exam, except for one outstanding matter.

'Have you heard from Carrefour?' I asked.

'No, but it's only been a week.'

'A week and two days, actually.'

I was starting to regret ordering a barbecue that was out of stock.

'You couldn't give them a ring, could you?' I asked.

Melanie could sense my frustration and rang them straightaway. I could tell from her responses that it wasn't good news. Not only was it still out of stock, but they couldn't tell her when they might have some. That left us with two options: wait or get a full refund and look for another.

'What do you think?' asked Melanie.

'Let's take a look at what else they've got.'

We simply couldn't risk waiting any longer.

Back at Carrefour, none of the other models were suitable.

'Let's get our money back and try somewhere else,' suggested Melanie.

I knew exactly where we could go: Brico Center on the outskirts of town. Once there, we made a beeline for the outdoor living section.

'What about that one?'

Melanie was pointing at a similar-sized model to the one we'd ordered from Carrefour, except this one had four burners: three for the grill and one for a combined hotplate and griddle.

'It's ideal, but have you seen the price?'

The point of sale read "€256".

'But if it's what you want.'

Having found one I was happy with at half that price, it pained me to spend so much but, on closer inspection, it was obvious why it was more expensive. Everything smacked of quality. The heavy-duty grills were coated in a similar material to that you'd find on a gas hob, and the burners were made of stainless steel rather than cheaper galvanised metal. If only we had more time, I would have searched further afield, but we didn't; Richard and Yvonne would be here in a matter of days. With that in mind, we bit the bullet and handed over the cash. At least that was one less thing to worry about.

I waited until the following morning to start assembling it. Every component had been fabricated from high quality steel and manufactured to the highest standards but, an hour into the build, I spotted a catastrophic flaw. The largest and aesthetically most important component, the lid, had a significant dent in it. I had no option but to dismantle my work, box it up, and return it.

By the time I was ready to leave, Melanie still hadn't returned from Slawit's morning dog walk, but I had a good idea where to find her. I loaded the barbecue into the back of the car and drove down into the village. As I suspected, Melanie had stopped to talk to Meli.

'What's the matter?' she asked.

'The barbecue, it's going to have to go back. The lid has a whopping great dent in it.'

'Oh dear. Look what Meli gave us.'

With guests on the way, a dozen freshly laid eggs would definitely come in handy.

'*Muchísimas gracias* Meli (Thank you very much).'

'If you take us home, I'll come with you,' said Melanie.

'OK.'

As usual, Slawit was reluctant to get in the car. Melanie dragged her into the footwell and off we went. Having taken the eggs inside and left Slawit in the garden, we set off to Ourense. The last thing we needed was an 85-kilometre round trip, but what choice did we have?

The woman at customer services was very helpful. She glanced at the offending lid, and checked their stock on the computer.

'I think we might be out of stock,' she said.

Could things get any worse?

My hangdog expression prompted a response.

'Wait here and I'll ask someone to do a physical stock check,' she added.

'What are we going to do if they haven't got one?' whispered Melanie.

I hadn't a clue.

A few minutes turned into five. How long could it take to check the stock? If nothing else, living in Spain had taught us the art of being patient. After what felt like an eternity, I caught sight of another member of staff walking towards us carrying a large box.

'*Señor* Bricks?'

'*Si.*'

'*Esto es para ti* (This is for you).'

What a relief; they'd managed to find one.

In situations like this, it would be nice to hear an apology, but that's rarely the case. That aside, we weren't going anywhere without checking the contents. Thankfully, everything was in order.

On the drive home Melanie's phone pinged notifying her of a text message.

'You'll never guess who this is from.'

In that case, why ask?

'Who?'

'The agricultural college in Monforte. Our licences are ready collect.'

'Crikey! I'd forgotten all about them.'

'Me too.'

'How long has that taken?'

'Only four months,' she replied, with more than a hint of sarcasm.

By the time we got home, another morning had disappeared. I had hoped to do some revision before my Spanish lesson, but it wasn't to be. Once again, I left Andrea's brimming with confidence.

On my return, it took me the best part of two hours to assemble the new barbecue and I couldn't have been happier with the result. That evening, I put it through its paces with chicken fillets and thick pork sausages. Both cooked beautifully, but a little more practice wouldn't go amiss. With Richard, Yvonne and the kids arriving shortly, I'd get plenty of opportunities to hone my skills.

'You haven't forgotten that we're meeting Carol and Gerry for lunch today, have you?' asked Melanie.

Of course I had.

'That's today, is it?'

'*Tsk!* Yes.'

What would I do without Melanie keeping track of our social calendar?

Carol and Gerry were only here for a fortnight, and we'd arranged to meet them at Restaurante Casa Antonio in the village of Goián at 1:30 pm. The place does an excellent three-course *menú del día* for only ten euro a head.

'Would you like to come back to ours for a drink?' I asked, after we'd finished.

Gerry jumped at the chance. Poor Carol, when it comes to driving, she always draws the short straw.

Back home I pulled the cork on a bottle of white wine and poured Carol a glass of squash.

'So, where is he?' asked Gerry.

'He's a she. Slawit!' I called.

'Not the dog.'

I looked at him quizzically.

'Wolfie's been dying to meet him,' he added.

'Dying to meet who?'

Gerry has a tendency to go off on a tangent that only he can follow.

'Terry, of course. Wolfie can't wait to meet him.'

Right on cue, Carol handed Gerry a carrier bag. He peered inside and, with all the theatre of a magician pulling a rabbit from a top hat, dipped his hand inside and pulled out a garden gnome. Unlike Terry, this little chap was wearing the colours of Gerry's home team, Wolverhampton Wanderers, more commonly referred to as Wolves.

'So, where is he?' he asked.

I couldn't quite believe it. I thought Melanie and I were bonkers taking Terry on tour, but Gerry and Carol had brought their beloved Wolfie all the way from England to meet him. The least I could do was bring him out to say hello.

It's fair to say that Gerry was slightly envious of Terry's larger size and clay construction; Wolfie was made out of cheap plastic, but the two gnomes got on like a house on fire. Needless to say, Carol had been monitoring Terry's tours on my Facebook page.

When Melanie had first suggested dusting him down and taking Terry on tour, I'd had my doubts but, if Carol had enjoyed the posts, I felt confident others would have.

At 8:30 pm on the 11th of July, Richard, Yvonne, Mason, and Erren descended on *El Sueño* in a flurry of excitement. They'd spent the afternoon exploring the city of Braga in Portugal on a Segway safari. The kids, now teenagers, had loved every minute. As for Mum and Dad, they'd survived unscathed.

Melanie had prepared pasta bake and tear 'n' share garlic bread for dinner. Pudding was a very luxurious chocolate torte.

'Would anyone like a few rounds of cards?' asked Melanie, after everything had been cleared away.

'Aw yeah,' replied Erren.

Playing cards is something of a tradition during their stay. By the time we called it a night, the clock had ticked around to one in the morning.

The following day, the 12th of July, marked my birthday. Another year older but none the wiser. Melanie's gifts included a new mouse mat sporting the logo "I love pork pies", and a matching coaster. My sister Julie had bought me a blue T-shirt with the message "We Are Premier League" emblazoned across the front, a less than subtle hint to Huddersfield Town's historic promotion to the top flight, but best of all was the gift from Richard, Yvonne, and the kids. At great personal risk to themselves, they'd managed to smuggle an enormous pork pie through customs, and I couldn't have been happier.

At lunchtime, I fired up the new barbecue and loaded the grill with pork sausages. Unfortunately, not even a birthday could recuse me from going to my Spanish lesson.

In my absence, the kids spent most of the afternoon messing about in the pool. The adults had been roped in to blowing up a host of inflatables which included a bright-yellow banana, a one-person dinghy, and a cross between a killer whale and a dolphin. My personal favourite was a smaller version of the long-since departed Gary Gator. It was pleasing to see they'd remembered him and, who knows, maybe one day Mason and Erren's kids will have their own version of this holiday favourite.

'Let's go to the bar on the Malecón for a birthday drink,' suggested Melanie.

Paseo Malecón is a one-way street running parallel to the río Cabe in Monforte de Lemos. During the summer months, a riverside bar, Cervecería Anchoas, serves refreshments and tapas. It's a beautiful location, in the heart of town. They also serve my favourite beer, Estrella Galicia 1906, on draught. Half an hour later, we were heading into town.

We parked on the opposite side of the river to the bar and made our way on foot. It wasn't until we were halfway across the bridge that we noticed the *paseo* had been blocked off and the bar was closed.

'I bet they're getting ready for the wine fiesta,' I said.

At which point Richard's ears pricked up.

'Wine fiesta?'

'Yes, it starts this Friday. Perhaps we ought to go.'

'That's a good idea,' he replied.

'Cantón de Bailén is open,' said Melanie.

The setting at Bar Cantón de Bailén wasn't quite as relaxing, but they do serve Estrella Galicia 1906 on draught, and their tapas are excellent. A few drinks later, we headed home for dinner. I much preferred a barbecue with friends than a meal in a restaurant.

When all the food had been eaten and everything cleared away, Melanie introduced us to a card game from her childhood, Newmarket. Betting pennies for fun was hardly gambling, and the kids loved it. So much so that, when we finally called it a day, the clock had ticked around to three in the morning. I really couldn't have wished for a better birthday. It's strange how, as we get older, the simple things in life become the most precious.

The next day, everyone had a lie-in and, despite doing my best to squeeze in some last-minute revision, there were far too many distractions for me. I figured if I wasn't ready by now, I never would be. That evening, we took things a little easier and had a relatively early night. Tomorrow was our date with destiny, and both Melanie and I were keen to be as sharp as possible.

At 5:30 am on Friday the 14th of July, we were rudely woken by a blaring alarm clock. The drive to Santiago de Compostela would take an hour and a half, and the exam was scheduled to begin at 8:15 am. For months we'd been gearing up for this day and, while the citizenship exam hadn't exactly been a walk in the park, the language exam was on a completely different level, and I for one was feeling apprehensive.

By the time we arrived on campus, the clock had moved round to 7:45 am. We found a parking space without a problem and made our way to the test centre.

'This is it,' I said.

'It looks deserted.'

She wasn't kidding.

We climbed the steps to the entrance and went inside. The building was eerily quiet. We checked a noticeboard for information.

'There's nothing here,' said Melanie. 'Are you sure this is the right building?'

I checked the registration form.

'That's what it says here. Let's see if we can find someone to ask.'

We walked down a corridor trying every door, but they were all locked. If I wasn't anxious before we'd arrived, I was now.

'It can't be here,' said Melanie.

She was right; wherever the exam was being held, it wasn't here.

'What are we going to do?'

I checked the time. We'd already wasted ten minutes.

'Did you bring your phone?' I asked.

'I forgot to pick it up.'

I couldn't say anything; mine never leaves the house.

'Come on, there must be somebody somewhere.'

Out on the street, there wasn't a soul in sight. I couldn't help thinking that an out-of-term university campus would make an excellent location for a post-apocalypse movie.

'Which way?' I asked.

'I don't know. What about up there?'

Turning right seemed as good a plan as any. Melanie set off at marching pace and I struggled to keep up.

'Come on,' she said.

It was alright for her; she wasn't keeping an eye out for marauding zombies.

When we reached a crossroads there were still no signs of life. Anxiously, I looked at the time. Another few minutes had slipped away.

'Where now?'

'We might as well go straight ahead.'

We crossed the road and continued on.

'There's someone,' said Melanie.

At last. I could only hope they weren't looking for some fresh meat.

We crossed over and picked up the pace. Please, please, please let them know where it is.

'Excuse me, we're here for the DELE language exam, but the address we've been given isn't correct. Is there an information office on campus?' asked Melanie.

'There is but it's closed outside of term time.'

My heart sank, but at least they hadn't tried to eat us.

'Did you say DELE, the language course?' they asked.

'That's right.'

'Well, I don't know if it's the place you're looking for, but the language department is over there. Go to the end of this road and turn left. You can't miss it.'

My heart skipped a beat. We weren't out of the woods yet, but it seemed reasonable to assume that a language exam would take place in the language department. We thanked them and headed off at pace. At the end of the street, we turned left and continued on. A bead of perspiration trickled down the back of my neck. Neither of us had expected a workout when we left home.

'Over there,' said Melanie.

At last, more people. As we neared a building, students were milling around the entrance and others were coming and going.

'This must be it,' I said.

At least I hoped so; I couldn't keep this pace up for much longer. Inside, the place was alive with students. There was a desk along one wall with a notice taped to the front which confirmed we were in the right place. What a relief. Once again, the receptionist requested our registration form and photo ID. With less than ten minutes to spare, we'd made it.

The exam conditions were very different to those of the citizenship exam. The term free-for-all sprang to mind. We found ourselves waiting in a corridor along with other candidates. Moments before the exam was due to begin, an invigilator stepped out of a classroom and, rather than call each entrant individually, everyone was ushered inside together. Younger students had little regard for age but, when no quarter was asked, none was given, and Melanie and I pushed our way inside along with everyone else. The layout of the classroom was also completely different to the academy. Individual desks had been pushed together to form long rows and candidates were told to use every other chair. Once we were seated, papers were handed out and instructions issued. Chief amongst them was the need for silence.

First up was the reading module. The time allotted to this part of the exam was sixty minutes. I checked my watch and turned over the paper. As I did, the person sitting behind me began reading the questions to themselves; quietly enough not to attract the attention of the invigilator, but loudly enough to be a distraction. Soon after that the questions started.

'What do they mean by…?'

'Can we use a dictionary?'

'Do you have another pencil, mine's broken?'

I felt like standing up and shouting, 'What part of silence don't you understand?' Thankfully, the invigilator reminded everyone, although the person behind me paid no heed. Seventeen minutes into the exam, the classroom door burst open.

'Sorry I'm late, I thought it started at half past,' said the mystery entrant.

To my surprise, the invigilator allowed them to stay. Distractions aside, when time was called, I'd answered all the questions and even had time to check my answers. I wasn't exactly brimming with confidence, but it could have been worse.

Next up, a thirty-five-minute listening exam. At this point I'd expected to be given a set of headphones. I wasn't exactly relishing the idea of using a secondhand set, but anything was preferable to the din we'd endured so far. To my amazement, no such headphones were forthcoming.

'And your time starts now.'

To my astonishment, three ceiling-mounted speakers delivered the audio with all the quality of an old gramophone. Within seconds of it starting, every man and his dog had a question. The commotion was so bad the invigilator was forced to stop the tape and tell everyone to keep quiet. By this juncture, I was a nervous wreck. I pinned my ears back but, try as I might, I couldn't understand a word. For all I knew the narration could have been spoken in Klingon. Minutes of audio slipped by before I regained a modicum of composure. When the tape finished, I wasn't sure how many questions I'd answered, never mind if I'd answered them correctly or not.

At that point we were given a break. Answer papers had to be left on the desk, and we were asked to return in fifteen minutes. We followed the crowd into a communal area, and I bought us an overpriced and underflavoured coffee from a vending machine.

'Well?' asked Melanie.

'I did terrible on the listening. I couldn't hear a thing.'

Melanie could see how deflated I was feeling and did her best to lift my spirits. I pride myself on being a cup half-full kind of person, but I'm also a realist. The overall pass mark was sixty percent, but each module accounted for a different percentage of the total score. I felt reasonably confident I'd achieved at least that on the reading, but I'd be lucky to get anywhere near that on the listening. Dwelling on the past was futile. I dusted myself down, tossed the empty coffee cups into the waste bin, and we made our way back to do battle with the Spanish writing module. That contest was scheduled to last fifty minutes. Let the game begin.

When we entered the classroom, I could hardly believe my eyes. At least three candidates were hastily completing their answer papers from the previous modules. It's said that cheats never prosper, but who are they kidding? A firm rebuke from the invigilator stopped them in their tracks; however, they were still allowed to submit their papers and, as far as we were aware, they were accepted.

For obvious reasons, the answers on the writing module were not multiple choice. This made assessing how we'd fared virtually impossible. That said, Melanie seemed much more confident with her performance than I was with mine. If I had to guess, my chances of success were currently in the balance. In five days, we would have to return for the fourth and final module: speaking. Perform well in that, and who knows; underperform and failure was inevitable.

Land of Rivers and Trees

We arrived home in time for a late lunch. Richard and the kids had spent most of the morning messing about in the pool while Yvonne relaxed in the sunshine with her nose in a book.

'Are we going to the fiesta tonight, Uncle Craig?' asked Erren.

I suspected Richard had primed her to ask, but the answer was still the same.

'I don't see why not.'

'Let's have dinner in town as well,' suggested Melanie.

When guests come to stay, Melanie draws the short straw at meal times. I figured she deserved a night off from cooking, and everyone agreed.

At eight that evening, with the sun still high in the sky, we headed into Monforte de Lemos. Parking spaces would be scarce, but I had an idea we might find some in Rúa Corredoira. My hunch paid off. Not only were we able to park, but we were less than a hundred metres from Paseo do Malecón, focal point of the two-day wine fiesta.

From the footbridge spanning the river, we had a clear view of the *paseo*. Along its length, purpose-built booths had been constructed to house local wineries who were exhibiting their wines and offering tastings to potential customers and visitors. Having crossed the river, we made our way to the stand where souvenir glasses and tasting tokens were being sold.

'You might like to try this one, Richard.'

I'd stopped at Adega Cachin, one of our favourite winemakers in the Ribeira Sacra. Their wine, Peza do Rei, was selected by President Barack Obama to serve at a White House dinner to celebrate Hispanic

Heritage Day, and the owner, César Enríquez, was invited to attend. Today, his son, also called César, was serving behind the counter. Richard was almost as impressed with my knowledge as he was with the wine.

When the setting sun had scaled the tallest apartment blocks, we left the fiesta and headed to Restaurante Cardenal on Rúa Cardenal Rodrigo de Castro. This pedestrianised thoroughfare, in the heart of town, was a hive of activity.

'Could we have a table for six?' asked Melanie.

'Do you have a reservation?'

We hadn't thought to book.

'No.'

'Would you like to dine inside or out?'

On a warm summer evening it would have been a travesty to eat inside.

'Out.'

'You'll have to wait, but that table has already asked for their bill,' he said.

We were happy to wait, and a few minutes later took our seats. Pizzas and pastas were the order of the day. On a warm Spanish evening, nothing compares to an alfresco dinner with friends.

In years gone by, the kids would have taken a midnight dip before going to bed. Nowadays, they're more interested in playing cards. Mason and Erren had caught the Newmarket bug and, once again, it was three in the morning before we turned in.

'We can play again tomorrow,' said Melanie.

We oldies needed some sleep.

17

Parple Rain

When Richard, Yvonne, and the kids were last here, we'd introduced them to a nearby river beach known locally as Playa A Cova. It's situated in an idyllic location on the river Miño and, as well as a sandy beach, it also boasts a very good restaurant with stunning views over the river, the beach, and the surrounding valley. Before leaving us, Richard and Yvonne were keen to treat us to lunch, and the restaurant at A Cova would be ideal. The outside terrace is very popular at this time of year so Melanie rang to make a reservation.

Shortly after 12:30 we left Slawit in the garden and headed off. The weather had been fabulous during their stay and today was no different. I chose the entrecote steak in cheese sauce for my main course, and very nice it was too.

'Who'd like to go to a fiesta this evening?' asked Melanie.

The village of Anllo was hosting its annual rock fiesta: Rock Anllo. The line-up read like a who's who of local amateur rock bands including Maskarpone, Os Desviaos (The Deviants), and D.J. Nacho Morales on the decks. Headlining the event was Vera Lynn, a well-known band from Monforte de Lemos whose bassist, Marcos, is most often found serving behind the trade counter at Ramón Otero builder's merchant.

'Well?' asked Yvonne, of the kids.

When you're a teenager, sounding enthusiastic about anything is simply not cool but, when they found out it didn't start until midnight, they were more than up for it.

I doubt we'll ever get used to leaving home at 11:30 pm to go to a fiesta, but that's exactly what we did.

The village of Anllo brings a whole new meaning to the phrase off the beaten track. It's literally miles from anywhere, and it came as no surprise to find the designated parking area less than half-full. The sound of music led us from there to the village hall or *local social*. A temporary stage had been erected on the village green, and D.J. Nacho Morales was doing his best to breathe life into proceedings.

At midnight, the first act took to the stage. Os Desviaos by name and deviants by nature. It's fair to say their music was something of an acquired taste. Next up, Vera Lynn. Years of performing in public had given them a very professional edge, and their English-speaking playlist read like an anthology of rock legends. Some of their pronunciation left a bit to be desired, but at least we could sing along. At one in the morning, following a rendition of Prince's *Purple Rain*, we called it a night and headed home. Alas, once you've heard it sung as parple rain, it's impossible to unhear.

'Can we play cards?' asked Mason.

'It's a bit late,' replied Yvonne.

'Aw go on, just a few hands,' pleaded Erren.

Yvonne looked at us; how could we refuse?

'Go on then, but just a few rounds,' said Melanie.

Late mornings had been a recurring theme during their stay, and the following day was no different.

'Can we have that rice thingy for lunch, Uncle Craig?' asked Mason.

Mason was referring to paella, a holiday favourite. As this was their last full day and the weather conditions were perfect, I was happy to oblige. There's something uniquely Spanish about paella, a great meal designed for sharing. Melanie did most of the heavy lifting; all I had to do was cook. When the last of the liquid had boiled away and the rice had started to catch, I switched off the burner and presented it to my drooling audience.

'I think it's one of the best I've ever made,' I said, as everyone tucked in.

'It's delicious,' said Melanie.

While we ate, Slawit waited patiently in the hope of scraping out the pan. Unfortunately, she was out of luck.

'There's nothing left,' I said, showing her the empty pan.

The poor dog looked devastated.

'Come on, I'll get you something,' said Melanie.

A hide dog treat took the edge off her disappointment.

The kids spent the afternoon soaking up the rays. It had suddenly dawned on them that today was their last chance to top up their tans before heading back to Blighty. In years gone by, that would have been the last thing on their minds. How times had changed.

'What's Slawit done with that treat?' I asked, midway through the afternoon.

'She had it a minute ago,' replied Melanie.

'Don't tell me she's buried it.'

Slawit has this terrible habit of burying half-chewed hide sticks and, more often than not, we're the ones to find them. Imagine digging up a lump of decaying flesh while repotting your petunias; it's absolutely disgusting.

That evening we played cards for the final time. In the space of a week, the kids had gone from Newmarket novices to beating us hands down.

On their final morning, golden tans played second fiddle to the swimming pool, and it was nice to see they hadn't lost their sense of playfulness. After lunch they readied to leave, but not before presenting Melanie with an enchanting windchime and a beautiful scarf. As for me, I wouldn't have swapped my pork pie for anything. At 3:30 pm, we wished them a safe journey home and waved them goodbye. We'd had a fabulous week, but it was time to catch up on some much-needed sleep.

I had hoped that today's Spanish lesson would be my last but, given my exam performance, I suspected it might not be. Failure was a real possibility, and the thought of having to resit it was quite depressing.

'How did you get on?' asked Andrea, on my arrival.

I explained how nerves, noise, and general disruptive behaviour had conspired to unsettle me. As always, she managed to put a positive spin on events, and I left with a renewed, if unwarranted, sense of optimism. On reflection, if I had to continue my lessons, I couldn't have wished for a better teacher. If only I'd started sooner, the outcome might have been very different.

'How did it go?' asked Melanie on my return.

'OK. Anyway, I've been thinking.'

'Oh yes. What about?'

'After the speaking exam, let's go into Santiago for lunch.'

'That would be nice.'

'I thought we could go to that Italian place in the square.'

I was referring to La Piccola Italia, a cosy pizzeria in Praza de Fonseca. We'd stumbled across it a few years ago while playing tour guides for Cathy and Ema-Lee. They'd been staying at *Campo Verde* at the time and, when their rental car failed to materialise, we'd offered to ferry them around.

The next morning, we readied ourselves for the fourth and final part of the Spanish language exam. Every candidate had been allotted a different start time, staggered at fifteen-minute intervals. Having the same surname meant that Melanie and I would be starting one after the other. I was scheduled to go first at half past twelve. As a consequence, we didn't leave home until 10:40 am, ample time for our nerves to get the better of us.

'What are you doing?'

We were just about to leave when Melanie picked up Terry from the dining room floor.

'I thought we could take him with us to Santiago.'

I had a feeling I might live to regret agreeing to take Terry on tour.

Unlike our previous visit, the campus was a hive of activity when we arrived and there wasn't a parking space in sight.

'There must be a place around here somewhere. Keep your eyes peeled,' I said.

Every turn took us further away from the language department.

'There!' said Melanie.

The space was a bit tight, and further away than I would have liked, but we couldn't drive around forever.

'I'm going to be late,' I said, as we stepped out of the car.

'You go and I'll find the payment machine,' said Melanie.

'Are you sure?'

'Certain.'

'Do you know where you're going?'

'I'll find it. Now go!'

There wasn't a moment to lose. I left Melanie in the street and dashed off. My trek to the language department left me out of breath and feeling hot and bothered. I rushed across to the registration desk only to be informed that exams were currently running thirty-five minutes behind schedule. By the time Melanie caught up with me, my heart rate had returned to normal.

'They're running late,' I said.

'Yes, the woman on reception said.'

'How much time did you put on the parking?'

Getting towed away was the last thing we needed.

'An hour and a half.'

Fingers crossed, that would be enough.

When I arrived, two other candidates had been waiting. Shortly after that, a third came out of the exam room and left. Five minutes later, an invigilator called one of the other two into a second room. When another person left, the second candidate had been called. I wasn't sure what was going on, but I was next up.

'Cryig Bricks,' called the invigilator.

I jumped to my feet.

'Good luck,' said Melanie.

She led me into an office and asked me to choose between two pictures, a clothing retailer or a railway station. My limited lexicon of railway terminology was only bettered by my lack of clothing vocabulary, so I opted for the station.

'You have ten minutes to prepare, starting from now,' she said, and then left.

As to what I was preparing for, that was anyone's guess. The next ten minutes were the quickest of my entire life.

'Cryig, would you like to follow me.'

Startled by her sudden entrance, I jumped to my feet and followed her into a classroom next door.

Another invigilator was already seated. It was her job to assess my performance. I took a seat and filled my lungs. As I did, she asked me a question.

Other than knowing it had nothing whatsoever to do with a railway station, I hadn't a clue what she'd asked. My bewildered expression prompted her to repeat the request. Once again, I was dumbfounded and, while she waited for a reply, my anxiety levels went through the roof. Red blood cells filled my cheeks, and I was powerless to stop them. It wasn't until she rephrased the question that the penny dropped. Out of courtesy she was asking how I would like to be addressed, formally or informally.

Her question smacked of exam etiquette. Something you're probably taught on official courses. Alas, the course notes I'd purchased from Amazon didn't include such niceties.

'Just call me Craig,' I replied, which produced a faint smile.

No wonder they were running late.

Formalities aside, I had three minutes to describe what I could see in the picture of the railway station. In the time it had taken me to walk from one room to the next, the shortest ten minutes of my life had been replaced by the longest three minutes. Within sixty seconds of opening my mouth, I hit the vocabulary equivalent of a brick wall. Things were not going well and the invigilator could sense my feeling of hopelessness. To her credit, she covertly pointed out elements of the picture I'd failed to mention. For example, the TGV engine waiting in the station, except her reaction suggested it wasn't.

'*Alta velocidad* (High speed),' I blurted out.

Only afterwards did I realise the TGV is a French engine and the Spanish equivalent is the AVE. I guess two words out of three ain't bad.

If my preparation for the first part of the exam had been sketchy, the second part was non-existent. Nowhere in the course notes had it mentioned anything about role play yet here I was, buying the wrong ticket and trying to exchange it. Had I been auditioning for a comedy sketch I might have stood a chance, but I wasn't. I couldn't help thinking that if I was relying on the speaking module to claw back some marks, I was deluding myself.

In the final part of the module, candidates were required to talk about themselves. I decided it was time to put my cards on the table, bare my soul, and hope they took pity on me. I began with telling her where I was from, how I'd got here, and why I wanted to stay. I loved Spain, the warmth and generosity of its people, and the outstanding natural beauty of the Ribeira Sacra. Would it make any difference? Who knows, but at least I'd given it my best shot.

When it was finally over, I felt exhausted. Melanie had already entered so all I could do was sit and wait. Fifteen minutes later she appeared.

'Well, how did you get on?' I asked.

Like me, Melanie had chosen to answer questions on the railway station, the inference being that we don't do enough clothes shopping. She thought she'd fared quite well on the picture and the role play, but had struggled with freestyling. It seems she doesn't like talking about herself as much as I do.

'What about you?' she asked.

Listening to Melanie left me feeling even more deflated.

'You'll be fine, and if we need to resit it, then that's what we'll have to do,' she said.

In this instance, I suspected the royal we meant me.

'Anyway, we can't change anything now so let's get some lunch,' she added.

Melanie was right. We'd given it our best shot; only time would tell if our best was good enough.

Twenty minutes later we were standing in front of the city's iconic cathedral. From there we headed for Praza de Fonseca and the restaurant La Piccola Italia. Once again, the food was excellent.

After we'd eaten, we strolled into Praza da Quintana de Mortos at the rear of the cathedral. Melanie couldn't wait to get Terry out and frame him in front of the iconic twin towers.

'Take him over there,' she said, offering him to me.

A group of tourists had stopped at the monastery of San Martiño Pinario to listen to their tour guide. Melanie wanted Terry and me to tag along.

'No chance. Give me the camera and you join them.'

Not for one minute did I expect her to do it, but she did.

While Melanie and Terry pretended to be part of the tour group, I took a few snaps. Strangely enough, not one person paid a blind bit of notice to a garden gnome joining their tour.

'Over there,' whispered Melanie.

Why she was whispering was anyone's guess.

'What?'

'Put him on the tourist train.'

Even the pilgrimage city of Santiago de Compostela isn't immune to the demands of tourism. During the summer months, a bright-yellow, road-going tourist train, with seating for sixty, departs from the Praza do Obradoiro every fifteen minutes for a tour of the city. As passengers queued to buy their tickets, Melanie perched Terry on the engine and snapped away. Representing Huddersfield Town AFC was a proud moment – unofficially, of course.

The following morning felt a bit cooler than it had been but, given I'd rarely shown my face before midday, I couldn't say for certain. Melanie spent most of the morning in and out of the laundry room washing bedding. I mowed the front lawn, topped up the swimming pool, and made a start on weeding the vineyard. It wasn't until after lunch that Melanie found an email in her inbox.

'I've got my result,' she said.

'What result?'

'For the citizenship exam. They've sent me an email. Have you got one?'

I hadn't the last time I'd checked.

'What time did it come?'

'Just now.'

'And?'

'I've passed.'

'Well done. I knew you would.'

I rushed into the office to check my inbox and there it was, an email from the Instituto Cervantes. The result was in an attached pdf file. I opened it and read the certificate: "*Resultado obtenido en la prueba CCSE – APTO*" (Result obtained in the CCSE test –

PASS). I couldn't have been happier. Whatever the results of the language exam, at least we wouldn't have to resit this one.

'Well?' asked Melanie.

'I've passed.'

That evening we afforded ourselves a pat on the back and a celebratory drink. One down and one to go.

A few days later, I made a start on book five in The Journey series. Louise was still working on the fourth book but, when it comes to writing, there's no time like the present.

'Come and look at what Pepe gave us,' said Melanie. She and Slawit had just returned from their morning dog walk.

Pepe lives in the village with his wife Milucha and his mother Pilar who last year turned a hundred. His *huerta* or vegetable garden is the pride of the village. I saved what I was working on and followed her into the kitchen.

'Crikey!'

Sitting on the worktop was the largest *calabacín* (courgette) I'd ever seen.

'What are we supposed to do with that?'

'I've no idea, but it nearly broke my arms carrying it home.'

'I'm not surprised. How much does it weigh?'

'I don't know.'

Melanie took out the kitchen scales and placed the enormous vegetable on top. At just over six kilos it was a monster.

'We'll never eat all that.'

Despite efforts to the contrary, we're yet to find a good use for a *calabacín*, but that won't stop us trying. One recipe we had invented was *calabacín* pizzas: centimetre-thick rounds, drizzled with olive oil, sprinkled with rock salt, topped with sliced tomatoes and grated cheese, and cooked on the barbecue. At lunchtime we did just that.

Later in the day, Melanie made two loaves of zucchini bread, one for Pepe and the other for us, and dozens of carrot and courgette muffins which she distributed equally between Pepe, Marisa, and Pilar and Ignacio. They were over the moon, but little did they know, they were actually doing us a favour.

18

Where's Jesus?

Within days of our visitors departing, normal service was resumed. Melanie would start the day taking Slawit on her morning walk, and I would check my inbox before catching up on world events. On her return, we'd take breakfast on the terrace and then I'd go into the office to continue writing.

'You're not going to believe this.'

Melanie had burst into the office with a face like thunder.

'What?'

'A chuffing bird has eaten the first tomato.'

'Oh no.'

'Oh yes.'

Melanie had been watching its progress for weeks and was really looking forward to picking it. We did have others, but this would have been our first.

Land of Rivers and Trees

A few days later, our second tomato went the same way and we weren't alone; our neighbour Lino had experienced a similar problem. He thought a fox might be to blame, but we had our doubts. To get into our garden, a fox would have to open the gate or vault the fence, neither of which seemed likely.

That evening the weight of suspicion shifted.

'What's Slawit found?'

You get to know when your dog has found something interesting. In Slawit's case it's usually edible so we went to take a closer look.

'Slawit, leave it!' called Melanie.

On closer inspection, she'd found a hedgehog.

'You grab the dog and I'll get a shovel,' I said.

'Aw, you're not going to kill it, are you?'

'Of course not, but I'll need something to pick it up with.'

Melanie grabbed the dog, and I got a shovel from the shed.

'Before you do that, just hold Slawit for a minute,' said Melanie.

I took her collar and Melanie marched off towards the house.

'Where are you going?'

'I won't be a minute.'

Within seconds she was back, and she wasn't alone.

'Really?'

'Why not? You'll be able to write about it. I can see the headlines now: "Terry the terrier apprehends Canabal tomato thief".'

'Do hedgehogs eat tomatoes?' I asked.

'I don't know.'

We weren't even sure if they were carnivores or vegetarians.

Melanie placed Terry on the grass next to the hedgehog and took a few snaps. Photoshoot complete, I set about relocating our prickly friend into the adjacent field.

'According to Google, hedgehogs eat insects and worms although they're quite partial to fallen fruit.'

While I'd been away, Melanie had done some research.

'Tomatoes are fruits,' I said.

It hadn't gone unnoticed that the two we'd lost were both low hanging. That's why we'd first suspected a bird but, in light of this new evidence, the hedgehog became our prime suspect. As if to confirm our findings, from that point on, we didn't lose a single tomato.

They do say be careful what you wish for. Within weeks of buying a super-duper barbecue, I was beginning to question that decision. In practical terms, four burners were two too many and the powder-coated grills, of which there were six, were really difficult to clean. Ideally, they needed to be soaked overnight, but ours were too long to fit in the sink. If only we had a long shallow bucket.

'What about one of those plastic storage boxes they sell at the Chinese bazaar?' suggested Melanie.

It pays to involve an expert in these matters.

'That's a great idea. Come on then.'

'What, now?'

'Why not? We can call at the agricultural college on the way and pick up our licences.'

'Give me five minutes and I'll be with you.'

Five minutes inevitably turned into ten.

Having collected our licences, we drove across town to the Chinese bazaar and found exactly what we were looking for. It was a bit more expensive than I would have liked, but beggars can't be choosers.

After a long soak in soapy water, I had hoped the baked-on grime would simply wipe away, but no such luck. It took me ages to get them clean. Perhaps upgrading the barbecue hadn't been such a good idea after all.

Since Easter, we hadn't taken a single booking for *Campo Verde*. As a consequence, our letting season wouldn't get underway until this Saturday, the 29th of July. To date, we'd only taken five bookings for a total of seven weeks. Even including the two Easter weeks, it was hardly enough to cover our operating costs, never mind make a profit. If nothing else, it reinforced the argument for selling.

'You do realise we haven't been to the Guardia to find out what we're supposed to do about the guests?'

'I know. Perhaps we ought to call in this afternoon.'

We'd planned to go up to the house today anyway. There was the gazebo to set up and the garden furniture to take out of storage.

'Do you know where it is?' I asked.

'What?'

'The *casa cuartel* (police station) in Escairón?'

'Not exactly, but I'm sure I've seen a sign for it on that roundabout opposite the town hall.'

That was as good a starting point as any and, if we couldn't find it, we could always ask. Before then, I wanted to do some online research to get an idea of what to expect. An hour or so later, I'd found exactly what I was looking for. Other than adding a few additional questions to our existing booking form, the only other requirement was to submit those details to the Guardia Civil within twenty-four hours of the guests arriving. Better still, that information could be submitted online.

Finding this out came as quite a relief. I'd had visions of having to make wholesale changes to our operating procedures. At the moment, we left the house keys in a secret location and guests let themselves in. It saved us having to hang around for them to arrive. The following day, we called at the house to welcome them and answer any questions. In those circumstances, supplying the Guardia Civil with their details within twenty-four hours of their arrival would have been virtually impossible. Submitting them online would make things much easier.

'That doesn't sound too bad,' said Melanie.

'No, but we do need a password to access their online system.'

'And where do we get that from?'

'We need to take this to the police station.'

I'd printed off an application form from their website. 'Can you give me a hand to fill it in?'

After lunch we completed the paperwork and readied to leave. By the time we reached the village of Escairón, the clock had ticked around to ten past two.

'There,' said Melanie.

As she'd suggested, there was a sign on the roundabout. A few minutes later, we were pulling up outside a building that looked more like a small block of flats than a police station.

'It looks closed,' I remarked.

On closer inspection it was. A timetable on the door indicated the opening times were between 9:00 am and 2:00 pm. We'd missed them by ten minutes. Time was now of the essence. Tomorrow was Friday, and the guests would be arriving the day after that.

'We'll have to come back tomorrow.'

From there we continued on to *Campo Verde*. When I pulled into the entrance, Melanie hopped out to open the gate. As she did, I could hardly believe my eyes. The lawns looked absolutely terrible, and I couldn't understand why. Even when guests aren't staying, lawn sprinklers keep the grass looking green and healthy. These looked like they hadn't seen a drop of water for months. Something was wrong.

'The grass looks dry,' said Melanie.

As the house had been stood empty for a while, Melanie went upstairs to load the dishwasher while I checked the programmer in the *bodega*. When I switched on the light, the power was off. If the circuit breakers had tripped out, that would explain why the lawns hadn't been watered.

'The power's off,' called Melanie from upstairs.

'I know.'

When I looked, the main circuit breaker had tripped off. I flicked it back on and everything seemed fine.

'It's back on,' I called.

Breathing life into the lawns wouldn't happen overnight, but at least I could make a start.

'What's wrong with the sprinklers?'

Melanie had come downstairs to give me a hand with the gazebo.

'What do you mean?'

'They don't seem very strong.'

By strong, I assumed she was talking about the water pressure. I stepped outside to take a look. It wasn't just low, it was virtually non-existent.

'That's strange,' I remarked.

The lights in the *bodega* were still on. The only other thing it could be was the individual circuit breaker for the water pump. I went inside to take a look, and that's exactly what it was. Problem solved, or so I thought. When I tried to switch it on, it just kept tripping out. I couldn't believe it.

'There must be something wrong with the pump. You'd better call Ramón.'

Melanie made the call.

'He's busy at the moment, but he'll call back tomorrow.'

'Did you tell him it's urgent?'

'Of course I did, but if he's busy, he's busy.'

Life without water was unthinkable, but no pump meant no water. In less than two days, a family of four would be arriving expecting to spend a week in a luxury farmhouse with running water. As things stood, we couldn't offer them a drop. At times like this it's important to accept the things we cannot change and focus on those we can. Before heading home, we assembled the gazebo, took all the garden furniture out of the *bodega*, and gave it a thorough clean.

The next morning, we went back to the police station in Escairón. A Guardia Civil vehicle suggested someone was home. You know you're getting older when policemen start looking younger, and the officer on duty looked like he should have been at school. To his credit he listened patiently while Melanie explained.

'We need a password to use the online system,' she said, showing him the form we'd filled in.

To our surprise, he knew all about the new regulations, but still couldn't help us.

'I don't have the access code for the computer,' he said, pointing at the monitor on the desk. 'You'll have to come back on Tuesday and speak to my boss.'

'We've got guests arriving this weekend,' said Melanie.

'Write down their details and drop them in when you're passing.'

We thanked him for his insight and left.

'I told you we should have done it earlier,' I said.

'No, you didn't.'

'Anyway, have you heard from Ramón?'

We knew from experience that if he hadn't rung by 9:30 am, we were unlikely to hear from him until lunchtime, and so it proved. When he did call, he arranged to meet us at 4:00 pm.

At five past the phone rang.

'Where are you?' asked Ramón.

'We're here.'

'Where?'

'At *Campo Verde*.'

He'd got his wires crossed and had gone to Canabal. Could things get any worse? Half an hour later he pulled onto the driveway. Ramón is nothing if not thorough. After a lengthy investigation, our worst fear was realised. The pump was to blame.

Borehole water pumps are very different to surface pumps. Rather than drawing water from the well, the pump is lowered to the bottom where it pushes the water out. As a result, it would have to be hauled 200 metres to the surface before it could be checked. A specialist would then determine if it could be repaired. If not, we'd need to buy a new one. Unfortunately, none of this work could begin until Monday morning.

'But we have guests arriving tomorrow,' I explained.

Ramón suggested asking a neighbour if we could run a hosepipe from their house to ours. I wasn't convinced. Water is a precious commodity in villages like Vilatán, especially during the summer months. The only reason we had a borehole was because the communal supply, from a *depósito de agua* (water storage tank) in the mountains, was only available to homeowners who had paid for its initial construction some fifty years ago. At the time, only half the village had contributed; the others had been left to their own devices.

'We could ask Luis,' suggested Melanie.

His house was the only one close enough to run a hosepipe from. Unfortunately for us, his family had chosen not to contribute to the communal supply, and they didn't have enough water for two houses. There had to be another way.

'Do you have a *depósito*?' asked Ramón.

Ramón was referring to the type of container used in the chemical industry. They're generally square in shape, made of white plastic, and capable of holding one cubic metre of liquid.

'I'm afraid not.'

His expression suggested he was out of ideas.

'Does Ramón Otero's sell them?' I asked.

He didn't know but it couldn't harm to ask. When he called them, they could only offer us a 250-litre plastic container.

'We've almost got that much,' I replied.

A few years ago, we'd had to buy two plastic containers to store some wine in. The largest was 125 litres and the other 100 litres, and that's when it dawned on me. We had much more storage capacity than that.

'What about wine vats, would they do?' I asked.

Ramón smiled.

'They'd be perfect. We can use the plastic containers to fetch some water from my house and then transfer it to one of the vats,' he said.

As luck would have it, we kept the trailer at *Campo Verde*. I hitched it to the back of the car and we followed him home. An hour or so later, we were back.

Melanie helped me push the trailer into the *bodega* and I pumped the water from the two storage containers into the largest wine vat. While I did that, Ramón rigged up a temporary pump to feed water from the vat into the household pipework. It was genius. Four hours after arriving, running water had been restored. All we had to do now was keep the vat topped up.

On the day that guests arrive at *Campo Verde*, Melanie and I have a very busy morning. Today we had the added pressure of filling the two storage containers with water before leaving home. Given the problems we'd had with the car over the last few years, I was reluctant to put too much strain on the engine, but what choice did we have? Including the weight of the trailer, we would be hauling the best part of half a ton. To make matters worse, the 23-kilometre journey from home to *Campo Verde* was almost entirely uphill. In an effort to reduce the strain on the engine, I took it slowly and drove in a low gear.

Readying the house went well. Melanie had done most of the cleaning yesterday while waiting for Ramón to finish. I transferred the water into the vats which brought the total amount available to 450 litres.

'Where's Jesus when you need him?' I joked.

'Who?'

'You know, that bloke who turns water into wine.'

'Wouldn't that be nice?'

I'd written a note for the new arrivals explaining the situation and asking them to use the water sparingly. It wasn't ideal, but it was better than nothing. We could explain in more detail when we called to see them tomorrow.

The next day, I wasn't taking any chances. Before leaving home, I refilled the containers and we hauled another load up to *Campo Verde*. While I transferred the water into the vats, Melanie explained the situation.

'How much had they used?' she asked, on the drive home.

'About 200 litres.'

'I'm not surprised. Before coming to us they spent a week camping at the coast. The first thing they did was put the washing machine on and have four showers.'

That night, Melanie set the alarm clock for 7:30 am. We'd arranged to meet Ramón at 9:00 and I wanted to refill the containers before setting off. My poor little car was really suffering.

Ramón arrived on the dot, accompanied by two of his lads. Hauling a water pump out of a borehole is no mean feat, especially when it's 200 metres deep. As well as the weight of the pump, there's also 200 metres of polypropylene water pipe to drag to the surface, all of which was attached to a steel cable. Within minutes of them starting, it was obvious the garden simply wasn't big enough to accommodate all that pipework.

'Can we use that field?' asked Ramón.

The adjacent field belonged to Pablo's father-in-law, also called Ramón. I was sure he wouldn't mind, but it's always better to ask permission in these situations. I told him to carry on while I went to have a word. As expected, he didn't mind. Within an hour, they'd dragged the torpedo-shaped pump to the surface.

'That's the problem,' said Ramón.

Having separated the electrics from the main body, he'd discovered some charring around the wires.

'What's caused that?'

'Probably an electrical storm.'

Power surges during electrical storms are a common occurrence in Spain.

'Do you think the pump specialist will be able to fix it?'

'I'm not sure but as soon as I know anything, I'll let you know.'

On that note they left, taking the offending article with them. Melanie and I did our best to make the garden look as unmolested as possible before heading home.

That evening, I suddenly remembered we hadn't taken the guests' details to the police station.

'It's too late now. We'll have to go in the morning,' said Melanie.

Another day, another fifty-kilometre round trip, and another half-ton load. Would it ever end?

19

Well I Never

When is a change not as good as a rest? When it involves filling containers with water and hauling them twenty-three kilometres across country every morning. Over the last four days, that's exactly what we'd been doing.

'What time are we setting off?' asked Melanie over breakfast.

'I thought we'd go a bit later today.'

The job was difficult enough without having to negotiate our way around the guests' car. Unloading had been a masterclass in ergonomics. My inability to reverse the trailer had resulted in me pulling forwards into the driveway, unhitching it, and pushing it past two parked cars before reversing back out, turning around in the village, and reversing back in to rehitch the empty trailer. Talk about a faff, and wouldn't you know it, when we did eventually leave home, our arrival at *Campo Verde* coincided with the guests departing. Trying to reverse the trailer fifty metres up a winding lane was out of the question.

'You'd better say hello,' I said.

Melanie hopped out. I had no choice but to drive through the village and back round. On lanes that are little wider than footpaths, that was no easy task. I could only hope I didn't meet anything coming in the opposite direction. When I finally got back to where I'd started, Melanie was seconds away from sending out a search party.

'Where have you been?' she asked.

'Trying to get back here in one piece.'

Little by little, we were getting on top of the water situation. After emptying today's containers, two wine vats were full to the brim and a third one was nearly half-full.

On the way home we stopped at the police station but, once again, the place was deserted. They'd no doubt be hiding in a hedgerow somewhere waiting to snare unsuspecting motorists who happened to be travelling half a kilometre over the speed limit. At least it wouldn't be me. Falling foul of the law was the last thing we needed. Our applications to become Spanish citizens were dependent on a clean record.

The following day, we'd arranged to meet friends for lunch.

'Are we going to *Campo Verde* this morning?' asked Melanie.

'I thought we'd go this afternoon.'

'Oh, OK.'

After yesterday's fiasco, I was keen to avoid bumping into the guests. Besides which, the vats were nearing capacity and, with a bit of luck, we might only have to make one more trip. Which reminded me: we still hadn't heard from Ramón.

'I think we ought to ring Ramón this afternoon if we haven't heard from him by lunchtime,' I said.

After a long lazy lunch, the last thing either of us wanted to do was load the trailer with water and drive up to *Campo Verde* but, as we couldn't risk the main vat running dry, we had no choice.

'Will you ring Ramón while I fill the containers?'

Melanie picked up the phone and I went outside to make a start. At last, some good news: the pump would be ready tomorrow. With any luck, this would be our last delivery.

When we arrived at *Campo Verde*, the guests were out and we were back home within the hour. That evening, we retired to the far end of the garden with a glass of wine and watched the sun setting behind the woody knoll.

A new day brought renewed optimism. We'd just finished breakfast when the postlady pulled into the entrance and tooted her horn.

'I'll go,' I said.

A letter needed signing for.

'What is it?' asked Melanie.

'It's from the council in Escairón.'

'What do they want?'

'Give me a chance.'

I sliced open the flap and pulled out the letter.

'I think it's something to do with the bank account.'

Letters from the council are always written in galego which makes translating them that bit trickier.

'What bank account? Give it here,' said Melanie.

She didn't exactly snatch it, but wasn't in a mood to wait.

'Well?' I asked.

'I think it's something to do with our bank account.'

'*Tsk!* That's what I said.'

'We'll have to call at the town hall and find out what they want.'

One more job to add to the list.

As soon as we'd finished breakfast, we headed off to the police station in Escairón. When we arrived, the place was closed. Who knew the local constabulary would be this busy? Had we not known better, we might have thought they were avoiding us.

'Where next?' asked Melanie.

'Let's go to *Campo Verde* and call at the town hall on the way home.'

Even though we weren't delivering any water, we had to make sure the main vat was topped up. As soon as we'd finished, we drove back to Escairón.

'We've received this,' said Melanie, sliding the letter across the counter.

Our translation wasn't far off the mark. For reasons no one could quite explain, sixteen months ago, when we'd changed banks, the wrong account details had been transferred to the council. As a consequence, we were now in arrears with our annual refuse collection to the tune of twenty euro. An error we were happy to rectify but, when I offered to pay, we were steered in the direction of the nearest bank. We should have known. After queueing for what felt like an eternity, we finally settled the account. Talk about bureaucracy gone mad.

It's a measure of the positive impact moving to Spain has had on my life that, given everything we'd been through over the last week or so, I'd managed to remain calm. With a bit of luck, we'd have running water tomorrow and things could finally get back to normal. As for the Guardia Civil, I'd had an idea.

'Perhaps we ought to email them.'

'Who?'

'The Guardia Civil.'

We'd just gone to bed, and I was about to switch off the light.

'Saying what?'

'I don't know. Something about them never being there and seeing if they can email us a password. Would you mind?'

'Oh, I see, you want me to do it.'

'You're better at that sort of thing than I am.'

On that note, I switched off the light and went to sleep.

'Are we taking some water to *Campo Verde* this morning?' asked Melanie.

If we hadn't heard from Ramón by lunchtime we'd have to, but midway through the morning he rang. He'd meet us first thing after lunch, but it wasn't all good news. On closer inspection the old pump was beyond repair and he'd had to buy a new one. It wasn't his fault but, given how long we'd had to wait, the outcome was rather galling.

It wasn't until we sat down for lunch that I remembered last night's discussion.

'Did you email the Guardia?' I asked.

'Of course.'

At least Melanie was on the ball.

'And?'

'They haven't replied yet.'

At 3:00 pm we left home for *Campo Verde*. Shortly after we arrived, Ramón's van pulled onto the driveway. He'd brought a co-worker with him, but I helped where I could: holding this and pulling that. Melanie sat on the garden wall watching.

'Craig,' she called.

When I turned to face her, she tipped her head towards the gate. I looked around, to see two officers of the Guardia Civil stepping out of their car. The last time officers had visited *Campo Verde* was during the renovation work. On that occasion, they'd fined the builder for not wearing a hard hat. To make matters worse, neither Ramón nor his colleague was wearing one. Was a bad situation about to get even worse?

I looked at Melanie and flicked my head. Together, we went to meet them.

'Smile,' I whispered as we walked up the driveway.

Two Brits grinning from ear to ear. What must they have thought of us?

'Melani Bricks?' asked one of the officers.

Why is it that policemen can make the most innocuous question sound like an accusation?

'Yes,' she replied, still grinning like a Cheshire cat.

'I'm Sergeant Lopez. You sent me an email.'

Perhaps it hadn't been such a good idea after all, but his mood suggested otherwise.

'If you come to the station on Sunday lunchtime, I'll definitely be there providing there isn't an emergency,' he added.

Asking him to define an emergency might have been pushing our luck, so we thanked him for calling and assured him we'd be there.

It took Ramón and his co-worker the best part of three hours to install the new pump but, by the time they left, running water had been restored. As for the guests, they'd be leaving tomorrow morning, but our role as water carriers had ensured their taps had never run dry.

Throughout the afternoon, we'd watched with interest as the area's main water bomber flew backwards and forwards overhead. Somewhere nearby, the countryside was ablaze. The twin-engine Canadair CL-415 is based at Santiago Airport and had spent all afternoon collecting water from the *embalse de Belesar* (Belesar reservoir). This huge amphibious aircraft is capable of dropping 6000 litres in one pass, and its bright yellow and red livery is instantly recognisable. On the drive home we saw why it had been so busy: a huge conflagration filled the distant horizon and plumes of thick grey smoke were rising towards the heavens.

Within half an hour of returning home, the phone rang.

'It's the guests,' said Melanie, holding her hand over the microphone.

I feared the worst.

'What do they want?'

'They haven't got any water.'

My heart sank. Just as we thought everything was back to normal, events had conspired against us. At times like this, it feels like the whole world is against you.

'Tell them we're on our way.'

Before leaving home, Melanie rang Ramón. He was as flummoxed as we were, but agreed to meet us at the house. Wouldn't you know it, by the time we'd driven to *Campo Verde*, the water had started flowing again. Ramón suggested an airlock might have been to blame. Thank heavens for that. We'd all had a wasted journey, but rather that than the alternative.

That evening we sat out in the garden watching distant flames flickering in the night sky. Darkness had long since silenced the drone of aircraft engines. From now until sunrise, firefighting ground crews would do their best to keep everyone safe. Given the size of the conflagration, it was the best they could hope for. In the dead of night, the flames seemed much closer than they probably were. Just in case, we packed a few essentials before turning in.

By the time we woke, the aerial firefighters were already at work, and confidence was high it would soon be extinguished.

'Is that your phone?' I asked.

We were sitting up in bed enjoying our first cuppa of the day. Melanie jumped to her feet and sprinted into the lounge. Slawit, who'd been curled up between us, opened one eye and then went back to sleep. I glanced at the clock. The time read 8:42 am. Who on earth would be ringing us at this time in a morning?

'It's the guests,' said Melanie. 'They haven't got any water.'

I was lost for words. Was it possible another airlock was to blame?

'Tell them we'll be there as soon as we can.'

Their stay at *Campo Verde* seemed destined to end as it had begun: waterless. I dragged myself out of bed and laced up my boots.

'We'd better call Ramón,' I said.

'I'll wait until nine. After all, it is the weekend.'

She had a point. As soon as I'd dressed, I hitched the trailer to the back of the car, secured the two plastic containers, and filled them with water. I had hoped the car could have a well-earned rest, but no such luck.

'Are you ready?' asked Melanie impatiently.

'Ready when you are.'

A few minutes later, we were off. En route the clock ticked past nine. Melanie rang Ramón, and he agreed to turn out as soon as possible. We did hope the guests might have left by the time we got there; I was all out of excuses and saying sorry was wearing thin. Alas, they'd stayed behind to apologise for being unable to wash their breakfast dishes. Some people are just too nice.

In Ramón's absence, Melanie and I made a start readying the house for the next guests. Thankfully, we had some water left over in the wine vats but, as the temporary pump had been disconnected, I had to ferry bucketfuls of water from the *bodega* to the first-floor accommodation as and when required.

Two hours later, Ramón turned up, and he wasn't best pleased. Weekends are reserved for the family in our neck of the woods. As time ticked on, his patience wore thin. Finding the cause was proving elusive. It wasn't until he removed the cover for the wellhead that he found the culprit. A brass fitting securing the polypropylene water pipe to the wellhead had sheared off and fallen down the borehole, taking the water pipe with it.

Ramón looked devastated. With the light from his phone, he peered into the abyss. In the darkness, a glimmer of hope. The top of the water pipe was clearly visible, yet tantalisingly out of reach.

'What can you do?' I asked.

'I'll have to drag it out again.'

That meant starting again on Monday.

Before leaving, he reconnected the temporary pump to the wine vat. At least the new arrivals would have an emergency supply. After a morning of setbacks, Melanie and I drove home to lick our wounds and have some lunch before returning with two more containerfuls of water. Would this nightmare ever end?

On the drive home, Melanie had a question.

'Haven't we had any enquiries for the house yet?'

The answer was no, but I knew why she was asking. This saga had taken its toll on all of us.

The house had been on the market with Michelia Property since the 3rd of April. We'd opted for a monthly subscription plan at a cost of twenty pounds per calendar month. Since then, we hadn't had a single enquiry, and I was starting to think we were wasting our money. As soon as we got home, I logged on to the website to check the listing. Everything looked in order; the description was appealing, the photos excellent, and the house was listed in the correct region and country. I had hoped my offer of "try before you buy" might have generated some interest. Perhaps it hadn't been such a great idea after all.

It wasn't until I clicked on the heading "Your Account" that I realised I'd made an almighty blunder. I'd wrongly assumed that all enquiries would be forwarded to my personal email address, but that wasn't the case. The only way to check for them was by logging in to our account. I couldn't believe I'd made such a stupid mistake. Staring back at me were eight unanswered enquiries.

'You're not going to believe this.'

I had no choice but to come clean.

'What?'

I explained my glaring oversight. Melanie was surprisingly understanding. The earliest enquiry dated back to the 8th of June, almost two months ago. All I could do was reply to them all and hope they'd forgive my tardiness.

The following morning, we were back at *Campo Verde* to welcome the new arrivals. Leaving them a note about the water had been a complete waste of time. They'd used more in eighteen hours than a family of four had used in the previous forty-eight. At this rate we'd be up and down like yoyos. Providing the car lasted that long.

Having conducted the meet and greet we drove to the police station in Escairón and, hallelujah, someone was home. The sergeant on duty was able to access their system and, after completing a host of online forms, presented us with a password to the Guardia Civil website and a second password enabling us to enter the required information. I'd like to say we were delighted, but exhausted would be nearer the mark.

At 11:00 am, on Monday the 7th of August, our nightmare finally ended. What I'd thought might be a tricky and time-consuming job turned out to be a piece of cake. With the aid of a long piece of wire, Ramón fished out the water pipe and replace the broken fitting. Such was his confidence that he disconnected the temporary pump from the wine vat, and loaded it into the back of his van.

From discovering the problem to reconnecting the supply had taken ten days, and ten years off our lives. As for the car, she'd performed flawlessly, but I couldn't help thinking there'd be a price to pay for her service.

The following morning, I logged on to the Michelia Property website and found three new enquiries. It looked like our twenty quid subscription might have been worth it after all. Having sent replies, I continued working on book five. While I did that, Melanie caught up with some household chores. How quickly our lives had returned to normal.

Two days later I was in the office when a phone call broke my concentration. Moments later, Melanie walked in.

'It's the guests,' she whispered, handing me the phone.

My heart sank. Communications with guests are rarely good news. Perhaps they'd broken a wine glass or something equally insignificant.

'Hello,' I said, trying to sound upbeat.

'Hi, I'm afraid we haven't got any water.'

Had I not been made of sterner stuff, I would have dropped to my knees and cried.

'I'm really sorry about that, we'll be with you in half an hour,' I replied.

Before involving Ramón, I wanted to check a few things.

When we arrived at *Campo Verde*, the guests were waiting for us. Doing anything in the glare of others is never ideal. I began with the outside tap, and watched in horror as water came gushing out. Had we driven all this way for nothing?

'It definitely wasn't working when I rang you,' said the guest.

As if on cue, the gushing water slowed to a dribble and then stopped altogether. Opening the tap had simply drained the system. Perhaps the circuit breaker had tripped off again. Alas, it wasn't going to be that straightforward.

'You'd better ring Ramón,' I said.

Melanie made the call.

'He'll call in first thing after lunch.'

That gave Melanie and I just enough time to drive home and have ours before returning.

Ramón got there shortly after 3:30 and spent the entire afternoon trying to diagnose the problem. In the end he had to concede defeat.

'I'll have to come back tomorrow and drag the pump out,' he said.

His air of resignation mirrored our emotions. Thankfully, he'd come prepared, either that or he hadn't had time to take the other pump out of his van. Before leaving, he reconnected it to the wine vat. Our days of transporting water were set to continue for a while yet.

The next day, Ramón's mood had lifted. Overnight, he'd had an idea. Before hauling the pump out of the borehole, he replaced the condenser with one with a slightly higher rating. It took a matter of minutes and the result was instantaneous. As if by magic, water came gushing out of the tap.

'Is it fixed?' I asked.

'*A ver* (We'll see),' he replied.

For the next hour, Melanie and I waited anxiously while a thousand-plus gallons of water drained into the lawns as he tested the system. Eventually, he declared the problem solved. Perhaps now, our lives really could get back to normal.

20

Table Toppers

Throughout the year, the village of Sober hosts a number of fiestas. Chief amongst those is the wine fiesta held on the weekend of Palm Sunday. The second most popular celebration is the annual *rosca* fiesta, and this weekend marked its twenty-second anniversary. A *rosca* is a traditional Spanish cake with a doughy texture and is baked in the shape of a bagel.

Festivities were scheduled to begin on Friday evening with the mayor hosting an event aimed at local residents. This year's programme included a new attraction, the imaginatively named Túnel do Vino or Wine Tunnel. The main event is held on Saturday lunchtime when people from far and wide descend on the village to sample some 2000 slices of free *rosca*.

It's a great weekend of entertainment, but Melanie and I much prefer the intimacy of Friday's programme to the crowds on Saturday. As for the Túnel do Vino, we weren't sure what to expect. A few phone calls later and the usual suspects had been rounded up.

On Friday evening we arrived in Sober at 6:30 pm. Unusually for us we were the first to arrive, but we didn't have long to wait. From there we strolled across the newly resurfaced Plaza del Ayuntamiento towards the Túnel do Vino. Housed in a large marquee, it gave local wineries the opportunity to promote their wines. Inside were four rows of tables draped with white cotton tablecloths, and on each row were sixteen different wines. Entry into the marquee cost the princely sum of €2.50 and included a souvenir wine glass. Once inside, visitors could taste as many wines as they liked. The only limiting factor was time. The marquee opened at 7:00 pm, and would close an hour later.

'What's the catch?' I asked.

'That's what I was wondering. Surely we can't just help ourselves to as much wine as we want,' said Gerry.

There was no catch, and that's exactly what was on offer. It's surprising how quickly an hour passes when you're tasting wine. At 8:00 pm the curtains closed and everyone was politely but firmly ushered outside where another surprise awaited us. The mayor, Luis, had arranged a cooking demonstration from one of the area's top chefs, Carlos J. González of Restaurante Merenzao. Little did we know that all his recipes involved breathing new life into stale *rosca*. By the time he'd finished, we were glad we'd booked a table at Restaurante O Xugo.

Most fiestas have a staggered timetable which allows attendees to enjoy a meal with family and friends before returning later in the evening. They're called *descansos* or breaks: *primero descanso, segundo descanso* (first break, second break) etc. Having finished our meal, we made our way back to the square for the second part of the evening's festivities.

'Look,' said Melanie, pointing into the crowd.

She'd spotted our neighbours, Marisa, Pilar, and Ignacio so we went over to say hello. The number attending this part of the festivities was higher than earlier but was still fewer than two hundred. Once word of the Túnel do Vino spread, I suspected next year's figure would be considerably higher.

Tonight's entertainment came from Cé Orquestra Pantasma, an act we first saw two years ago at this same event. He'd gone down a storm on that occasion, and he hadn't lost any of his appeal. Back in the 70s, one-man bands were quite popular on TV talent shows, but tastes change and performers retire. Cé Orquestra Pantasma harped back to an era when a one-man band could top the bill.

During a brief intermission, the mayor and his staff served slices of *rosca* accompanied by *licor café*.

'This is awful,' said Melanie.

The *licor café* wasn't up to our usual standards.

'What do you expect for nothing? Anyway, it's not that bad,' I replied.

By that time of night, taste was a secondary consideration.

'In that case, you won't mind finishing mine,' she said, handing me her cup.

On his return, Cé Orquestra Pantasma dazzled the audience with his humour and musical prowess, and ended his act to rapturous applause and shouts of bravo. We'd had a fabulous night, and the mayor Luis had done his chances of re-election no harm at all.

Saturday the 12th of August marked the start of the Premier League season and, for the first time in forty-six years, Huddersfield Town AFC would be part of it. Their first game was away from home against a well-established Crystal Palace side packed with internationals such as Benteke, Zaha, and Loftus-Cheek. To be fair, Town's owner, Dean Hoyle, had invested heavily in the squad during the summer. The team starting today's game was unrecognisable from the one that had gained promotion.

Throughout the afternoon, I'd kept a close eye on the BBC's two-minute updates. On twenty-three minutes, Town took a surprise lead, thanks to an own goal. Three minutes later, Steve Mounie, one of the new summer signings, scored a second. Perhaps the Premier League wasn't as difficult as people made out. The second half followed a similar pattern and, on seventy-eight minutes, Mounie scored his second and Town ran out 3–0 winners.

'Well?' asked Melanie, when I stepped outside.

She'd spent the afternoon lazing in the sun with her nose in a book.

'We won, 3–0. I can't wait to watch it on *Match of the Day*.'

We still hadn't taken the plunge and bought a TV, but I could stream Premier League highlights through the internet and watch them on the laptop.

Later that evening I got to see them in action, and the scoreline definitely flattered their performance. At the end of the programme, host Gary Lineker revealed the league table, and wouldn't you know it. After game one of the new season Huddersfield Town were top of the league. I couldn't resist taking a photo for posterity. Given their performance, it might be the last chance I'd get. To have any hope of surviving they'd have to improve and fast, but for the time being I'd savour the moment and enjoy their success.

In the week following Town's opening day win, we received another enquiry for *Campo Verde*. A man called Matt wanted to view the house. Needless to say, I replied immediately. Four days later he messaged again asking me to resend the details. Apparently, he'd deleted them in error. I guess I'm not the only person to make mistakes.

'That bloke emailed again,' I said.

'What bloke?'

'The one who wants to view the house.'

'Oh yes, and what did he want?'

'He'd lost my message.'

'Really?'

'I know, but he must be keen to email again.'

'I suppose so. Does he live in Spain?'

'No, the UK.'

Melanie rolled her eyes.

'Talking about viewings, are we going to make any wine this year?' asked Melanie.

A link might not seem obvious but, since moving wine production to *Campo Verde*, the two were inextricably linked.

Ideally, we needed a seven-day window when we could come and go in order to monitor the progress of the primary fermentation. For a second year in succession, a late frost had left us with little if any useable grapes. If we were going to make wine, we'd have to buy some.

'I'd like to, but where can we get the grapes from?'

Last year, we'd drawn a blank.

'I've seen a notice offering grapes for sale.'

'Where?'

'I'm just trying to think … Ah yes, it's on the way into town just past the hotel. You know, the one opposite the cemetery.'

'Hotel Terra Galego?'

'That's the one.'

'Are you sure?'

'Yes, why?'

'It's a bit early.'

Harvesting doesn't usually start until September.

'Perhaps they're just taking orders.'

'The next time we're passing we'll call in and find out.'

If we could get some grapes, we'd have plenty of time to make wine. The guests currently at *Campo Verde* were leaving on the 27th of August and the next ones wouldn't be arriving until the 12th of September.

It's difficult to imagine another place where the summers are more perfect than the Ribeira Sacra. While friends in southern Spain have to lock themselves away in their air-conditioned homes, prisoners to the extreme heat, we're able to sit in the sunshine and enjoy an al fresco lifestyle.

'I think the mole is back.'

Melanie had been pegging out the washing and noticed a trail of earthwork at the far end of the garden.

'Not again.'

Who would have thought that watering the lawns would attract such unwanted visitors? When the surrounding countryside is baked solid, excavating through moist earth must be a real treat. In an attempt to rid the garden of these troublesome critters, I enlisted the help of my Facebook followers. Three solutions were offered. The first, immortalised in a comedy sketch by Jasper Carrot, was a definite non-starter: I've never fired a shotgun and had no intention of starting now. The second involved purchasing mole traps, but the thought of digging even more holes in the lawn turned me off that idea. It was the third suggestion that grabbed my attention. It was so far left-field I figured it was bound to work. Who knew that the smell of mothballs was as repulsive to moles as rotting corpses are to humans and, more to the point, how did they find out?

'Mothballs,' I announced.

'Excuse me?'

'We need to get some mothballs to get rid of the mole.'

'Mothballs?'

Melanie's scepticism mirrored my own, but it had to be worth a shot.

'It's either that or a twelve-bore shotgun.'

'Mothballs it is then. Do you know where we can get some?'

That was a very good question. I wasn't even sure what a mothball looked like, never mind where to get them from.

'I don't. Do you?'

'I think I've seen them in Mercadona.'

Mercadona is Monforte de Lemos' premier supermarket and our personal favourite. Later that day, we drove into town to take a look.

'The place that sells grapes is coming up on the left,' said Melanie, as we drove into town.

Since we'd spoken about it, I'd been calculating how many we'd need. A lot would depend on the price, but 350 kilos would be ideal for the size of our vats. As we approached, I slowed down. A notice confirmed what Melanie had thought. They did sell grapes, but there was no mention of the variety or the price.

'We'll have to ring them. Have you got a pen?' I asked.

'No.'

'There's one in the glovebox.'

Melanie made a note of the number and we continued on. At the supermarket, I let Melanie take the lead.

'This is them,' she said, holding out a packet.

Printed on the front were the words *pastillas antipolillas* (mothballs). At a cost of one euro for twenty, it had to be worth a go. I wasn't convinced it would work but what did we have to lose?

Back home, I wasted no time deploying my secret weapons. Debra, the person who'd come up with the idea, suggested poking a hole in the top of each molehill and dropping in a mothball.

While I'd been busy mothballing the enemy, Melanie had made a call about the grapes. The chap she'd spoken to confirmed the variety as Mencia. He sourced them from the Bierzo region where harvesting had already begun. At a cost of eighty cents per kilo including delivery, we couldn't resist. As a rough rule of thumb, and taking into account our low-tech processing methods, a kilo of grapes would produce a bottle of wine. Eighty cents a bottle didn't sound bad at all. As for availability, he would call us as soon as he had them.

If anything, the mothballs proved to be more of an aphrodisiac than a deterrent. The following morning the mole had run amok and left a maze of earthwork running here, there, and almost everywhere. I could only conclude that Spanish moles had a less sensitive disposition, either that or Debra was having a laugh.

'Well, that was a waste of time,' I said.

'What was?'

'The mothballs.'

'Oh dear. What now?'

'I guess I'll have to use my powers of persuasion.'

Persuasion needs a persuader and mine was a ten-pound sledgehammer. I sat on a garden chair and waited patiently for it to raise its head. It took a while but eventually it couldn't resist coming back for more. With all the stealth of a ninja warrior, I raised the sledgehammer and watched as the earth began to lift. Slowly at first but, as it gained in confidence, the mound began to grow. I held my breath, took aim, and with all the force of a Yorkshire Luddite, brought the hammer crashing down. Only time would tell if I'd hit the mole on the head.

Since acknowledging my mistake, I'd been checking the Michelia Property website on a daily basis. We hadn't exactly been inundated with enquiries, but we couldn't complain. I'd always been confident that, providing we could get people to view it, the house would sell itself. In that regard, Galicia had turned out to be more popular than either of us had expected.

'We've got a viewing,' I announced.

Melanie's eyes lit up.

'From that chap who lost the email?'

'No, from a guy called Claus. Actually, it's his wife Anelise who's coming. She's flying into Galicia on the 5th of September and wants to view the house on the 6th.'

'That's great news.'

That same day, Louise returned the edited manuscript of *Opportunities Ahead*. It wasn't the end of the process, far from it, but every edit took me one step closer to publishing. I spent the next two days working on her suggestions before sending it back.

On Sunday evening, the 27th of August, we had a phone call from the grape supplier. He had a batch arriving tomorrow and would meet us at Vilatán at 8:30 am. That night we set the alarm for seven.

We'd arranged to meet him in a layby a short distance from the house. He arrived in a van pulling a covered trailer and followed us through the village to the house. Before unloading, he offered us a taste. Melanie declined; she's not a fan of seeded grapes.

'*Son muy dulces* (They're very sweet).'

He wasn't kidding.

Generally speaking, the sweeter the grapes the higher the sugar content, and the more alcoholic the wine. We'd ordered 350 kilos; 362.5 was close enough at a cost of 290 euro.

'Drop the empty crates off at the yard when you're done,' he said, before leaving.

By 11:30 we'd crushed the grapes, cleaned the equipment, and completed all the measurements and calculations. A specific gravity of 1103 was much higher than we'd ever achieved with our own grapes and, providing the fermentation ran through to complete dryness, would deliver a wine of at least 14% vol.

'What about the crates?' asked Melanie.

There was no way we could take them all in one go.

'Let's take half now and the others tomorrow. We'll be coming back to inoculate the wine.'

We loaded them into the back of the car and drove into Monforte de Lemos. When we arrived, the yard was deserted and the gates padlocked. We had no choice but to toss them over the fence.

While Melanie prepared lunch, I checked my inbox before moving on to Michelia Property where I found another enquiry from a couple in the UK, Ronnie and Marlene.

'You're not going to believe this,' I said.

'What?'

'We've had another enquiry and they want to try before they buy.'

Perhaps it hadn't been such a bad idea after all.

'That's great news, when?'

'They're not sure but probably in early October.'

Over the next five days, I exchanged eighteen correspondences with Ronnie culminating in a reservation from the 7th to the 14th of October. The couple weren't just keen, they were positively obsessed. It went without saying that everything was dependent on the outcome of Anelise's viewing, but having two prospective buyers was a nice position to be in.

Within twenty-four hours of adding yeast to the grape must, it had started bubbling and burping, and all the numbers were heading in the right direction: temperature, specific gravity, and pH.

More good news followed. On the last day of August, Louise sent me the final edits of *Opportunities Ahead* and I wasted no time uploading the manuscript to Amazon. Since my last book launch, Amazon had introduced a preorder option allowing readers to order the book before launch day, so I decided to give it a go. The book would be available from midnight on the 7th of September with the launch date a week later on the 14th. I wasn't sure what, if any, advantage there would be but nothing ventured, nothing gained.

The excitement and anticipation of launching the fourth book in The Journey series was overshadowed by some very sad news.

'I've had an email from Cristina,' I said.

'Oh yes, how is she?'

'She's not too good; her mum passed away this morning.'

'Aw no.'

Cristina was the daughter of Christina and Barry, a couple we'd met almost five years ago when they bought a house in the area to renovate. On retirement, they'd moved here permanently and we became close friends. They really took to their new lives in Spain until the unthinkable happened. In July last year, Barry had a heart attack and died. Following his passing, Christina had been determined to stay in Spain but it wasn't to be. On a trip to the UK to see her daughter and grandson over Christmas, she'd been taken ill and, on the 31st August, lost her fight for life. Cristina's news wasn't altogether unexpected, but it was no less upsetting, and we spent the rest of the day in quiet reflection.

21

What's for Dinner?

Seven days after adding yeast to the crushed grapes the specific gravity had fallen to 1033, and we were back at *Campo Verde* to press the must. It's a messy and time-consuming job, but well worth the effort. Three and a half hours after arriving, we'd transferred 250 litres of red wine into a clean vat for the final stage of fermentation, proving once again that a kilo of grapes produces a bottle of wine, *más o menos* (more or less).

'I've heard from Cristina again.'

Melanie was in the kitchen preparing dinner.

'How is she?'

'As you'd expect. She's sent me a copy of the funeral announcement.'

'When is it?

'Thursday the 28th at 1:30 pm. She asked if we'd raise a glass in her mum's memory.'

'That's nice.'

'Perhaps we should organise lunch for those who knew her. What do you think?'

'I think it's a good idea. I'll have a phone around.'

Given what we knew about Christina and Barry, that was exactly what they would have wanted us to do.

If I had to guess, I'd say we'd used the alarm clock more often this year than in the previous fifteen put together but, having waited five months to get our first viewing, we had no intention of being late. We'd arranged to meet Anelise in the layby on the outskirts of Vilatán at 8:45 am. Within five minutes of our arrival, a car pulled up alongside.

'Anelise?' I asked.

'Yes, sorry I'm late.'

'No problem. Would you like to follow me; it's not far?'

Two minutes later we were pulling into the driveway at *Campo Verde*. Anelise had flown into Santiago de Compostela yesterday and viewed another property that same day. After that viewing, the owners had invited her to join them for dinner and, by her own admission, she'd had a bit too much to drink.

'Do people usually serve that many after-dinner liqueurs?' she asked.

'That's Galician hospitality for you,' I replied.

It wasn't until I opened the *bodega* door that we realised exactly how fragile she was feeling.

'I'll have to give the cellar a miss,' she said.

In her present condition, the aroma of fermenting wine was too much to handle, and none of us wanted to see what last night's dinner looked like. Other than that, the viewing couldn't have gone any better. She loved what we'd done with the house. So much so that at one point she stopped to stroke one of the internal exposed stone walls.

'This is lovely,' she said.

Whatever floats your boat.

Before leaving she said that her husband would want to see the place before they could make a decision. At that point I thought it only fair to tell her we had another interested party. It's tricky in these situations. I didn't want her to think that we were trying to pressure her but, if she was serious about the place, I didn't want her to miss out on it either. We made it clear that the house would be sold on the basis of first come, first served.

The 15th of September started like most days. Melanie took Slawit out for her morning walk and I went into the office to check my emails and catch up on world events before starting to write. What I didn't expect to find was an email from the Instituto Cervantes. The subject line read "*Diplomas* DELE. *Convocatoria de julio de 2017 Publicación de calificaciones*" (DELE Diplomas. July 2017 session. Publication of grades). The result of my Spanish language exam was one click away.

Since I'd taken the exam there'd been no let-up in my studies, such was my conviction that a resit was inevitable. Nervously, I opened the email. An attachment contained a certificate detailing the result.

The four modules, reading, writing, listening, and speaking had been marked in two groups, and candidates had to score a minimum of thirty marks in each group to pass. In the first group, reading and writing, I'd scored 20.83 and 14.02 respectively making a combined total of 34.85, not exactly a glowing reflection of my hard work, but a pass nonetheless. Everything now rested on my performance in the second group: listening and speaking.

During the exam, the listening module was a real low point for me. The sound quality of the recording had been appalling and interruptions from other candidates were wholly unacceptable. A score of 14.17 was a fair reflection of those concerns. Everything now rested on the final module, speaking. On the day of the exam, I'd got off to the worst possible start when asked how I'd like to be addressed, formally or informally. I could only hope my heartfelt ad-libbing had won the day. I scrolled down to the result. Was a mark of 15.83 enough?

Mental arithmetic suggested it was. I reached for the calculator and punched in the results: 14.17 + 15.83 = 30. Talk about a close call. With scores calculated to the one-hundredth of a point, I'd achieved the exact pass mark. I knew it was going to be close; I just didn't realise how close. When Melanie got home, I couldn't wait to tell her.

'That's fantastic news. I'd better check my inbox.'

She too had her results but, unlike me, she'd sailed through with an overall score of 77.23.

More than anything, these results meant we could press ahead with our goal of becoming Spanish citizens. If we managed to achieve that, it wouldn't matter what politicians in Westminster were able to negotiate; our rights as Spanish citizens would be enshrined in national and European law.

One of the last fiestas in Sober's festive calendar is the *festas do* Carme. This year it would run from the 15th to the 18th of September. The majority of holidaymakers had long since left the area making it one of the quieter fiestas. During the fiesta, most days begin with a church mass followed by a religious procession and then vermouth. We saved our attendance for the final evening, and the Grand Paella in Plaza de Ayuntamiento.

When we arrived in the square, Pepe Arias was hard at work cooking tonight's enormous paella. He's something of a celebrity in the world of grand paellas, travelling around the area with his specialist equipment cooking paella at various events and fiestas.

The offer of free food is always a popular attraction and, by 8:45 pm, a long queue had formed stretching across the square and halfway down Rúa do Comercio. In an effort to keep everyone happy, the mayor handed out cups of wine. When service began, Melanie's shellfish allergy forced her to abstain, but I ate enough for both of us.

After everyone had eaten their fill, the entertainment began. Tonight's performers were a duo called La Hora Bruja (The Witching Hour). As singers go, they weren't that bad. What caught my attention was the vehicle they'd arrived in. Most of the top performers have a significant entourage. While the group prepare for the concert, a crew of roadies transform an articulated lorry into an enormous stage complete with lighting and sound system. This couple had rolled up in a Ford Transit. Between them they'd dropped one side of the cargo bay to create a small but perfectly formed stage. Talk about cute.

Within half an hour of them starting, most of the paella-loving audience had headed home, and we weren't far behind. As for The Witching Hour, perhaps three-quarters of an hour would have been more appropriate.

Fifteen months after the UK had decided to leave the European Union, Melanie and I were finally in a position to take back control of our own futures by applying for Spanish citizenship. To date we'd spent the best part of a thousand euro in pursuit of our goal. We'd requested copies of our birth certificates and marriage certificate from the General Register Office and asked the Criminal Records Office for our police certificates, all of which had to be officially translated and notarised. We'd also applied to the local authorities for a Spanish police certificate and passed both the CCSE citizenship exam and the DELE A2 language exam. All that remained was to complete the application form. With that in mind, we'd arranged to meet our adviser, Paula.

'You'll need to apply online,' she said.

'OK.'

'We can do it now if you'd like. Do you have all the documentation with you?'

'I think so.'

Paula logged on to the government website and, starting with Melanie, completed the application form and uploaded copies of all her documents before doing the same for me.

'How do you want to pay?' asked Paula.

'How much is it?'

'One hundred and one euro, each.'

More expense.

A bank transfer completed the process. After everything we'd been through, the final step felt somewhat underwhelming.

'What now?' I asked.

'You'll have to wait.'

'How long?'

According to Paula, we couldn't have chosen a worse time to apply. Austerity measures introduced in the wake of the global financial crisis had led to major delays at the Department of Justice. To compound this, in October 2015, the government passed a decree allowing descendants of Sephardic Jews, expelled from Spain in the fifteenth century, the right to apply for Spanish citizenship without going through the usual application process. To date, they'd received over 50,000 requests. All other applications were currently taking years rather than months to process. On the 1st of February 2020, the UK would leave the EU. It wasn't essential to hear before then, but it would be nice. We thanked Paula for her help and headed home for lunch.

On the 28th of September, nine friends of Christina and Barry met for lunch at Restaurante Casa Antonio. In life, it had been one of their favourite eateries and a place we'd enjoyed many happy lunches together. At 1:30 pm, we raised a glass to them both in the sure and certain knowledge that it was exactly what they would have wanted us to do.

The last guests of a disappointing season left *Campo Verde* on the 3rd of October. If this was to be our final year, it couldn't have been much worse. In total we'd had seven weeks of paying customers. Ronnie and Marlene would make that eight but, if they decided to buy the house, we'd agreed to deduct their rental fee from the asking price. In addition to all the usual running costs, marketing, insurance, utilities etc, we'd also spent over six hundred euro on a new water pump, to say nothing of the extra time and effort Melanie and I had put in, but we couldn't complain. We'd had a good run over the past nine years and, in the main, loved every minute of it. Providing quality accommodation for the discerning traveller had been challenging and fun, but the time had come to hang up our marigolds, turn the page, and write a new chapter in our lives.

Before then, we had to ready the house for Ronnie and Marlene and hope they fell in love with the place. In a way, we were glad they'd taken up our offer to try before you buy. Moving abroad is a huge undertaking often taken on the spur of the moment while wearing rose-tinted glasses. Some people even buy off plan without ever seeing the finished property. At least Ronnie and Marlene would have a whole week to road-test their potential new home and explore the area.

On the morning of the 7th, we left home at our usual time of 9:30 to prepare the house for their arrival. We didn't say as much, but I think we were secretly hoping it might be our final clean. Before leaving, I left them a note. As with all our guests, we would call the following morning to introduce ourselves and welcome them properly.

That evening saw the start of Music in Autumn, a series of five concerts to be held in the *casa de cultura* in Sober. The first performer was a guitarist, David Antigüedad Mangas from Salamanca. At this time of year, the number of concert goers are even fewer than normal due to the mayor's refusal to heat the auditorium. Fortunately, the weather this October had been particularly kind so we wrapped up warm and drove up to Sober. The programme included pieces by Johann Sebastian Bach, Joan Manén, Fernando Sor, and Antonio José Martínez Palacios. David's playing was exceptional and, by the time he'd performed an encore, we were glad we'd made the effort.

Having braved the elements, we decided to make a night of it by going into Monforte de Lemos for dinner. For weeks, our neighbour Marisa had been singing the praises of Portovelo restaurant. The place was under new management and, according to her, they served the best pizzas in Monforte de Lemos. We'd pretty much tried all the pizzerias in the area and none of them were to our liking. We prefer our base thin and crispy; those made locally are usually thick and stodgy.

What we hadn't expected to see was a familiar face. The new owner was none other than Sergio, a young man we'd met shortly after arriving in Spain. At the time he'd been working elsewhere as a waiter. Originally from the Dominican Republic, his beaming smile and conscientious work ethic set him apart from his co-workers, and it was no surprise to find him running his own place.

'*Hola, qué tal* (Hello, how are you)?' he asked.

We hadn't seen him for years yet he greeted us like long-lost friends. When he asked if we'd made a reservation, it hadn't crossed our minds.

'No problem, follow me,' he said.

In common with many local eateries, the place was first and foremost a busy bar serving a wide range of tapas. The dining room was at the rear. Sergio led us to a table and handed us a menu. It's fair to say that the décor, furniture, and even the crockery and cutlery had seen better days, but he was obviously doing something right. The bar area was packed and the dining room busy. It's often the case that new management take over a business lock, stock, and barrel from an absentee owner. Sergio would be able to put his own stamp on the place as finances allowed. In the meantime, his priorities were food, service, and price. If he got those right, he'd be well on the way to running a very successful business.

One thing he hadn't compromised on was the food. We'd never seen such an extensive menu. Marisa had waxed lyrical about his pizzas and we were eager to try one. To that we added a bowl of macaroni alla puttanesca to share. At four euro a bottle, the house white was a very palatable Godello. Marisa was right about the pizza; it was delicious, and the portion of macaroni was enormous. When we asked for the bill Sergio offered us a *chupito* (shot) on the house, and we couldn't resist *licor café* on the rocks. The food had been excellent, the service impeccable; as for the price, let's just say I had change from a twenty euro note. Our experience at Portovelo left us in no doubt that Sergio was onto a winner, and we couldn't have been happier for him.

On Sunday morning we readied ourselves to welcome Ronnie and Marlene to *Campo Verde*. October's weather is often hit and miss, but we'd woken to a clear sky and bright sunshine. Try as we might, it had been almost impossible to keep our expectations under control. So far, I'd handled all the communications with Ronnie, and done my best not to build up Melanie's hopes. All that went out of the window when we met them. They'd fallen in love with the house and, within minutes of our arrival, had offered us the full asking price.

On the face of it, they seemed like a genuine couple, but there was a catch. For personal reasons, they didn't want to complete the sale until the following April and were hoping the offer of a deposit would encourage us to take the house off the market.

We had our concerns. This was their first visit to Spain, never mind Galicia, and they hadn't yet been here twenty-four hours. Taking everything into account, we thought it prudent to consider their offer before giving them an answer. In the meantime, there were a few practical issues to address. If they were serious about buying the house, they would both need a national identity number or NIE.

'How do we get one of those?' asked Ronnie.

'It's quite straightforward. The police station in Monforte de Lemos issues them.'

'Can you help us with that?'

'Of course. You'll also need a bank account.'

By law, funds used to purchase a Spanish property have to come from a Spanish bank.

'How much will that cost?'

'You can open one with next to nothing and pay in the balance when you're ready.'

'Can you help us with that as well?'

'We could speak to our bank manager if you like, or go elsewhere if you'd prefer.'

'No, wherever you think.'

Before leaving, we arranged to pick them up on Tuesday at 10:30 am and take them to the police station to apply for NIE cards. If everything went to plan, we could go to the bank afterwards and ask about opening an account. We didn't want to appear pushy, but they were only here a week and things don't always go to plan in Spain.

'If we do manage to get everything done on Tuesday, we'd be happy to show you around the area on Wednesday, if you like?' I said.

They jumped at the chance, and when I suggested a boat trip on the river Sil, they couldn't wait.

We'd always thought the house would sell itself, but even we hadn't expected it to be that easy.

22

Don't Mess with Lola

On Tuesday morning we drove back to *Campo Verde* to collect Ronnie and Marlene and take them to the police station in Monforte de Lemos. It was a measure of their eagerness that they were waiting in the garden when we arrived. From there we drove straight into town and found roadside parking nearby. As we made our way towards the police station we bumped into Raquel Arias Rodríguez walking in the opposite direction.

'*Buenos días*,' I said.

To which she reciprocated.

'That's the former mayor of Sober. She's now an MP in the Galician parliament,' I said.

Ronnie's expression gave nothing away, but it couldn't harm our credibility to be on first-name terms with the local MP.

The police station was much quieter than we'd expected. Melanie helped with translation and within fifteen minutes they'd completed the necessary paperwork and we were standing outside on the pavement.

'Is that it?' asked Ronnie.

'You have to pay this at the bank and then come back here,' I said.

Even policemen aren't trusted to accept payments.

'How much is it?'

It's easy to forget how little others understand.

'Nine euro and fifty-four cents.'

'Is that all?'

Twenty minutes later, they'd made the payment, returned to the police station, and were now in possession of their shiny new NIE cards. I could only hope such speedy service didn't give them a false impression of Spanish bureaucracy. They didn't have long to wait to see the other side of the coin. When we arrived at the bank, the manager, José Antonio, was out of the office and wouldn't be back until 12:30 pm.

'What now?' asked Ronnie.

We did what any self-respecting Spaniard would do and went for a coffee. When we returned, José agreed to see us, and was more than happy to open an account for them. By the time we left, the clock had ticked around to 2:00 pm and, although we would have to return on Friday to collect their debit cards, the morning's events had gone much smoother than we could have imagined.

'Thank you so much, we really do appreciate it,' said Marlene.

'You must let us buy you lunch to say thank you,' added Ronnie.

There was no need but they insisted.

By the time we'd eaten, dropped them back at *Campo Verde*, and driven home, the time had moved on to 5:30. It had been a long day, but Ronnie and Marlene seemed as enthusiastic as ever at the prospect of buying the house and moving to Spain. That evening we retired to the far end of the garden with a glass of wine to unwind and watch a beautiful sunset.

The following morning, we were back at *Campo Verde* for 10:30 am. As if to reinforce their enthusiasm for a new life in Galicia, their questioning had shifted from practical matters such as water and waste, to more aspirational ones about growing their own vegetables and acquiring more land. We hoped today's tour would further strengthen their desire to move here.

For many people, the Ribeira Sacra means absolutely nothing. For those in the know, it's an area of outstanding natural beauty, inhabited by warm and generous people, and home to unique traditions and fabulous cuisine. Melanie and I were keen to show them as many of its treasures as possible.

'We thought we'd start with coffee at the Parador,' I said, as we drove towards Monforte de Lemos.

Their response suggested this luxury chain of state-run hotels was new to them. The Parador in Monforte de Lemos would provide the perfect introduction. Housed in the former Palace of the Counts of Lemos and the Monastery of San Vicente do Pino, no expense was spared in its renovation.

Located atop a hill in the centre of town, visitors are treated to unparalleled views over the town and surrounding countryside.

'This is beautiful,' remarked Marlene.

Over the last few days, we'd got to know Ronnie and Marlene a little better. Ronnie seemed very focussed, quietly spoken, and kept his emotions in check. In contrast, Marlene was more needy and insecure, and wore her heart on her sleeve. After wandering around the Parador, and taking coffee in the cafeteria, we continued on.

From Monforte de Lemos we headed towards the village of Doade. A trip to the Ribeira Sacra wouldn't be complete without visiting the viewing point at Pena do Castelo. I parked in the forest carpark and we walked the 500 metres or so to the top of the valley. Whatever the season, the views are always spectacular. From the banks of the river Sil to the tallest peak, vineyards climb the steep valley slopes on narrow terraces. At this time of year, we were treated to a display of autumnal colours: rusty browns and intense purples blanketed the valley. Such was the vastness of the panorama and beauty of the foliage that even Ronnie was struggling to contain his emotions.

'I've never seen anything like it,' he said.

'That's where we're going next,' I said, pointing down the valley.

Excursions on the road-going tourist train had finished for the year, but the route it follows was definitely worth driving. It wasn't the most direct way to our chosen lunchtime eatery, but it was the most picturesque. We thought a traditional three-course *menú del día* at restaurant O Xugo in Sober would give them an idea of the food they could expect.

Lunch proved a bit tricky as they were both vegetarians, but they seemed to enjoy what they'd ordered and were overwhelmed by the size of the portions.

After lunch we made our way to the embarkation point for a cruise along the river Sil. From the moment they stepped aboard to the time we disembarked, Ronnie and Marlene didn't stop smiling. The beauty of the Ribeira Sacra had once again worked its magic and, by the time we dropped them off, they were more convinced than ever that this was the right destination to start a new chapter in their lives.

Two days later, we met them at the bank to make sure they collected their debit cards without a hitch. Afterwards, they followed us home to sign a deposit agreement. In exchange for taking the house off the market, they agreed to pay a ten percent deposit with the balance due within twelve months. I'd originally suggested six, but they were worried everything might not fall into place in time. Ronnie had a house to sell in the UK and, although he was confident they'd be in a position to complete by the beginning of April, he was nervous about losing his deposit. As we'd decided not to involve solicitors, we saw no reason not to take them at their word and extend the time period to a year. The next time we saw them they'd be here to complete the deal. Between now and then, we promised to keep in touch.

The following morning, when we went to collect the dirty laundry from *Campo Verde*, they'd left us a box of biscuits to say thank you. It wasn't much, but it's always nice to feel appreciated. Above all, we hoped we'd given them an insight into what their new life could be like.

Six days later, our bank confirmed receipt of the deposit. There was some way to go before all the i's had been dotted and the t's crossed, but everything was moving in the right direction. In some ways we felt quite sombre. We're not ones to get sentimental about a property, but we'd put our hearts and souls into creating a home from home for international travellers, and it would be sad to see it go.

Over the weekend, we called to see our neighbour Toño to ask if he could service the car before we drove south and take a look at the temperature gauge. While we'd been out and about with Ronnie and Marlene, I'd noticed that it would inexplicably soar into the red before falling back to normal. Given the symptoms, I thought a sticking thermostat might be to blame. I'd had a similar problem with my first car, a bright-yellow Ford Cortina mark II.

For a one-car family, their collection and drop-off service is invaluable.

'Can you leave it with me on Monday evening?' he asked.

'No problem.'

Toño would take it to the workshop on Tuesday and get his brother to have a look at it.

On Monday evening, Melanie came with me. It's not far but at least I'd have someone to talk to on the walk home. When we got there, she hopped out and rang the doorbell.

'There's no one home,' she said.

'How do you know?'

Toño's house was surrounded by a two-metre-high wall and, from the moment she'd stepped out of the car, Roy, the family's German Shepherd, hadn't stopped barking.

'If they were in, they would have answered by now,' she replied.

It looked like we'd have to come back.

'What are you doing?' I asked.

Melanie was about to open the gate.

'Toño won't mind if we leave the car on the drive and post the key through the letterbox.'

'Perhaps not, but Roy might.'

'He'll be fine.'

In rural Galicia there are three main reasons for owning a dog: protecting livestock, deterring predators, and guarding homes. Roy had met both of us before and, in the presence of his owners, was as soft as a brush. That said, I had no doubt that if we scaled the wall and entered the garden, he would happily rip our throats out. I could only hope he was a little more understanding when Melanie opened the gate.

Thankfully, the minute he saw her, he trotted outside and snuggled up, seeking some attention. While Melanie distracted Roy, I drove inside, locked the car, and posted the key through the letterbox. Getting him back inside proved slightly more difficult, but we got there in the end.

The following evening, when Toño dropped the car off, it wasn't good news. Hauling half-ton loads of water from home to *Campo Verde* had come at a price; the cylinder head gasket had gone again. To make matters worse, in a little over a month we'd be driving over one thousand kilometres for our winter break. This was the last thing we needed.

'How much will it cost to repair?' I asked.

He'd have to ask his brother to prepare a quote.

'And how much do we owe you for the service?'

Toño handed me an invoice.

'Pay me later,' he said, before heading off into the village.

'What are we going to do?' asked Melanie.

'I'm not sure.'

This would be the second time in two years the head gasket had failed. It seemed reasonable to assume that the engine was reaching the end of its useful life. We couldn't really complain; the car was fifteen years old and had covered over 350,000 kilometres, the equivalent of over eight times around the planet. She'd been a reliable workhorse over the years, but daily driving had taken its toll, and she'd gone from being a thoroughbred racehorse to an overworked pit pony. We had two options: repair her or replace her.

Fixing the head gasket would probably be the least expensive. Two years ago, it had cost us 1325 euro. The question was, would we be better off putting that money towards a new car? The problem with replacing her was the timeframe, but it couldn't harm to take a look at what was available.

Over the next few days, I scoured the small ads looking for a possible replacement. Given the size of our budget and the short timeframe, I decided to concentrate my efforts on Renault Meganes. The model wasn't without its flaws but, having experienced most of them, I knew what to look out for. I didn't say anything to Melanie because I wasn't convinced it was the right course of action.

In the Catholic calendar, the 1st of November represents All Saints' Day, sometimes referred to as All Hallows' Day. It's a time when all saints, known and unknown, are supposed to be remembered and honoured. It's also the day when the village of Canabal holds my favourite fiesta of the year, *magosto*.

We woke to a thick frost and icy mist, but the day ended with clear skies and bright sunshine. At 5:45 we left Slawit in the garden and wandered down the lane into the village. Meli had been watching for us from her kitchen window and we walked together to the *local social*. Preparations were well underway when we arrived with chestnuts roasting over an open flame.

'Let's eat outside,' suggested committee member Estevo.

At the moment, it was warmer outside than in but, once the sun had set, temperatures would plummet. Meli and Lola were having none of it.

'We're not eating out here,' said Meli.

'And you can put the fire on as well,' added Lola.

It would be a brave man to go against Lola's wishes.

Attendance was relatively low which was hardly surprising for a Wednesday evening. Despite that, we had a great time. The chestnuts had been perfectly roasted and the local wine went down a treat.

A week after Toño had dropped the car off, he still hadn't brought us an estimate. Time was slipping away and we needed to make a decision.

'Let's go and have a word with Toño,' I suggested.
'OK.'

As expected, he didn't have a quote but promised to speak with his brother in the morning.

'If we haven't heard anything by tomorrow, we'll call at the workshop and speak to his brother in person,' I said, as we walked home.

Every passing day took us closer to our trip south.

We weren't that surprised when we didn't hear anything the following day; it's just how things are. Undeterred, we called at the workshop and, to his credit, his brother dropped what he was doing and prepared an estimate there and then. The final price would depend on what he found when he removed the head, but the job would cost somewhere between five and six hundred euro. This was a game-changer. Even his top estimate was less than half what we'd paid two years ago.

'If we did go ahead, how soon could you do it?' I asked.

'If I start on Monday, I should have it finished by the end of the week.'

We couldn't ask for much more than that. We thanked him for his time and went away to consider our options.

'What do you think?' asked Melanie, on the drive home.

'It's a good price.'

'But?'

'I'm just not sure it's the right thing to do.'

Ideally, the car needed replacing and, had we not been going away, we would have taken a chance on the head gasket surviving until we'd found another, but we were. With that in mind, we decided to bite the bullet and get it repaired.

On Monday lunchtime we dropped the car off at Toño's, and spent the rest of the day tidying the garden. I raked up leaves while Melanie weeded the gravel beds and then we pruned the roses.

'I think we ought to dig up the holly bush,' I said.

'The rhododendron has had it as well,' said Melanie.

It was a shame really. We'd bought both of them the year we moved in, and although neither had truly flourished, the rhododendron did flower, albeit every other year. After a long hot summer, they'd finally given up the ghost.

On Thursday we had an unexpected visitor. Toño's brother called to see us, and it wasn't good news.

'Look,' he said.

He'd taken some photos of the cylinder head on his phone and was pointing at the screen.

'Can you see it?' he asked.

I hadn't a clue what I was looking at.

'There,' he said, having zoomed in.

He'd found a flaw on the surface of the cylinder head. It wasn't very long or deep but, in his opinion, it would almost certainly compromise the integrity of the gasket.

'What can we do?' I asked.

There were two options, neither of which was very attractive. We could hope for the best and let him finish the job, or he could try and source a replacement engine.

'If you did replace the gasket, how long would it last?' I asked.

He shrugged his shoulders.

'Are we talking days, weeks, or months?'

He was reluctant to say but thought it would be months rather than weeks, and possibly even longer. As for finding a new engine, that was equally unpredictable. Not only would it cost considerably more, but the replacement might not be any better than the one we had.

If only we were back in the UK. The country is littered with small engineering firms that would be more than capable of skimming the head (eliminating the score by removing a thin layer of metal), but here in Spain, a country that for all intents and purposes missed out on the industrial revolution, that wasn't an option. Talk about being stuck between a rock and a hard place. I stared at Melanie.

'Don't look at me. I haven't a clue.'

On my head be it.

Given the choices, replacing the gasket seemed the least bad option. Only time would tell if I'd made the right decision.

The final bill came to 510 euro which, given the work involved, seemed fair and reasonable. When Toño dropped it off on Saturday morning, I couldn't wait to take her out for a spin.

How quickly the problems of the past are forgotten when you're sitting behind the wheel and everything is working as it should. We could only hope it remained that way until we'd sold the house and had the cash to replace her. Between now and then, there was the small matter of a round trip to Andalucía to undertake.

23

Bumps in the Road

By mid-November, daily temperatures had reached the point of no return, but we couldn't complain. Overall, we'd had an exceptional year. Only when the office became too cold to type in did I concede defeat and turn on the heating.

On Saturday the 18th, the mayor of Sober hosted another concert in the Music in Autumn series at the *casa de cultura*. The day had started out damp, overcast, and bitterly cold but improved throughout the day. By two o'clock the clouds had cleared and it felt comfortably warm in the sunshine. We knew from experience that the auditorium would feel like the inside of a fridge but if people don't attend these events, they'll stop staging them.

At 7:20 we left home in anticipation of a 7:30 start. As expected, the *casa de cultura* was absolutely freezing. Tonight's performer was a pianist, Susana Gómez

Vázquez from the university town of Alcalá de Henares in the province of Madrid, a town famous for being the birthplace of Miguel de Cervantes, author of *Don Quixote*. Susana was a graduate of the Royal Academy of Music in London and had performed at prestigious events all over Europe, the United States, and South America, and yet here she was, entertaining forty or so folk in the municipality of Sober. Despite the Arctic-like conditions, her performance, which included pieces by Schubert, Dean, Granados, Gómez, and Ginastera, was exemplary, and we were delighted we'd made the effort.

On Wednesday morning, temperatures hit a low of -4°C.

'It's freezing out there,' said Melanie, having returned from her morning dog walk.

Slawit wasn't bothered; her fleecy dog coat had kept her toasty warm. I can only imagine what the neighbours must have thought. Most village dogs don't even live inside.

'This was in the mailbox,' said Melanie, handing me an official looking letter.

I slipped the letter opener under the flap and sliced across the top. The correspondence was a payment demand from Sober Council for water and refuse collections. Despite having our own borehole, we'd kept the connection to the municipal water supply, just in case. The demand was for a staggering 141 euro. That might not sound a lot, but it was way more than our usual demands.

'Can you remember how much we pay for water and bins?' I asked.

'They're two separate bills.'
'I know, but how much are they?'
'I'm not sure, why?'
'According to this we owe 141 euro.'
'You're joking. That can't be right.'
'Look,' I said, handing her the letter.
Melanie studied it carefully.
'This includes a *multa* (fine),' she said.
'What for?'
'I don't know.'
My constant questioning was starting to annoy her.
'Let's go up to the town hall and find out what's going on,' I said.
'Can we have our breakfast first?'
'Of course.'
After we'd eaten, we jumped in the car and drove up to Sober. We handed the letter to the receptionist who studied it carefully.
'According to this, you haven't paid your water bills or refuse collections for the last two years and they're due again,' she said.
'That can't be right; they're paid direct from the bank,' I replied.
'Hmm, have you changed banks recently?'
As soon as she mentioned the bank, I knew exactly what had happened. It wasn't just the payment to Escairón Council they'd cocked up; it was here as well.
'How much is the fine?' asked Melanie.
The receptionist checked the details on her computer.
'One euro.'
Melanie and I looked at each other and almost burst out laughing; even the receptionist cracked a

smile. I couldn't help thinking that fines are meant to deter late payment; this one was almost an incentive.

'I suppose we have to pay this at the bank,' I said.

'That's right, but can I make a note of your new bank account details before you go?'

We gave her the account number and walked across the square to the bank. It's difficult to put a value on peace of mind, but one euro seemed a small price to pay.

As the clocked ticked down to our winter getaway, the weather worsened. I don't usually look forward to going away but, once we're there, I don't look forward to coming back. This year, however, I was ready for some winter sun.

With seven days to go until we were due to leave, we drove to *Campo Verde* to rack (clean) the wine and rake the lawns one last time. We don't have any trees, but those in our neighbours' gardens keep us more than busy at this time of year. As for the wine, that would need filtering again on our return and then it would be ready to drink. Initial indications were very good. At over 14% proof it certainly packed a punch, but the fruity notes and mild tannins made it very smooth. Before heading home, we unplugged all the electrical appliances and made sure the bins had been emptied.

'Can we nip into town on the way home?' asked Melanie.

'What for?'

'I want to get some chorizo.'

While we're away, we stock up on food essentials we're unable to buy in Galicia. Over the years, that list has become shorter and shorter. Nowadays, the reverse is true, and we wouldn't dream of leaving home without packing some Galician chorizo. How times had changed. Our butcher of choice is Carnicería Real on Rúa Real in Monforte de Lemos. They're a specialist pork butcher who sell some of the best chorizo in the area.

Before we knew it, I was readying the car for an early start. I began by checking the tyre pressures and adding some air to compensate for the extra weight and high-speed driving. After that I checked the oil level and coolant, both of which were spot on. Last but not least, I topped up the screen wash. A few days earlier I'd bought a litre of oil and the same of coolant to keep on hand just in case. Fitting everything into the back of the car was as challenging as usual, but we got there in the end. I even managed to leave enough space for my laptop which would be packed first thing in the morning.

That night, Melanie gave me a hand to lay a towel across the windscreen. If the forecast was correct, we were in for a cold start, and so it proved. What I hadn't anticipated was moisture freezing the tailgate to the car. Try as I might, I couldn't open it. The laptop would have to travel in the cabin with us.

Neither Melanie nor I said a word about the head gasket. The last thing we wanted to do was tempt fate. I did, however, keep a watchful eye on the temperature gauge throughout the entire journey. So much so that I drove straight past the petrol station we usually top up at. That aside, we couldn't have wished for a better run, which was more than could be said on our arrival. After a ten-and-a-half-hour drive, the last thing we needed was to find the apartment's allotted parking space occupied.

New laws requiring rental owners to register their properties with the local authority had spawned a whole new industry along the Costa del Sol. Property management companies had sprung up here, there, and everywhere flooding the market with competitive offers to manage rentals. Unfortunately, not all operators were as professional as they should have been.

The owners of this apartment had chosen a confident young man by the name of Ben. According to him, ensuring the parking space was vacant on our arrival was not his responsibility. Undeterred, we unloaded the car and I parked on one of the access roads. Having dispatched Ben, we settled down to a well-earned Teatime Taster. There's something quite satisfying about leaving home in subzero temperatures, driving 1100 kilometres, and ending the day sitting outside with a glass of wine on a comfortably warm evening with stunning views over the Mediterranean Sea.

Sunny days, warm temperatures, and clear blue skies made it easy to settle in to our new yet familiar surroundings. We enjoyed meals on the terrace and afternoon strolls along the coastal boardwalk. In the evenings we would marvel at amazing sunsets as pastel pinks became intense purples or bright oranges smouldered into flaming reds.

Visiting Málaga's magical Christmas lights has become something of a tradition in the Briggs household; even Slawit seems to enjoy the experience.

On Wednesday the 13th of December, we wrapped up warm and set off for Málaga city. I had hoped the roads would be a little quieter midweek, but they were absolutely chocker. A forty-minute journey took well over an hour, but it was worth the effort. The Christmas decorations had transformed Calle Marqués de Larios into a magnificent cathedral of light complete with stained-glass windows, lancet arches, and a central dome.

The following morning, we were treated to another wondrous sight. Across the Mediterranean Sea, at the edge of infinity, the continent of Africa appeared on the horizon with the morning sunshine reflecting off the snow-capped peaks of the Rif Mountains.

On the Monday before Christmas, we headed out to do our Christmas shopping. As usual we'd allotted ourselves twenty euro to buy each other as many gifts as possible. In previous years, we'd found everything at the open market in La Cala. This year we decided to have a break with tradition and go to the Miramar shopping centre in Fuengirola. Unbeknown to Melanie, that wasn't the only break with tradition. Prior to leaving Galicia, I'd bought her a brand new, all-singing, all-dancing digital camera.

Back in May, when I'd bought her a beat-up old Sony, I couldn't have imagined how much use she would get out of it. Every morning, she would return from having walked the dog with photos of things she would previously have walked straight past. It used to be Melanie who would have to wait while I stopped to take snaps, and now it was the other way around. When we take the time to look, it's amazing what's hiding in plain sight, and I couldn't have been happier that she'd started seeing the world through a different lens.

On reflection, leaving the Christmas shopping until the last minute wasn't such a good idea and I was relieved I'd bought her a surprise. The items available in the shopping centre were either not suitable or too expensive. In the end I spent just fifteen euro on a tin of Christmas biscuits, a pack of four Ferrero Rocher chocolates, a new diary, and a pack of elasticated hair ties.

On the run-up to Christmas the weather couldn't have been better. Cloudless skies, bright warm sunshine, and not a breath of wind. All that changed on Christmas Eve. Clouds rolled in and although it didn't rain, it felt much cooler. Tomorrow's traditional barbecue looked in jeopardy.

On Christmas morning, Melanie took Slawit outside for her morning constitutional and returned with two mugs of coffee. One by one, we opened our Christmas gifts, and I saved the best until last.

'Oh wow! When did you get this?' she asked.

Though I had cheated, Melanie approved of her new camera. I think it was the bright pink body as much as anything.

As for me, it's not often I get excited about a new coffee mug, but the one my sister Julie had bought me was very special indeed. After the first game of the Premier League season, Huddersfield Town were top of the table. Julie had captured that moment and had it transferred onto a coffee mug. Town's reign as league leaders had been short-lived, although they had managed to stay there for one more game. From that point on, their fortunes had been mixed but, with half the season left to play, they were sitting in eleventh spot with a realistic chance of retaining their Premier League status. Only time would tell how that went.

'What are we going to do about lunch?' asked Melanie.

We'd woken to a thick layer of cloud, and if we couldn't have a barbecue Melanie would have to improvise.

'Let's wait to see if it improves.'

A special day called for an equally special breakfast, and a sausage sandwich certainly hit the spot. After that, we drove down to the boardwalk for a stroll along the front. By lunchtime, the weather had improved sufficiently to light the barbecue, and breaks in the clouds made it feel comfortably warm.

The weather over the next few days was mixed. On Wednesday, Slawit broke her dewclaw and, given the inflated prices of everything in this part of Spain, we thought twenty euro was a fair price to have it trimmed.

On Thursday, I suggested a change of scenery for our afternoon dog walk.

'Would you like to go to Cabo Pino this afternoon?'

'Why not?'

Prior to the boardwalk opening, we would often go for a stroll around the marina. Unlike Slawit, Jazz had loved being close to the water.

As things turned out, we couldn't have chosen a better day to go. In the bay adjacent to the marina, twenty or more kitesurfers had taken to the water.

The talent of some people never fails to amaze me. Kitesurfing is similar to windsurfing except surfers strap an enormous kite to their torso. Using the power of the wind, they're able to reach phenomenal speeds and very often take to the air. Watching them bouncing over the waves at breakneck speed, it was surprising they didn't collide with one another.

We decided to stay in on New Year's Eve. Melanie cooked an Indian feast of poppadoms, onion bhajis, and chicken Madras. At midnight we wrapped up warm and braved a chilly sea breeze to watch fireworks light up the night sky. An hour later we welcomed in the New Year for a second time from the comfort of the sofa when the chimes of Big Ben initiated a spectacular fireworks show over the river Thames.

Another twelve months had slipped away, and last year's future was now its past. Forlorn hope had turned into euphoric elation when Huddersfield Town exceeded expectations and gained promotion to the Premier League. My writing had continued apace with the publication of the fourth book in The Journey series, and I was making good progress on the fifth. We'd enjoyed a fabulous mini-break and visited some amazing places, and who would have thought that thirty-six years after leaving school, we'd be back to learn new skills in an unfamiliar language. Our quest to become Spanish citizens had tested our resolve. Exams had been passed and documents secured. Only time would tell if our adoption papers would be accepted. There'd been a few bumps in the road, and I doubted the car would ever recover from its water-carrying exploits, but at least the sale of *Campo Verde* was progressing well. What we would do then was anyone's guess, but where's the fun in knowing what the future holds?

HASTA LA PROXIMA

What Next?

If you've enjoyed *Land Of Rivers And Trees* and the other books in The Journey series, rest assured there are many more adventures to come. Until then, why not immerse yourself in Craig's debut novel.
Set in Galicia, *PANDORA'S BOX* is a cosy crime with a hint of romance.

Here's a taste of what's in store.

Pandora's Box

CHAPTER 1

A raised voice broke my concentration. Dave had been wittering on about politics for the last ten minutes – same tune but different lyrics. Don't get me wrong, I'd got a lot of time for Dave. We'd been best mates since our first day at infant school but when he started with politics I tended to switch off. For someone who chose not to vote at the last general election, he certainly had a lot to say on the matter. Beside which, the conversation on the adjacent table was much more interesting. A group of university students were boasting about their gap year plans.

For as long as I cared to remember, Dave and I had spent Thursday evenings in the Rose and Crown. Living in a university town was a double-edged sword. The local economy thrived but the presence of students provided a slap in the face for those of us excluded from Britain's educational elite. To them we're little more than local yokels, too thick to go to university and too frightened to step outside of our comfort zone. But as Dave was fond of reminding me, 'By the time these muppets leave university, the only thing most of them will have is a lifelong debt.' He had a point, but while the likes of him and me were struggling to make ends meet on a government funded building apprenticeship, this lot would be heading off into the wide blue yonder for the next twelve months.

Two of the group were flying to Vietnam on a trekking experience through Southeast Asia. Another three were embarking on a grand tour of Renaissance Italy in Rupert's soft-top Beemer. Both trips sounded great, but what really piqued my interest was the ambitions of an attractive blonde they'd nicknamed Bubbles. She was one of those southern types born with a silver spoon in her mouth and an inherited air of superiority.

'I've decided to work my way through Belgium, Germany, Austria, Switzerland, and France,' she announced.

'You, work!' scoffed a lanky lad with a Birmingham accent.

Her friends seemed flabbergasted.

'That's right. I've signed up to become a GapEx.'

'Tom!' Just as things were getting interesting, Dave nudged my arm.

'What?'

'I asked if you were going to the match on Saturday?'

'Of course I am.'

'The lads are meeting up in the Plumbers at one. I'll pick you up at a quarter to.'

Raucous laughter boomed out from the next table. It seemed I'd missed the punchline.

'They don't serve champers, you know,' chimed one of the Beemer boys.

Another burst of laughter filled the room.

'You'll be lucky to get bread and water,' commented another.

It seemed the joke was on Bubbles.

'Don't forget to pack your toolbox.'

Each wisecrack sent Bubbles' companions into fits of laughter and left me wondering what she'd signed up to become. Whatever it was, her fellow students couldn't envisage Bubbles being one.

'It's not all building walls and fixing roofs, you know. You get to stay with real people and experience the true romance of a place.' Her remarks only served to encourage her entourage.

'Well?' asked Dave.

I'd switched off again.

'Well what?'

'What's wrong with you tonight? I asked if you wanted a lift into town.'

'Yes please. What time?'

'I knew you weren't listening. A quarter to one.'

'Right, of course, that would be great. Cheers.'

'Are you having another?' asked Dave, having downed the dregs of his pint.

I glanced at the time, 10:39 p.m., and decided against it; we both had college in the morning. Dave offered me a lift home but I decided to walk.

I couldn't help noticing Rupert's convertible as I

strolled through the carpark. As well as being the only BMW, his personalised plate was a bit of a giveaway: RUP 87T. If nothing else, the pretentious registration helped disguise the car's true age.

The weather over the last few days had been pretty good for the back end of April and tonight was no exception. A cloudless sky had sent the mercury plummeting, but I'd rather that than rain. Within a few minutes of me leaving the pub, Rupert's Beemer came flying past. The back window was steamed up and the thumping beat of the sound system melted into the cool night air as it sped away. Had I witnessed my life as a metaphor? Rupert and his university chums speeding along in life's fast lane while I trudged in their wake.

This July would mark a milestone, a quarter of a century, and all I had to show for it was eight grand in the bank and a twelve-year-old Ford Focus. I wouldn't mind, but seven and a half of that was an inheritance from Aunt Flo. To make matters worse, since splitting up with Kirsty, I'd moved back in with Mum and Dad and hadn't had a steady girlfriend for over a year. The closest I ever came to university was thumbing through a prospectus. After two years at sixth form college, I'd had enough of education.

A career in retail loomed, thanks in no small measure to a full-time vacancy opening at Tesco within weeks of me finishing my exams. I went from Saturday boy to trainee manager without so much as an interview, which was hardly surprising as the only difference was the number of hours and the job title. After three years stacking shelves and taking orders from idiots with half my brains but twice the experience, it was time for a change. If I was ever going to make anything of myself, it wouldn't be as a lackey for someone else.

From supermarkets I entered the world of insurance, or assurance to be more precise. Another fancy job title followed, financial adviser for one of the lesser-known insurance companies, Knight Shield Life. The position was sold as a halfway house between employment and self-employment. Selling life insurance, on a commission-only basis, was nothing if not cut-throat. Unlike many new recruits, I managed to ride the ups and downs but life was a struggle. When Dave asked me to join him on a government funded building apprenticeship, I jumped at the chance. He had dreams of us going into business together, but I was never convinced. He'd always been more of a talker than a doer. 'We'll make a fortune,' he'd boasted. Eighteen months in and his enthusiasm had waned. We'd be lucky to find employment when we qualified, never mind working for ourselves.

The walk home had done nothing to lift my spirits. I pushed open the garden gate and counted the ten paces from the pavement to the front door of 39 Castlegate Road. I wiped my feet on the way in and went into the front room.

'I'm back,' I announced.

'Hello love. Kettle's just boiled if you fancy a brew,' said Mum.

Dad didn't say a word. He was too wrapped up in the night's movie.

'No thanks, I'm going up.'

'Is everything alright?' she asked.

'Yeah, I'm just a bit tired. It's been a long day.'

'Will you be here for tea tomorrow?'

'Of course I will.'

'Don't be cheeky to your mother,' snapped Dad, without diverting his gaze.

Fish and chips on Friday was a family tradition. Dad picked them up from the Ginnel chippy on his way home from work. Yet one more routine to my uneventful life.

I said goodnight and trudged upstairs. With the exception of sharing a bedsit with Kirsty for six months, I'd spent the last twenty-four years of my life in this six-foot by twelve-foot box. I kicked off my shoes, flopped onto the bed, and stared at the ceiling. A *ping* alerted me to new posts. Social media never sleeps. Dave had posted some political memes, none of which sparked any interest but I "liked" them anyway.

If only I had a gap year to look forward to.

My eyes wandered through the patterns on the embossed anaglypta, trapped in an endless maze of swirls.

What was it Bubbles had signed up to become?

I racked my brain trying to remember. If Dave hadn't been so eager to interrupt my eavesdropping, I'd have been paying more attention. Was it JobEx? I typed it into Google. The result was an online digital recruitment firm. My next guess, TravelEx, turned out to be a currency exchange company. That's when it hit me, GapEx. Things were going from bad to worse. Top result for that search was an eye clinic in Armenia. I could have sworn she'd said GapEx. I scrolled down the page and there it was, GapExchange – volunteer work in exchange for accommodation and meals in private homes and lifestyle enterprises. I clicked on the listing. The homepage read as follows:

GapExchange is an online platform dedicated to matching host providers with work participants, in a variety of different accommodation opportunities including hotels and hostels, farms, domestic homes, and even Dutch barges. GapExchange facilitates cultural exchanges for gap year students and travellers seeking a unique work and holiday experience.

So, it wasn't just for students. I continued reading:

Typically, the participant will work a four-hour day in exchange for free accommodation and meals. This may vary depending on the provider's requirements. The specifics of each individual arrangement will be agreed prior to work commencing. Participants frequently stay in the homes of their providers and are encouraged to participate in day-to-day duties.

GapExchange offers two membership levels, Free or Premium. At a cost of 10 euros per annum, Premium membership allows participants unlimited access to all areas, including contact details of all providers, their full profile, and reviews from previous participants.

Regardless of your membership choice, all providers must register before posting their

work vacancies. Once a registration is approved, providers can update their profile at any time and view the profile of all participants.

We encourage participants to provide a comprehensive biography including previous experience and trade skills such as building, joinery, electrical, plumbing, and general skills such as farming, agriculture, gardening, and landscaping. If you have previously worked with animals state your level of expertise and experience.

Providers and participants should clearly state their expectations before agreeing to an exchange, and participants should never arrive without prior agreement.

Was this for real? I was struggling to get my head around the concept of travelling the world for as little as four hours' work a day. Was it a scam?

A tab below the header read "Find Provider". The dropdown menu allowed users to refine their search.

Right then, where would I like to go on my gap year vacation?

Australia looked interesting, but how would I get there? I decided to try a bit closer to home – Europe. Somewhere warm and sunny – Spain. I hit the search button and was staggered by the number of listings. Page after page of providers looking for participants. Didn't people want to travel the world for free? I could talk. I was the one working my nuts off for the privilege of living at home with my parents.

I swiped down the listings, envious of the opportunities I was missing out on. On the second page one photo caught my eye. A beautiful stone farmhouse surrounded by green pastures and distant mountains, set against a backdrop of a cloudless blue sky. The property was in a place called Galicia and the description read as follows:

> **Hello participant. My name is Samantha. I live in a small village in the south of Lugo province in Galicia, Spain. I've lived in this beautiful area for more than three years. Over the next twelve months I am aiming to develop a holiday retreat for those wishing to explore this undiscovered corner of Spain.**
>
> **I am looking for help to restore and renovate several outbuildings that can be used for guest accommodation. I would prefer a long-stay participant but would consider short stays. The ideal candidate will be a qualified tradesperson or have extensive experience renovating older properties on a budget. In exchange for a four-hour working day, or twenty-four-hour week, I will provide you with your own independent room with private bathroom facilities and three meals per day.**
>
> **The house is located two kilometres from the nearest village where you'll find a restaurant/bar. The nearest town is seven kilometres away and the beautiful coastline and beaches of Galicia are about an hour and a half by car. There are many countryside walks in the area and the house is located on the winter route of the Camino de Santiago pilgrimage trail.**

I fell backwards and searched the ceiling for an escape route through the swirling ripples in the anaglypta. What was I waiting for? This listing could have been written for my skillset. I'd never given much credence to fate. It struck me as a bad excuse for making poor decisions. As far as I was concerned, everyone was the master of their own destiny. Some people take the opportunities life presents them and others don't. We either reach for the stars or scrabble around in the dirt. The question was, did I have the courage to take control of my own life, create a profile, and make an enquiry?

Self-doubt is the denier of opportunity, but what did I have to lose?

I was three months away from completing my apprenticeship. I'd be a fool to throw in the towel now. Perhaps I should wait until I'd qualified. The voice of parental reason echoed around my head. I knew exactly what they'd say.

If I didn't do it now, I probably never would. I was young, free, and single, but in reality, the shackles o expectation kept me bound to predictability. It was time to stand on my own two feet and trust in my own ability. For someone who held fate in such low regard, I was placing a great deal of faith in it deciding my future.

Forget fate, I was determined to create my own destiny. I completed the registration form and sent an enquiry.

AVAILABLE NOW
EXCLUSIVELY FROM AMAZON

About the Author

Craig began writing a weekly column for an online magazine in 2004. He has written a number of articles for the Trinity Mirror Group and online publications such as CNN, My Destination, and Insiders Abroad.

In 2013 he published his bestselling travel memoir, *Journey To A Dream*. It told the story of a turbulent first twelve months in Galicia. Since then he has added *Beyond Imagination*, *Endless Possibilities*, *Opportunities Ahead*, *Driving Ambition*, *The Discerning Traveller*, *A Season To Remember*, *An Excellent Vintage*, *Life In A Foreign Land*, *The Accidental Explorer*, *Seasons To Be Cheerful*, *Here To There And Back Again*, and *Land Of Rivers And Trees* to The Journey series.

As well as writing, Craig is an enthusiastic winemaker and owns a small vineyard.

Printed in Great Britain
by Amazon